When industrialization began in the United States, both free and bound labor supplied the commodities whose flow was dominated by merchant capital, while the legacy of the Revolution made possible the inclusion of white males from society's lower strata in the active citizenry. The voting rights and freedom of association enjoyed by workingmen hastened the dismantling of personal forms of sub-ordination, most dramatically in the brief moment when African Americans claimed those rights after the destruction of slavery. Never-theless, neither white nor black workers fashioned the new rules for a society based on wage labor. Both the shaping of economic develop-ment and the allocation of poor relief were effectively insulated from democratic control, while new forms of social domination disguised as freely contracted market and familial relationships were sanctioned by the courts, restructured police and military forces, and the criminalization of unemployment. Workers' use of their access to political power on behalf of their visions of the commonweal chal-lenged, but never defeated, the new style of class rule, which both strengthened government and limited its sphere of action.

Citizen Worker

Citizen Worker

*The Experience of Workers in the United States
with Democracy and the Free Market
during the Nineteenth Century*

David Montgomery

Yale University

CAMBRIDGE
UNIVERSITY PRESS

Published by the Press Syndicate of the University of Cambridge
The Pitt Building, Trumpington Street, Cambridge CB2 1RP
40 West 20th Street, New York, NY 10011-4211, USA
10 Stamford Road, Oakleigh, Melbourne 3166, Australia

©Cambridge University Press 1993

First published 1993

First paperback edition 1995

Printed in the United States of America

Library of Congress Cataloging-in-Publication Data is available.
A catalogue record for this book is available from the British Library.

ISBN 0-521-4205-7 hardback
ISBN 0-521-48380-8 paperback

To Sam and His Grandma

Contents

Acknowledgments

This book had its origins in the Tanner Lectures, which I presented at Brasenose College, Oxford, on April 29, May 3, and May 6, 1991. I am deeply indebted to the Tanner Lectures on Human Values for making possible my initial research into the subject of workers and citizenship, for assembling eminent scholars to discuss the lectures, and for granting me permission to reproduce portions of those lectures as part of this book. David Lord Windlesham, principal of Brasenose College, provided warm and memorable hospitality on that occasion. Joyce Appleby and John Saville prepared extensive commentaries. Valuable observations and criticisms were also offered by Anthony Badger, Timothy Breen, W. R. Brock, Clive Bush, Bruce Collins, Edward Countryman, Anthony Dworkin, Laurence Goldman, Howell John Harris, David W. Harvey, Eric Hobsbawm, Deian Hopkin, David Howell, Maldwyn A. Jones, Neville Kirk, Peter Parish, Harry G. Pitt, J. R. Pole, Stanley Trapido, J. D. Walsh, and Gavin Williams. Dorothy Thompson and Edward P. Thompson contributed memorably both to the discussion and in the hospitality of their home. Without the historical imagination and organizational efforts of John Rowett the entire affair would never have occurred. I am also indebted to Yale University for providing the leave of absence needed for the preparation of the lectures.

The contribution of many able historians to the ideas incorporated in this work will be evident to any reader and will be made explicit through the citation of their work. I should also like to offer special thanks to Jane Levey, Holly Allen, Tara Fitzpatrick, Paul Foos, and Kathleen Clark for their contributions to research seminars, which enriched my knowledge of the period. Julie Saville's doctoral dissertation on the transition from slave to wage labor in South Carolina, Amy Dru Stanley's dissertation on wage and marriage contracts in the nineteenth century, Christopher Tomlins's writings on the law of master and servant, and Iver Bernstein's book on the draft riots in New York City charted paths of investigation that I found especially inspiring. So too did Robert Steinfeld's history of the evolution of the law of free labor, which he kindly permitted me to use before it had been published.

The staffs of the Philadelphia City Archives and Yale's Sterling Memorial Library and Beinecke Rare Book and Manuscript Library gave gracious and indispensable assistance. The unforgettable knowledge and understanding of the late Susan Steinberg eased many a quest for books and other sources.

Portions of this work were discussed with participants in gatherings organized by the Vermont Labor History Society, the University of Minnesota History Department, the Five College Seminar, and Trinity College. An early version of the manuscript was read in its entirety by Bruce Laurie, Christopher Tomlins, and Allen Steinberg. Their criticisms guided many subsequent revisions, though on some important points we continue to disagree.

My special thanks go to Frank Smith and Martel W. Montgomery, each of whom in a different way grasped what this project was about and greatly expedited its completion.

Introduction

Workers in every industrializing country of the nineteenth century fought for civil and political rights within the national polity. In autocracies, where any popular mobilization could be regarded by the authorities as subversive, even strikes over economic issues frequently activated demands by workers for freedom of speech and association and for access to the decision-making power of government. Although social democratic parties proclaimed collective ownership of the means of production as their ultimate objective, and anarchists held all forms of government and all patriotism in contempt, the greatest mass mobilizations and general strikes of European workers before 1914 demanded political rights: the vote, civil liberties, and the end of autocracy. Where male workers could and did influence government by casting their ballots and were also free to form unions, as was the case during the last two decades of the century in France and the United States, they denounced the frequent intervention of soldiers in disputes between laborers and their employers as flagrant violations of that equality of rights on which republics were supposedly founded.

"In the end, it is the political context as much as the steam-engine, which had most influence upon the shaping consciousness and institutions of the working class," wrote E. P. Thompson. While England underwent the momentous social transformation of its industrial revolution, he explained, its political *"ancien regime* received a new lease of life,"* in reaction to the French Revolution and Napoleonic Wars, so that the working people "were subjected simultaneously to an intensification of two intolerable forms of relationship: those of economic exploitation and those of political oppression."[1]

The contrast between their situation and that found in the United States, where the democratic impact of the eighteenth-century revolution had preceded the country's industrialization, was often noted by Britons who had battled for universal manhood suffrage and annual parliaments. "*Here,*" proclaimed Irish-born John Binns from Philadelphia, "the *people* are sovereign." Thomas Ainge Devyr had expressed

1 E. P. Thompson, *The Making of the English Working Class* (New York, 1963), 197–9.

1

the same belief when he was arraigned in Newcastle before "their masquerading lordships in their black gowns and white wigs." One of them reproached Devyr and his Chartist associates for "committing not only a crime but a folly, in assuming that the mass could govern, instead of being governed." To which the irrepressible Devyr replied:

> It is a glorious sunset streaming through that gothic window. Did your lordship ever hear of a great country lying away in the direction of that setting sun? Did you hear that its people assume to govern themselves? Actually do the very thing that your lordship informs us cannot be done?[2]

Nevertheless, from the moment he landed on American shores until his death some four decades later, Devyr was locked in battle on behalf of tenant farmers and wage earners on the western side of the Atlantic, whose ability to "govern themselves," he concluded, was jeopardized by an emerging economic system propelled by the quest for private profits within the parameters set by market forces. The more that active participation in government was opened to the propertyless strata of society, the less capacity elected officials seemed to have to shape the basic contours of social life. Ray Gunn has written of the state of New York that by the 1840s "the economy was effectively insulated from democratic control."[3]

In the industrializing regions of the United States social priorities were set by people whose accumulated wealth proved decisive in determining the uses to which factors of production were put. Moreover, the economic power exercised by that wealth was underwritten by the coercive power of the police, armed forces, and the judiciary (or, more appropriately, as we shall see, the legal profession), and by privatized administration of poor relief. In addition, the inexorable grip of urban real estate owners on the decisions of local government persuaded Devyr and such successors as Terence V. Powderly and Henry George that monopolized access to land was the primary source of new forms of mastery of some human beings over others, which had become by the end of the century as onerous as those of the old regime.

Investigating the experience of workingmen and women with the simultaneous evolution of political democracy and a capitalist economy between the Jeffersonian triumph of the 1790s and the con-

2 John Binns, *Recollections of the Life of John Binns: Twenty-Nine Years in Europe and Fifty-Three in the United States* (Philadelphia, 1854), 227; Thomas Ainge Devyr, *The Odd Book of the Nineteenth Century, or, "Chivalry" in Modern Days* (Greenpoint, N.Y., 1882), "Irish and English Sections," 185–6.
3 L. Ray Gunn, *The Decline of Authority: Public Economic Policy and Political Development in New York, 1800–1860* (Ithaca, N.Y., 1988), 9.

solidation of business' power in the 1890s provides an opportunity to assess just what advantages political democracy provided workers in "the land beyond the setting sun," in comparison to those in industrialized portions of the Old World. Of the major industrial states in the 1880s only France had extended voting rights to virtually all its adult male population, while also securing freedom of the press and of association for its working people. The inclusion of workers in a French polity, which was still dominated by rural values and interests, placed severe restraints on the country's capitalist development, in the view of Gérard Noiriel, and "forced successive governments into compromises aggravating the rigidity of the labor market."[4] Neither democracy nor the indisputable political might of rural values and interests effectively restrained capitalist development in the United States, any more than it was impeded by autocracy in Germany or highly restricted franchise in England.

The contrast between the two sides of the North Atlantic had been more pronounced during the first half of the century than it was by the final decades. The United States had opened the franchise to propertyless white males in the northern states between the 1790s and the 1840s, and to black males in the southern states in the 1860s. In Europe the broad expansion of the suffrage achieved by the revolutions of 1848 had survived in few states outside of Switzerland and southern Germany.

During the 1860s the British Parliament had cautiously allowed the most prosperous of urban workingmen into the electorate, and the French Republic had bestowed the vote on virtually all adult males thirteen years after the suppression of the Paris Commune. By this time, the extension of voting rights, after workers' rebellions had been put down, appeared to many governments a promising way to enlist popular support for pending or probable wars. The German Empire offered its workers a frustrating blend of electoral privileges and authoritarian rule. All males over twenty-four years of age could vote for representatives to the imperial parliament, but the parliament could not overrule the kaiser and the government he selected. Its most industrialized state, Prussia, retained a three-class voting system for its own elections, while other states, such as Baden and Bavaria, boasted a more egalitarian franchise. After the demise of the oligarchical National Liberals early in the 1890s, however, voter participation and electioneering in both rural and urban regions of Germany had assumed an exuberant and populistic quality rivaling that found in American campaigns, while the powerful Social Democrats proved

4 Gérard Noiriel, *Les ouvriers dans la société française* (Paris, 1986), 134–5. My translation.

reluctant to resort to mass action on behalf of parliamentary rule. Elsewhere in Europe social conflict over voting rights reached new heights at the end of the century. Austria, Italy, Belgium, the Netherlands, Norway, Sweden, Spain, Russia, and Finland all produced huge mobilizations of workers demanding one man, one vote (in the Finnish case, one person, one vote) during the first decade of the twentieth century. Only in the aftermath of those struggles could the secretary of the Socialist International write with misplaced confidence, "No one doubts that within a few years democracy will triumph in all countries of European civilization."[5]

Important as they were, therefore, formal voting rights do not provide the only point of contrast, or even the most consequential one. Outside of the slave states, the formation of popular associations was subjected to far less police supervision in the United States than it was in Europe, and the culture of mass politics both encouraged popular assembly and lent the rights of assemblage a profound racial twist. The land of liberty was also the land of slavery. Political rights were identified as the privilege of white men everywhere in popular imagination, and in all but a few New England states by law. Consequently, the most intense and sanguinary battle waged by its working people for citizenship and suffrage was that by African Americans in the South after a war in which they had been enlisted on the winning side and slavery had been destroyed.

Democratization of the polity did have an impact on American economic development. It hastened the replacement of older forms of physical and legal coercion – such as imprisonment for debt or for "absconding from the service" of their masters, and the post–Civil War southern Black Codes – by the legal doctrine of "freedom of contract." Blatantly visible styles of domination and exploitation yielded to new forms, which were disguised as commodity exchange and justified by the ascendant discourse of equal rights and freely contracted arrangements. Amelia Sargent wrote in 1846 that when a worker first entered a textile mill, she

> receives therefrom a Regulation paper, containing the rules by which she must be governed while in their employ; and lo! here

5 Dick Geary, *European Labour Protest, 1848–1939* (London, 1981), 59–65, 103–18; David Blackburn and Geoff Eley, *Peculiarities of German History: Bourgeois Society and Politics in Nineteenth-Century Germany* (Oxford, 1984), 256–7, 275; Geoff Eley, *Reshaping the German Right: Radical Nationalism and Political Change after Bismarck* (New Haven, 1980), 21–4; Marcel van der Linden and Jürgen Rojahn, eds., *The Formation of Labour Movements, 1870–1914* (two vols., Leiden, 1990); Göran Therborn, "The Rule of Capital and the Rise of Democracy," *New Left Review*, 103 (May–June 1977), 11–17; Emile Vandervelde, *Socialism versus the State* (translated by Charles H. Kerr, Chicago, 1919), 61. Vandervelde wrote this important book in 1914.

is the beginning of mischief; for in addition to the tyrannous and oppressive rules which meet her astonished eyes, she finds herself compelled to remain for the space of twelve months in the very place she then occupies, however reasonable and just cause of complaint might be hers, or however strong the wish for dimission.[6]

Sargent sought the remedy for this new form of bondage "through the Ballot Box." She summoned the "hardy independent yeomenry and mechanics," who had "daughters and sisters toiling in these sickly prison-houses," to "see to it that you send to preside in the Councils of each Commonwealth . . . men who will watch zealously over the interests of the laborer in every department [and] who will protect him by the strong arm of the law from the encroachments of arbitrary power."[7]

Sargent's appeal to legislatures elected by broad-based manhood suffrage for protection from the regulations imposed by her employers under the "free market" proved futile. The law of master and servant, which found no place in the statutes adopted by elected legislatures of the free states, reappeared in court decisions and in commentaries on the common law, to provide legal sanction for employers' authority. At the same time, control of relief for unemployed but able-bodied men and women was commandeered by bourgeois reformers who reshaped charity to reinforce industrial discipline. The contribution of legislatures, especially after the 1860s, was to enact increasingly draconic vagrancy laws that made it a crime not to have a job. As labor reformer George McNeill wrote in his famous protest of 1877: "When [the worker] is at work, he belongs to the lower orders, and is continually under surveillance; when out of work, he is an outlaw, a tramp, – he is a man without the rights of manhood, – the pariah of society, homeless, in the deep significance of the term."[8]

It would be a serious error of judgment, however, to conclude that the revolution of the eighteenth century had left no durable legacy of egalitarian practice. "Nothing is more striking to an European traveller in the United States," wrote Alexis de Tocqueville, "than the absence of what we term Government, or the Administration."[9] Even the mechanisms through which the business and professional strata tried to dominate the nineteenth-century cities and factories leaked like a sieve. Although popularly elected governments secured little

6 Philip S. Foner, ed., *The Factory Girls* (Urbana, Ill., 1977), 135.
7 Ibid., 137–8.
8 George E. McNeill, *The Labor Movement: The Problem of To-day* (New York, 1887), 455, quoting from his own editorial of 1877.
9 Alexis de Tocqueville, *Democracy in America,* translated by Henry Reeve (New York, 1838), 51.

effective leverage over economic and social life, civil society nurtured
community solidarities and a swarm of institutions such as fraternal
orders, trade unions, Catholic parishes, self-governing plebeian Protestant congregations, and political clubs, all of which obstructed bourgeois control of American life at every turn. For working people the
most important part of the Jeffersonian legacy was the shelter it
provided to free association, diversity of beliefs and behavior, and
defiance of alleged social superiors in society.

As Alfred Young demonstrated in his exegesis on the memoirs of
the shoemaker George Robert Twelves Hewes, the revolutionary
struggle against British rule profoundly bolstered the self-esteem of
the artisans who had taken part, and eroded their readiness to defer
to the judgment and personal authority of fellow citizens who exhibited greater wealth or education.[10] Hewes's political and psychological odyssey, and that of innumerable contemporaries, suggests
that workers' claims to citizenship, which derived from the revolution
of the eighteenth century, informed the heady boast inscribed on a
banner carried by bricklayers in Philadelphia's 1788 parade in celebration of the new constitution: "Both buildings and rulers are the
work of our hands."[11] The bearers of that banner believed that the
archetypal citizen of classical republicanism, the "accomplished" man
who commanded property and arms, had no greater claim to guide
the polity than the less eminent male whose labors contributed to its
material welfare.[12]

The claim of every white man to equal political rights had been
championed by the Jeffersonians against what the Democratic-
Republicans of New York in the 1790s called the "consummate and
overbearing haughtiness" of the postrevolutionary Federalist elite.[13]
Theirs was the political community into which John Binns of the
London Corresponding Society and the United Englishmen fit with
ease. Its doctrines framed nascent awareness of class conflict in the
vocabulary of patriotism, race, and rights. The legacy of the eighteenth century revolutions, which had characterized the patriot as a
determined enemy of the status quo and especially of "feudal" privilege, while perpetuating the subordination of African Americans,

10 Alfred F. Young, "George Robert Twelves Hewes (1752–1840): A Boston Shoemaker
   and the Memory of the American Revolution," *William and Mary Quarterly*, 3d series,
   38 (Oct. 1981), 561–623. The literature on deference and the Revolution is too vast
   to be cataloged here.
11 [Anon.], "Account of the Grand Federal Procession," *American Museum*, July 4, 1788,
   63.
12 On classical republicanism, see J. G. A. Pocock, *The Machiavellian Moment: Florentine
   Political Thought and the Atlantic Republican Tradition* (Princeton, N.J., 1975).
13 Quoted in Howard B. Rock, *Artisans of the New Republic: The Tradesmen of New York City
   in the Age of Jefferson* (New York, 1979), 50.

made this usage both easy and very durable. The bloody test of the Civil War reaffirmed for the victors the linkage of loyalty to a common nation-state with struggle against social injustice. In the midst of that contest almost four million slaves laid claim to the rights of citizenship, and thereafter the advocates of both black and white workers justified their claims in terms of defense of the nation against southern and northern reincarnations of slavery.

The citizen-producer was customarily depicted as male. "To be adept in the art of Government," wrote Abigail Adams to her husband John, "is a prerogative to which your Sex lay an almost exclusive claim."[14] Neither the unsuccessful challenges raised by upper-class women to the doctrine of *coverture,* which vested all property possessed by the wife in her husband and subsumed her political identity in his, nor the prominence of women among the workers employed by factory experiments of the 1790s, altered the reality that women were expected to obey the laws, but might have no part in making them. Like the "passive" citizens of the French constitution of 1791, whose status as domestic servants or inability to pay taxes equivalent to three days' labor disqualified them from voting, those American women who were not slaves or indentured servants could – as we shall see often did – bring criminal charges before the courts against other men and women, but they could not participate in the selection of government officials. Unlike the male "passive" citizen of France, however, women who married during the antebellum decades transferred their legal capacity to make contracts and own property to their husbands. In the words of the prestigious legal commentator Tapping Reeve, the marriage contract gave the husband dominion over everything she had acquired by "labor, service, or act," as well as the "person of his wife."[15]

Moreover, as Joyce Appleby has argued, it was not simply their political egalitarianism that distinguished the views of Jeffersonian Republicans from classical republicanism, but also the Jeffersonians' conviction that public needs were best met by private arrangements rather than by the actions of governments or incorporated bodies. Appleby added that the Jeffersonian ideological victory of 1800 was so complete that it drove all other styles of discourse from the national political arena.[16] Many a writer on "working-class republicanism"

14 Abigail Adams to John Adams, May 9, 1776, quoted in Linda K. Kerber, *Women of the Republic: Intellect and Ideology in Revolutionary America* (Chapel Hill, N.C., 1980), 269.
15 Kerber, 119–27; Tapping Reeve, *The Law of Baron and Femme, of Parent and Child, Guardian and Ward, Master and Servant and of the Powers of the Courts of Chancery* (Albany, N.Y., 1862), 482. On early factories, see this volume Chapter 1. On the French constitution of 1791, see Georges Lefebvre, *The French Revolution,* translated by Elizabeth Moss Evanson (two vols., London, 1962–4), vol. 1, 151–2.
16 Joyce Appleby, *Capitalism and a New Social Order: The Republican Vision of the 1790s* (New York, 1984).

would agree with that proposition, at least in part. From another point of view, the Jeffersonian ideological triumph left dependent classes – slaves, indentured servants, wage earners, married women – bereft of a political vocabulary suited to their experiences and desires. We will have several occasions in these pages to examine working people's appropriation of portions of the Jeffersonian discourse for their own use. Such appropriation required the infusion of collective action and mutualistic values into republican rhetoric. As Raymond Williams has argued, "Certain experiences, meanings, and values which cannot be expressed or substantially verified in terms of the dominant culture, are nevertheless lived and practiced on the basis of the residue – cultural as well as social – of some previous social or cultural formation."[17]

The point of departure for popular blendings of traditional values with claims to active citizenship was the conviction that there was a common good to be fashioned by both private and public behavior, and that it was nurtured by freedom of speech and action and by self-organization. Mutual benefit societies, lyceums, mechanics' institutes, cooperatives, trade unions, and workingmen's parties all clothed themselves in Jeffersonian celebration of diversity and popular initiative. "Let a thousand flowers blossom" – to borrow a phrase from Mao Zedong.

But not all those flowers could find a place in the garden of capitalism. As commodity exchange assumed its industrial shape, bourgeois reformers approached plebeian life in the spirit John Milton had attributed to Adam in the Garden of Eden:

> To-morrow, ere fresh morning streak the east
> With the first approach of light, we must be risen,
> And at our pleasant labour, to reform
> Yon flowery arbours, yonder alleys green,
> Our walk at noon, with branches overgrown,
> That mock our scant manuring, and require
> More hands than ours to lop their wanton growth.[18]

The expansion of wage labor and the reification of the wage relationship by the legal doctrine of freedom of contract severed all but monetary bonds between employer and employee, while encouraging new forms of discipline through work rules, public institutions, and police powers. The new impositions by no means went uncontested. The social networks of urban economic and neighborhood life, mass communication systems based on the printed word, interaction among peoples of diverse cultures and beliefs, and the Jeffersonian legacy encouraged

17 Raymond Williams, *Marxism and Literature* (Oxford, 1977), 122.
18 John Milton, *"Paradise Lost," The Complete Poems of John Milton, with Complete Notes by Thomas Newton, D.D., Bishop of Bristol* (New York, 1936), 119.

ordinary people to believe that destiny lay "not in our stars but in
ourselves." Working people sought to use their access to the powers of
government not only to defend their customs against unpalatable
innovations, but also to reshape social life according to their own
aspirations and their own sense of the priority of the common welfare
over individual advantage.

My interpretation of this contest owes much to two recent developments in the study of law. The first stems from the emergence of a
body of legal protections of the individual worker (rooted in an-
tidiscrimination legislation), which has recently amended legal application of free-market principles. This contemporary development
has awakened scholarly interest in what the rights, obligations, and
protections of individuals on the job were in the past. Previous scholarship on labor and the law was devoted primarily to legal regulation of
collective action and to the law of slavery.

The second influential development has been the maturing of
critical legal theory. This reexamination of American law and its
history has produced rich evidence on the role of courts and the legal
profession in the development of the state in the United States. In
tandem with renewed scholarly interest in the individual worker, it
admonishes those who call for "bringing the state back" into the
history of American labor to scrutinize carefully the nature of the
nineteenth-century American state, and not to exaggerate the "relative autonomy of the state" in that period.[19]

Moreover, critical legal theory has also forced historians to come to
grips with the notion of discourse as power. Much historical analysis
today focuses on the role of historically evolving styles of conceptualiz-
ing human and even physical entities and relationships in the molding
of social dominance and subordination. Denouncing the notion that
language and law simply reflect material reality, and seeking to "inter-
rogate" vocabularies used in the past as well as those of the present,
these historians have called into question Karl Marx's famous maxim,
"It is not the consciousness of men that determines their being, but,
on the contrary, their social being that determines their conscious-

---

19 Peter B. Evans, Dietrich Rueschemeyer, and Theda Skocpol, *Bringing the State Back
In* (Cambridge, 1985). Among many contributions to critical legal history, I am
especially indebted to Christopher L. Tomlins, *The State and the Unions: Labor
Relations, Law, and the Organized Labor Movement in America, 1880–1960* (Cambridge, 1985); William Forbath, *Law and the Shaping of the American Labor Movement* (Cambridge, Mass., 1991); Robert J. Steinfeld, *Invention of Free Labor: The
Employment Relations in English and American Law and Culture, 1350–1870* (Chapel
Hill, N.C. 1991); and Amy Dru Stanley, "Contract Rights in the Age of Emancipation: Wage Labor and Marriage after the Civil War" (Ph.D. diss., Yale University,
1990).

ness."[20] Some, like Joan Wallach Scott, would have us "acknowledge
'class' but locate its origins in political rhetoric."[21] Others, somewhat
more modestly, would argue, as does William Forbath, that the "language of the law, along with other discourses of the powerful, lays
down the very terms within which subordinate groups are able to
experience the world and articulate their aspirations."[22]

The historicizing of discourse has greatly enriched our understanding of the operation of what Antonio Gramsci called the hegemonic
ideas of any social order, and has helped us especially to appreciate
the power of the way of thinking that appears in a given historical
period as "common sense," in limiting ordinary people's sense of
which courses of action are realistic and which utopian, and in shaping their verbalization of their own aspirations.[23] Nevertheless, to
locate the origins of class merely "in political rhetoric" is to uncouple
historically specific ways of thinking from the relationships of exploitation that are embedded in creating the goods and services used in
everyday life, and also from capitalism's relentless compulsion to
disrupt the patterns of life it had earlier brought into existence.
Nineteenth-century men and women were set to thinking about social
conflict in terms of antagonistic classes by their encounter with new
forms of exploitation. These did not involve the simple commandeer-
ing of produce and persons that had characterized earlier societies
and that continued to thrive in southern states until the 1860s, but
instead disguised the generation of wealth and the economy's creative
and ruthless dynamism as market relations, in which everyone received some equivalent for what he or she had contributed.

Although my analysis of the transformation of the master-and-servant relation, of the effort to police people for the sake of market
freedom, and of the role of political parties in the lives of working
people, devotes close attention to the ideological categories with
which working people interpreted their own experience and formulated their goals, it does not reach the conclusion that the world of
ideas provided the driving force of social domination and change.

Moreover, to argue, as Forbath does, that "the very terms within
which subordinate groups are able to experience the world and articulate their aspirations" were laid down by "the discourses of the power-

20 Karl Marx, "Preface to *A Contribution to the Critique of Political Economy*," in Marx,
   Selected Works, (2 vols., New York, n.d.), vol. 1, 356. For a critique of discourse, which
   offers an informative survey of the history of this style of thinking, see Bryan D.
   Palmer, *Descent into Discourse: the Reification of Language and the Writing of Social
   History* (Philadelphia, 1990).
21 Joan Wallach Scott, *Gender and the Politics of History* (New York, 1988), 59.
22 Forbath, 170.
23 Antonio Gramsci, *Selections from the Prison Notebooks of Antonio Gramsci* (translated and
   edited by Quintin Hoare and Geoffrey N. Smith, New York, 1971), 195–6, 246–7.

ful," helps us understand the content and appeal of what many historians have called "working class republicanism" only if we add a caveat. To avoid the trap of a new consensus history, in which everyone becomes "republican" and working-class culture appears only as a mental legacy of bygone social formations, it is urgent to devote close attention to people's actions along with their words, and to what some students of women's literature have aptly described as "silences." We will encounter the limitations of Forbath's formulation most dramatically when we examine the post-Emancipation struggles of African Americans in the South. Virtually overnight former slaves pulverized the hegemonic ideology so eloquently described by Eugene D. Genovese in *Roll, Jordon, Roll,* while they acted on aspirations that would simply not fit into the terms of thought professed by northern Republicans. Pierre Bordieu's description of the ambiguous and often hostile response of subordinate classes to the very styles of expression employed by the dominant strata serves as a warning to historians to tread warily when interpreting popular uses of republican ideology:

> The dominant language discredits and destroys the spontaneous political discourse of the dominated. It leaves them only silence or a borrowed language, whose logic departs from that of popular usage but without becoming that of erudite usage, a deranged language, in which the "fine words" are only there to mark the dignity of the expressive intention, and which, unable to express anything true, real, or "felt", dispossess the speaker of the very experience it is supposed to express. . . . And often the only escape from ambivalence or indeterminacy toward language is to fall back on what one *can* appreciate, the body rather than words, substance rather than form, an honest face rather than a smooth tongue.[24]

Finally, wrestling with the meaning of citizenship to the nineteenth-century worker may also shed some light on contemporary issues, which have been made murky by the discourse of the 1990s. No two phrases come coupled together more often today than "democracy" and "a market economy." A front-page article in the *New York Times* even referred to Czechoslovakia's pending transition to a "democratic market economy."[25] How an economy can be democratic, or what a market economy is like in the age of multinational corporations, we are never told. Both notions are employed in a manner that is deliberately vague, and just how they are related to each other is even

24 Pierre Bordieu, *Distinction: A Social Critique of the Judgment of Taste* (Cambridge, Mass., 1984), 462, 465; Eugene D. Genovese, *Roll, Jordan, Roll: The World the Slaves Made* (New York, 1972).
25 *New York Times,* May 19, 1992.

more so. We can only rest assured that they are both Good Things. As Judge Anthony M. Kennedy wrote in his judgment against Washington State's comparable worth statute: "Neither law nor logic deems the free market system a suspect enterprise."[26]

There is much in the experience of workingmen and women in this country that should lead us to think more carefully and precisely about these two notions and the historical relationship between them. In important ways the meaning of citizenship and the freedom of economic activity from state control did expand together, though neither one turns out to have been a simple logical consequence of the other. Over the course of the century, however, both the contraction of the domain of governmental activity and the strengthening of government's coercive power contributed to the hegemony of business and professional men, which was exercised through both governmental and private activity. It was the working people who sought to preserve the community welfare through both spheres.

26 Ibid., Nov. 15, 1987.

1

Wage Labor, Bondage, and Citizenship

During the eighteenth century merchant capital had encouraged the production of commodities through a variety of labor systems, ranging from the total subjugation of the slave to such autonomy among artisans and yeomen as was seldom to be found in either previous or subsequent human experience. It also underwrote established privilege and power based on family lineage and personal access to the levers of government. The rural and urban popular mobilizations of the late eighteenth and early nineteenth centuries, which democratized the American political system, also undermined the personal forms of subordination that had bound many working people for shorter or longer periods to masters, but that had also obligated both masters and municipal authorities to care for basic needs of working people and those who could not work.

In the late eighteenth century hired labor had coexisted with and often been overshadowed by slavery, indentured servitude, apprenticeship, and other forms of bound labor. Moreover, the largest concentrations of wage earners had been found among merchant seamen, who were subject to physical punishments and for whom quitting during the period for which they had signed on was the criminal offense of desertion. By the 1820s, however, the swelling ranks of men and women dependent on wages for their livelihood and on rental for their dwellings had made wage contracts so commonplace that they provided a norm in terms of which other social and political relationships were defined. That norm was elaborated by jurists and legislators in the context of redefinitions of the rights of property and the exigencies of commodity circulation. Indentured servitude had virtually disappeared by the census of 1850, and a few years after that enumeration, the number of wage earners ten years of age and older for the first time surpassed the number of slaves more than ten years of age.[1]

1 Slaves accounted for 23 percent of the nation's labor force over nine years of age in 1850 and 21 percent in 1860. Although the number of wage earners is difficult to calculate precisely from census data, the labor force in manufacturing, construction, mining, transportation, and domestic service accounted for 21 percent of the total in 1850 and 23 percent in 1860. U.S. Department of Commerce, Bureau of the Census, *Historical Statistics of the United States, Colonial Times to 1970* (2 vols., Washington, D.C., 1975, hereafter cited as Census, *Hist. Stat.*), vol. 1, 139.

Nevertheless, factory employment still accounted for only a small, if growing, fraction of the men and women who were dependent on wages for their incomes.[2] The Reverend Joseph Tuckerman, in a prizewinning *Essay on the Wages Paid to Females for Their Labour*, written in 1829, reminded his readers:

> The classes are very numerous, of those who are wholly depend-ent upon wages. They would, indeed, be numerous, if we looked for them among those only who have no trade. . . . This large division includes shop, market, and other porters; carmen; those who are employed in lading, and unlading vessels; wood-sawyers, hod-carriers; house servants; those employed by mechanics in a single branch of the business; and multitudes, who are men and women of any work, occasionally required in families, as wash-ing, scouring, &c.; or on the wharves, or in the streets of the city. Besides these, the number is great of those, who are journey-men, and many of whom will never be anything but journeymen, in the various mechanic arts; and considerable numbers are also employed in the different departments of large manufactories.[3]

Between the 1770s and the 1840s every state redefined its voting qualifications to incorporate into the polity the adult white males among these wage earners. Tocqueville grasped the dynamics of the complex process by which partisan divisions in the ranks of the "high-er orders" after the Revolution had led "each of their several members to follow his own interest; and as it was impossible to wring the power from the hands of a people which they did not detest sufficiently to brave, their only aim was to secure its good will at any price." The consequence was that "the most democratic laws were . . . voted by the very men whose interests they impaired." No less aristocratic a state than Maryland led the way, amending its state constitution in 1801 to abolish property qualifications for voting and require ballots to be cast in secret.[4]

The changes were justified by the rhetoric of equal rights and popular sovereignty, which conformed neatly to the everyday exper-ience of the large rural smallholding element of the population, and may well have encountered relatively weak resistance outside of

2 See Jonathan Prude, *The Coming of Industrial Order: Town and Factory Life in Rural Massachusetts, 1810–1860* (Cambridge, 1983); Sean Wilentz, *Chants Democratic: New York City and the Rise of the American Working Class, 1788–1850* (New York, 1984); Bruce Laurie, *Working People of Philadelphia, 1800–1850* (Philadelphia, 1980); Iver Bernstein, *The New York City Draft Riots: Their Significance for American Society and Politics in the Age of the Civil War* (New York, 1990).

3 Joseph Tuckerman, *An Essay on the Wages Paid to Females for Their Labour* (Philadelphia, 1830), 8.

4 Tocqueville, 38; Carl B. Swisher, *Roger B. Taney* (New York, 1935), 47–8.

Rhode Island because the wage earners' numbers remained unthreatening in comparison to those of small proprietors. Tocqueville's observation that most of the gentry "did not detest" the people "sufficiently to brave" them is especially apt. A comparison with the venomous hostility displayed by southern plantation owners toward the enfranchisement of their former slaves in 1867–8 underscores the fact that a significant portion of the gentry, assembling under the Jeffersonian banner, were prepared to advance their own political fortunes by soliciting the votes of humble farmers and artisans.

The most obvious legacy of the Revolution, in fact, had been a dramatic expansion of proprietorship in agriculture, encouraged by attacks on inheritance practices through which great families had kept their estates intact, and especially by migration into territories west of Pennsylvania that had been annexed to the United States. As the patriot Noah Webster wrote, "An equality of property, with a necessity of alienation, constantly operating to destroy combinations of powerful families, is the very *soul of a republic.*"[5] The male smallholder, casting his ballot openly in the presence of neighbors, with whom he shared militia service and routine economic interaction, was still the average American voter.

State constitutions of the early nineteenth century, however, did more than simply bestow suffrage on many rural and urban householders: they explicitly enfranchised men who did not own farms, businesses, or even homes of their own. To be sure, the qualifications imposed on elections for members of Congress or state legislatures fell more rapidly than those controlling municipal offices, governors, and the upper houses in some states. In New York City memorials from artisans to the legislature demanded that renters as well as homeowners be allowed to vote, and indeed by 1814 more than 77 percent of the city's voters were renters. Democratic-Republican politicians, who courted the endorsement of mechanics' associations and militia companies, lent conspicuous support to those demands. They clothed their advocacy of equal suffrage in ardent nationalism, and during the tense years between Jay's Treaty and the War of 1812 accused their foes of wishing to bring back the British king. One New York election broadside of 1807 proclaimed:

The finishing
STROKE.
Every Shot's a Vote,
and every Vote
KILLS A TORY!

5 Quoted in Pocock, 534.

Do your duty, Republicans,
Let your exertions this day
Put down the Kings
and tyrants of Britain.[6]

Opponents of manhood suffrage employed two arguments drawn from classical republicanism. One was that people with no propertied stake in society were potential followers of wicked and ambitious demagogues who appealed, in the words of New York's Chancellor James Kent, to "a tendency in the poor to covet and to share the plunder of the rich; in the debtor to relax or avoid the obligations of contract; in the majority to tyranize over the minority . . . ; in the indolent and profligate, to cast the whole burthens of society upon the industrious and the virtuous."[7] The other objection was that agricultural interests needed to retain some constitutional defense against the growing voting power of the cities. This argument (interestingly) assumed that the urban poor would follow the political dictates of their employers. As Josiah Quincy of Massachusetts explained, "There is nothing in the condition of our country, to prevent manufacturers from being absolutely dependent upon their employers, here as they are everywhere else. The whole body of every manufacturing establishment, therefore, are dead votes, counted by the head, by their employer."[8]

Only in Rhode Island, where laws dating from the eighteenth century severely limited the legislative representation of the many rapidly growing factory towns, and also restricted the electorate to those men with $134 worth of real estate who had been chosen as "freemen" by vote of a town meeting, did landowners' resistance to a series of reform attempts from 1811 onward ultimately force a violent confrontation, in 1842. "Worth makes the man, but sand and gravel make the voter," protested the champions of the People's Convention, which created a rival government based on white male suffrage. Their armed clashes with the authorities, the debate over possible federal intervention, and the trial and incarceration of Thomas Dorr galvanized democratic sentiment against this flagrant exception to what had become the American rule.[9]

6 Rock, 62; on renters as voters, see Elizabeth Blackmar, *Manhattan for Rent* (Ithaca, N.Y., 1989), 40. On nationalism and popular democracy in Europe, see E. J. Hobsbawm, *Nations and Nationalism since 1780: Programme, Myth, Reality* (Cambridge, 1990); Linda Colley, "Whose Nation? Class and National Consciousness in Britain, 1750–1830," *Past and Present*, 113 (Nov. 1986), 97–117.

7 Merrill D. Peterson, ed., *Democracy, Liberty, and Property: The State Constitutional Conventions of the 1820's* (Indianapolis, Ind., 1966), 194.

8 "Debates and Proceedings of the Massachusetts Convention," quoted in Robert J. Steinfeld, "Property and Suffrage in the Early American Republic," *Stanford Law Review*, 41 (Jan. 1989), 358–9. Kent made much the same warning. Peterson, 196.

9 Marvin E. Gettleman, *The Dorr Rebellion: A Study in American Radicalism, 1833–1849* (New York, 1973). The quotation is on page 39. See also [anon.,] *Charters and Legislative Documents, Illustrative of Rhode Island History* (Providence, R.I., 1844).

This famous exception deserves close attention because of what it reveals about the general pattern whereby wage earners were admitted to the polity. It may be said that the issue was especially hard fought in Rhode Island because it was so important there. Rhode Island in the 1840s was the only state in the Union where the manufacturing population outnumbered the farming population. The Blackstone Valley, which reached northward from Providence into southern Massachusetts, was the domain of Samuel Slater. Between the 1790s and the 1840s it had become the nation's leading center of textile factories, staffed by migrant and immigrant workers. Moreover, the city of Providence, which was grievously underrepresented under the existing constitution, contained more than 28 percent of the state's manufacturing and trades population. A foe of manhood suffrage argued, "The virtuous and intelligent yeomanry which compose the majority of the people of the United States, are desirous, that, in the extension of the suffrage, this class of Rhode Island people should not be put down by the stranger and the sojourner."[10]

At stake was more than just the power to vote in state elections. As was also the case in neighboring Connecticut, no person could become a legal resident of a town without permission of the town's voters. Consequently, indigent strangers could be denied the town's charity, and women, who owned no property apart from their husbands, had no claim for relief even on the town of their birth, once they had ever been married. Rhode Island's law code of 1822 specified that any "unsuitable person" who disobeyed a town government's orders to leave could be bound out for servitude for one year to any citizen of the United States. Moreover, the business and professional classes of the growing cities also felt oppressed. Not only were their towns ridiculously underrepresented in the legislature, but, if they did not qualify as freemen themselves, they could not sue in court, secure a debt, or attach property unless a freeman endorsed their case.[11]

In practice, the disfranchisement of mill operatives in Rhode Island did not differ much from the experience of their counterparts in neighboring Massachusetts or in the Manayunk or Brandywine Creek regions of Pennsylvania in the 1830s. Jonathan Prude has found that operatives in Oxford and Dudley (in Massachusetts, but part of the

---

10 [John Pitman,] *A Reply to the Letter of the Hon. Marcus Morton by One of the Rhode-Island People* (Providence, R.I., 1842), 26. The calculations of manufacturing population are from Amy Bridges, *A City in the Republic: Antebellum New York and the Origins of Machine Politics* (Cambridge, 1984), 185, n. 13. On the Blackstone Valley, see Prude.
11 [John A. Bolles,] *The Affairs of Rhode Island, By a Member of the Boston Bar* (Boston, 1842), 16–7; Kerber, 142; Pitman, 16; [anon.,] *Facts Involved in the Rhode Island Controversy with Some Views upon the Rights of Both Parties* (Boston, 1842), 12.

economic hinterland of Providence) were routinely excluded from town meetings and had taxpayer and residency qualifications for voting rigorously enforced against them. True, the Working Men's Party won more than 21 percent of the votes in Dudley in 1834, but there, as in Pennsylvania textile towns, that party's support came from established local mechanics and members of preindustrial elites, not from factory hands. Moreover, no women could vote, and to the north in the Merrimack Valley women constituted the vast majority of operatives. For mill hands and townspeople generally, access to government may have taken on special importance in New England because everyday social and economic life was more closely regulated by the many elected officials of town governments than was the case elsewhere. The more the details of local affairs were the stuff of governmental deliberations, the more important it was to be part of the electorate.[12]

The decisive battle for manhood suffrage was initiated in 1832–3 by regional conventions of workers, who linked their demand expressly to petitions and strikes for the ten-hour day and to demands for direct election of public officials, abolition of imprisonment for debt, and equal and universal education. The radical housesmith Seth Luther used the mistreatment of young workers in the factories of both England and New England to rally working people to the cause. He described the abuse of Paulina Brown, a sixteen-year-old operative in one of Slater's mills, who had allowed a drive belt to slip off a spinning machine. In revenge an overseer had placed a ludicrous, battered old hat on her head and forced her for almost two hours to march past the other workers, then to stand on a stove in public view, while he yanked her hands away from her tear-stained face. After that he had taken her into a closed room known to the workers as the "whipping room" and beaten her hands with a leather strap. When Paulina's father charged the overseer before a local justice of the peace, the magistrate awarded the father ten cents in damages. Her enraged co-workers appeared en masse before a Providence court to support a successful appeal to a sympathetic jury for more substantial damages (twenty dollars). Brown's punishment, the magistrate's disdain, and the argument of the defense attorney that the overseer had but properly reprimanded a "hired servant" who had "refused to obey [his] directions" had all added fuel to the workers' campaign for political rights. Despite the prominence of women in the audiences at workers' meetings through-

12 Prude, 98, 117, 218; Cynthia J. Shelton, *The Mills of Manayunk: Industrialization and Social Conflict in Philadelphia, 1878–1837* (Baltimore, Md., 1986), 123–8; Thomas Dublin, *Women at Work: The Transformation of Work and Community in Lowell, Massachusetts, 1826–1860* (New York, 1979); Tocqueville, 60–5.

out the region, among the witnesses who testified on Brown's behalf in court, and in the ranks of textile strikers in 1834, however, Luther's speeches, the Brown protest, and workers' demands for the ten-hour day were all routinely couched in terms of empowering working-class men to protect the women of their families from abuse.[13]

The suffrage struggle in Rhode Island also highlighted the exclusion of African Americans from the polity. All states outside of New England shaped their constitutions "to meet the public sentiment," either by prohibiting African Americans from voting, or else by imposing on them special property qualifications like that enacted in New York in 1825, which only sixteen black men in the state could meet. Although Thomas Dorr, Rhode Island's most prominent advocate of manhood suffrage, was an abolitionist and favored nonracial voting qualifications, the workers' movement had been silent on the question, and the Suffrage Association, which resumed the fight under the auspices primarily of urban business and professional men and Democratic political leaders, called for "a liberal extension of suffrage to the native white male citizens of the United States, resident in Rhode Island."[14] Its formulation was adopted by the People's Convention, which drafted a new constitution for popular ratification in 1841 in defiance of the state government. That instrument, which proudly cataloged the political and civil rights of "the people," admitted to suffrage every "white male citizen of the United States, of the age of twenty-one years, who has resided in this State for one year, and in any town, city, or district of the same for six months, next preceding the election at which he offers to vote."[15]

Rhode Island's authorities defeated Dorr's followers militarily and pursued them with repressive "Algerine Laws" punishing offenses against the state. The conservatives had enlisted numerous African

13 Seth Luther, *Address to the Working Men of New England on the State of Education and on the Condition of the Producing Classes in Europe and America* (New York, 1833), 20; Luther, *Address on the Right of Free Suffrage* (Providence, R.I., 1833); "L*****" [pseud.] to *Working Man's Advocate*, Feb. 25, 1833; Brief of Aaron Whiteside, *Richmond* v. *Brown*, Providence Court of Common Pleas, November term 1832 (courtesy of Teresa A. Murphy); Peter J. Coleman, *The Transformation of Rhode Island, 1790–1860* (Providence, R.I., 1963), 234–5; Brother Joseph Brennan, F.S.C., *Social Conditions in Industrial Rhode Island, 1820–1860* (Washington, D.C., 1940), 53–6; Teresa Anne Murphy, *Ten Hours' Labor: Religion, Reform, and Gender in Early New England* (Ithaca, N.Y., 1992), 32. The working-class–based desire for the "protection" of women in this epoch is well analyzed in Christine Stansell, *City of Women: Sex and Class in New York, 1789–1860* (New York, 1986), 76–101, 143–51.
14 [George T. Curtis,] *The Merits of Thomas W. Dorr, and George Bancroft as They Are Politically Connected, By A Citizen of Massachusetts* (Boston, n.d.), 5; Steinfeld, "Property and Suffrage," 353–4; Blackmar, 156; Gettleman, 44–53, 129–30; Leon Litwack, *North of Slavery: The Negro in the Free States, 1790–1860* (Chicago, 1961), 75.
15 [Frances H. Greene McDougall,] *Might and Right; By A Rhode Islander* (Providence, R.I., 1844), 98.

Americans into the troops that put down Dorr's forces, and subsequently upheld the right of black men to vote in the revised constitution adopted by the so-called Landholders' Convention. Convened amid
the repression, that body abolished the freehold requirement for all
native-born men but retained it for citizens who had been born
abroad.[16] The prominent abolitionist William Goodell vehemently championed the People's Convention despite its racial qualifications for suffrage. He argued that the landholders had historically been the allies of
slavery, and that it had been the conservatives who had "raised the cry of
treason against the abolitionists, in 1834–5–6," while Dorr had led the
legislative fight to defeat a proposed bill to outlaw antislavery agitation.
White workers, immigrant and native, and African Americans, free and
slave, shared a common need for democratic government. "If popular
sovereignty was permitted at the *North,* the precedent would be
dangerous to the *South,*" Goodell wrote. "If the disfranchised majority of
Rhode Island could form a Constitution without leave of their masters,
the disfranchised majority of S. Carolina might do the same, and the
'peculiar institution' would be overthrown."[17] Although no such alliance
materialized between the slave and the wage worker, Goodell's argument
foreshadowed the use that former slaves in South Carolina would make
of their voting rights to resist a reimposition of legal subjugation a quarter
of a century later.

After 1842 Rhode Island's political life came to resemble that of other
industrializing states. Its battle to open suffrage, however, had attracted
the support of labor reformers and of popular politicians throughout the
Northeast. Mike Walsh, the famous voice of New York City's Subterranean Democracy, armed his Spartan Band and marched to the aid of
the government installed by the People's Convention. Indeed, the prosecution at Dorr's treason trial depicted Walsh and New York's Tammany
Hall Democrats as the driving forces behind the rebellion. All the denun-
ciations of landed aristocracy and of popular disfranchisement that had
resounded in Jeffersonian circles during the 1790s had now become the
rhetorical stock-in-trade of the workers' movement. When young factory
operatives marched through the streets of Providence in March 1845 to
celebrate the end of the season of working late under candlelight, a local
correspondent reported, "The little devils would give three cheers for
'Liberation' [of Dorr], themselves just liberated for a brief season from
within the walls of the factory."[18]

16 Gettleman, 129–30; McDougall, 155–90.
17 William Goodell, *The Rights and Wrongs of Rhode Island* (*Christian Investigator,* No. 8,
   Whitesboro, N.Y., Sept. 1842). The quotations are on pages 16, 51.
18 McDougall; Joseph S. Pitman, *Report of the Trial of Thomas Wilson Dorr for Treason
   against the State of Rhode Island* (Boston, 1844), 10–35; *Providence Daily Gazette,* March
   24, 1845, quoted in Brennan, 48; Wilentz, 327–35.

The suffrage qualifications adopted by the "Landowners Convention" had retained property requirements for foreign-born men. During the 1850s Massachusetts, Pennsylvania, and other industrial states also imposed restrictions on the political rights of immigrants, such as residency requirements and literacy tests. In contrast to such midwestern states as Michigan, Illinois, and Wisconsin, where immigrant men who had simply declared their intention to become citizens swelled the electorate, New York, Pennsylvania, and Ohio required completed naturalization (usually taking five years from the filing of first papers). Chinese immigrants to California, who constituted fully one-fourth of the state's wage earners by the 1870s, were denied the possibility of becoming citizens at all by state legislation, and after 1882 by federal law. It was not lack of property that disqualified workers from voting in many states, but foreign birth or unsteady residence.[19]

As Walter Dean Burnham, Paul Kleppner, and other historians of American electoral behavior have noted, the years between the dramatic voter turnout of 1840 and the Bryan-McKinley campaign of 1896 stand out as the period of the consistently highest level of voting in the history of the country. Between 70 and 82 percent of all eligible males cast their ballots in every presidential election during the last six decades of the century. After 1870, black men constituted part of that eligible electorate, between 92 and 94 percent of adult males were citizens, and thousands of noncitizens in states outside of the Northeast could also cast their ballots. It was only between the mid-1890s and the mid-1920s that new literacy tests, poll taxes, lengthened residency qualifications, increasingly widespread preconditions of full citizenship, and requirements that prospective voters register in person sharply reduced the size of the electorate in both southern and northern states, significantly offsetting the expansion of the electorate through statewide, then federal, authorization of women's suffrage.[20]

One widespread restriction on voting rights is noteworthy, more for its symbolic meaning than for its effect on voter turnout. Both the People's Convention and the Landholders' Convention had barred "paupers and persons under guardianship" from voting. Most of the states that had neither property nor poll tax qualifications prohibited paupers from voting, either by explicit constitutional provision or, as in the case of Pennsylvania in 1877, by a ruling of the state supreme

19 Edna Bonacich, "Asian Labor in the Development of California and Hawaii," in Lucie Cheng and Edna Bonacich, eds., *Labor Immigration under Capitalism: Asian Workers in the United States before World War II* (Berkeley, 1984), 162–5.
20 Paul Kleppner, *Continuity and Change in Electoral Politics, 1893–1928* (Westport, Conn., 1987), 164–76. An excellent summary of voting participation and restrictions by Walter Dean Burnham can be found in Census, *Hist. Stat.*, vol. 2, 1067–72.

court.[21] Defined by the Massachusetts Supreme Court as "persons receiving aid and assistance from the public, under the provisions made by law for the support and maintenance of the poor," paupers owed their labor to the towns or counties that sustained them, and could be hired or even auctioned out to individual citizens by the selectmen.[22]

Public relief was a routine part of the income of the nineteenth-century urban poor, and aside from the privileged few, virtually any woman living away from a farm and without a man's income was impoverished. So dependent were antebellum women outworkers in the clothing trades on poor relief that, as Mathew Carey observed, outdoor relief payments fixed the level of women's wages.[23] Destitute or not, however, they were excluded from suffrage by virtue of being women. Moreover, by the 1870s most poor relief in larger urban areas had been taken out of the hands of elected governmental bodies by privately directed charities. Consequently, the important development that is revealed by the pauper exclusion is ideological: During the half-century following the Revolution a man's wage contract had taken its place alongside property ownership and race as a badge of participation in the polity.

By the time of the Dorr Rebellion the new mass electorate of urban areas was mobilized by Democratic, Whig, and American Republican (nativist) parties alike with exuberant pageantry, patriotic displays, vigilance committees that enlisted ordinary residents in the mustering of the faithful, and open physical combat to control polling places on election day. But the political culture practiced by all these parties bore the imprint of chattel slavery. All three parties appealed to southern and northern voters alike. All three celebrated the republic as a white man's commonwealth. African Americans were banned from their pageantry, except as occasional water carriers. Popular festivities and entertainments, which served in America and Europe alike as platforms for lampooning the wellborn, also provided occasions in this country for demeaning black neighbors as fit only to hew wood and draw water at the behest of whites. If they tried to join, or (more often) to stage similar festivities of their own, they invited assault by irate white mobs. Whites masqueraded in blackface even as they barred black participants, and the theme of white supremacy was widely broadcast from the hustings at workingmen's meetings by

21 McDougall, 98. The exceptions were Vermont, Kentucky, Tennessee, Indiana, Illinois, Michigan, and Missouri. Steinfeld, "Property and Suffrage," 353–4, n. 59.
22 Steinfeld, "Property and Suffrage," 374. The quotation is from an 1832 ruling of the Supreme Court, upon the request of the state senate. 28 Mass. (11 Pick.) at 540.
23 Stansell, 11–20; Mathew Carey, *Appeal to the Wealthy of the Land* (Philadelphia, 1833), 13–15.

such leaders as the exiled British Chartist John Campbell in Philadelphia and the Subterranean Democracy's tribune Mike Walsh in
New York.[24]

Edward Pessen has shown that before the 1840s, expansion of the
electorate brought little change, if any, in the elite status of mayors
and council members in major cities. Nevertheless, partisan mobilizations became a characteristic form of plebeian male sociability in both
urban and rural settings. "In 1840, when nearly two and a half million
American men voted, only 250,000 were enrolled in churches," writes
Jean Baker, "and throughout most of the nineteenth century, party
rallies were better attended than Sunday services or even meetings of
itinerant preachers." During the 1840s and 1850s master artisans and
small retailers, though not laborers, began to fill seats on city councils.
Although the most prominent merchants, bankers, and lawyers remained deeply involved in party affairs, they used local parties primarily as avenues of access to influence in national and state capitals,
and chose to shape local urban life increasingly through nongovernmental benevolent and reform associations.[25]

Moreover, when urban workers organized their own parades they
no longer appeared in their work garb, even when they were grouped
by trade unions, but in street clothes, increasingly difficult to distin-
guish in style from those of the middle classes. Public processions of
artisans dressed for and performing their work, which had been
characteristic of the late eighteenth-century civic pageantry, had
been reduced by the 1830s to employers' advertisements of their
wares. Workers celebrating or demanding their rights were attired as
citizens.[26]

Chicago's police historian John J. Flinn captured the symbolism of
workers in mufti in his description of the infectious spirit of the great
strike of 1877: "Workingmen who had no earthly cause to complain,
who could not call to mind a grievance, threw down their tools, tore

24 David R. Roediger, *The Wages of Whiteness: Race and the Making of the American Working
    Class* (London, 1991); Alexander Saxton, *The Rise and Fall of the White Republic: Class
    Politics and Mass Culture in Nineteenth Century America* (London, 1990); Jean H. Baker,
    Affairs of Party: The Political Culture of Northern Democrats in the Mid–Nineteenth Century
    (Ithaca, N.Y., 1983); Susan G. Davis, *Parades and Power: Street Theater in Nineteenth-Cen-
    tury Philadelphia* (Philadelphia, Pa., 1986), 46; Paul A. Gilje, *Road to Mobocracy:
    Popular Disorder in New York City, 1763–1834* (Chapel Hill, N.C., 1987), 153–8,
    162–70; Frank J. Webb, *The Garies and Their Friends* (London, 1857). On Campbell,
    see Roediger, 75; Laurie, 165.
25 Edward Pessen, "Who Governed the Nation's Cities in the 'Era of the Common
    Man'?" in Pessen, ed., *The Many-Faceted Jacksonian Era: New Interpretations* (Westport,
    Conn., 1977), 242–60; Baker, *Affairs*, 269; Bridges, 36, 75–6, 127. On benevolent
    associations see Chapter 2.
26 Davis, *Parades*, 124–44, 176; Wilentz, 87–93.

off their 'overalls,' snatched up their coats and hats, shook their clenched fists at their employers, and – joined the nearest mob."[27]

Despite the preponderance of rural influence in nineteenth-century state legislatures, therefore, political dynamics in industrializing America were different from those, for example, of Sweden, where smallholder dominance in parliament provided the only advocates of the interests of disfranchised urban workers. White wage earners in the United States were assiduously courted by urban politicians. To be sure, American workers had *not* secured the universal right to vote for which their European counterparts were still contending on the eve of World War I. Even though racial disqualifications were removed from northern states by the Fifteenth Amendment to the U.S. Constitution in 1870, foreign citizenship, failure to meet residency and poll tax requirements, and above all gender, sharply curtailed the working-class vote. This was true despite the high turnout of eligible voters historians have found during the last half of the century, and the prominence of manufacturing towns like Homestead, Pennsylvania, where workers occupied almost every local office. Jean-Claude Simon concluded that in the textile city of Lawrence, Massachusetts, only 15 percent of the population were registered voters in 1880.[28] The many residents of unincorporated company towns had no elected local government. As Leon Fink has shown, factory towns where labor reform parties won local control tended to be quickly erased from the map by state legislatures in the 1880s. Even before southern states had formally disfranchised them, thousands of rural black laborers were kept away from the polls by intimidation, or "bulldozing," as it was then called.[29]

Despite these barriers to voting, between two-thirds and three-fourths of the country's adult males cast ballots in every presidential election between 1872 and 1896. Male wage earners, white and black (by then), rural and urban, had become an important constituency

27 John J. Flinn, *History of the Chicago Police Force* (Chicago, 1887), 165.
28 Paul Krause, *The Battle for Homestead, 1880–1892: Politics, Culture, and Steel* (Pittsburgh, Pa., 1992); Jean-Claude Simon, "Textile Workers, Trade Unions, and Politics: Comparative Case Studies, France and the United States, 1885–1914," (Ph.D. diss., Tufts University, 1980), 35. See also David Montgomery, *The Fall of the House of Labor: The Workplace, the State, and American Labor Activism, 1865–1925* (New York, 1987), 167–9. Historical accounts of high voter participation have also noted that the turnout in urban areas was consistently lower than that in the countryside. See Paul Kleppner, *The Cross of Culture: A Social Analysis of Midwestern Politics, 1850–1900* (New York, 1970). On Sweden, see Birger Simonson, "Sweden," in van der Linden and Rojahn, vol. 1, 85–102.
29 Leon Fink, *Workingmen's Democracy: The Knights of Labor and American Politics* (Urbana, Ill., 1983), 82–8; Nell Irvin Painter, *Exodusters: Black Migration to Kansas after Reconstruction* (New York, 1976), 19–27.

that aspirants to political office had to court, and their right to vote was not denied because of their role as propertyless sellers of labor power, but rather predicated upon that role.

The Right to Quit

Hand in hand with working-class exercise of political rights came destruction of legal sanctions binding a worker to a particular employer. Testifying before a royal commission on trade unions at the very time Parliament was considering amendments to the British master-and-servant law, American iron manufacturer Abram Hewitt asserted, "I have never known a master to go to court" to force a worker back to a job he or she had quit. He considered enactment by a state legislature of a law allowing such action both politically impossible and "very undesireable."[30]

Master-and-servant law in Britain and the United States shared the same roots in the labor legislation of Tudor England. The law imposed criminal sanctions against workers who left their employment without the master's permission. Those sanctions applied to wage earners as well as to slaves, indentured servants, and apprentices.[31] In 1823 the British Parliament renewed the law's provision that abandoning work could lead to criminal prosecution before a justice of the peace and a sentence of up to three months at hard labor, after which the workers still owed their masters all contracted labor time. The new British law did, however, eliminate the magistrates' powers of supervision over conditions of employment, which had been part of the Elizabethan law but had lapsed into disuse. Daphne Simon has calculated that during the 1860s an average of ten thousand men and women in England and Wales were prosecuted each year for leaving their jobs, most of them agricultural laborers, household workers, miners, and workers in potteries and cutlery trades.[32]

During recent years a serious debate has developed among historians concerning just when and how criminal sanctions against quitting ("specific enforcement of labor contracts") came to an end in the United States. Robert J. Steinfeld has argued that the British law was applied in the North American colonies, and that its elimination after the Revolution was inseparably bound up with the demise of

30 U.K., *Parliamentary Sessional Papers, 1867*, xxxii, c 3952, "Fourth Report of the Commissioners Appointed to Inquire into the Organization and Rules of Trades Unions and Other Associations" (London, 1867), 10.

31 Albert Matthews, "Hired Man and Help," *Publications of the Colonial Society of Massachusetts*, 5 (Transactions, 1897, 1898), 234; Richard B. Morris, *Government and Labor in Early America* (New York, 1946), 1–18.

32 Daphne Simon, "Master and Servant," in John Saville, ed., *Democracy and the Labor Movement* (London, 1954), 160–200. The statistics on prosecutions are on p. 160.

indentured servitude – a process that involved almost half a century. Sharon Salinger, in the best recent study of indentured servitude, contends that the practice was quietly and gradually terminated not by any legal process, but rather by the drying up of demand for white men and women bound to long-term contracts, when an abundant supply of workers who could be engaged and dismissed at the employers' will became available. Christopher Tomlins takes quite a different approach. He asserts that colonial law did not follow that of England, that wage contracts were not specifically enforced in any British North American colony after 1700, and, indeed, that the doctrine of master and servant did appear in United States law as an *innovation* by commentators on the common law, which lent judicial sanction to the authority of industrial employers.[33]

There is evidence, not from the illustrious courts of record, but from the dockets of the mayor's courts and the prisons in Philadelphia and Baltimore, that can help us resolve this important controversy. Before reviewing that evidence, however, let us note that the arguments of all three historians bear witness to the coexistence of wage and bound labor in the early republic. Tomlins's point of departure is the broad discretion in the use of their own time and talents that was enjoyed by yeomen, mechanics, and those who engaged to work for wages from time to time. In contrast not only to their predecessors who had toiled under the Tudor Code, but also to their successors who would face the factory rules and vagrancy statutes of nineteenth-century America, and above all to black slaves, they were surely free men. Their lives provided the meaningful point of reference of Jeffersonian Republicanism.

At the same time, from New York southward the fields around them were often worked by slaves, and within the towns those men and women who had emigrated from the British Isles or German states had probably been purchased as indentured servants. During the 1750s, when a third of the urban work force was not free, master mechanics were more likely to employ a black slave (in New York) or a white indentured servant (in Philadelphia) in their shops than a free journeyman. By the 1790s, however, the great majority of the working people of both cities were neither owners of property nor the property of someone else. Sharon Salinger has calculated that there were but 422 indentured servants and 105 slaves in the city of Philadelphia by

33 Steinfeld, *Invention;* Sharon Salinger, *"To Serve Well and Faithfully": Labor and Indentured Servants in Pennsylvania, 1682–1800* (Cambridge, 1987); Christopher L. Tomlins, "Law, Labor and Ideology in Colonial and Antebellum America," paper presented at the 1992 meeting of the Organization of American Historians. This paper is a preview of Tomlins's forthcoming book, *Law, Labor and Ideology in the Early American Republic* (New York, 1993).

1795, and together they constituted only 4.3 percent of the work force. Nevertheless, city magistrates continued to be deeply involved in enforcing the subordination of bondspeople, apprentices, and seamen to their particular masters, while the municipal almshouse provided the city's first factory operatives, and vagrancy prosecutions threatened poor people who were simply too free – those who had no master of any kind. The disciplinary role of municipal authorities cast a long shadow over working-class life. It was to be reduced by popular struggles, only to rise again by midcentury in new forms.[34]

The records of the mayor's court and penitentiary of Philadelphia reveal that masters regularly resorted to legal incarceration to discipline their servants in the 1790s. The mayor was elected each year by the fifteen aldermen, who in turn had been chosen every other year by a ballot of the property owners. The mayor, clerk of the court, and aldermen all served as justices of the peace, and four times a year the mayor assembled with the clerk and two aldermen as a mayor's court to hear minor offenses. Offenses committed outside of the city limits were remanded by the mayor to a court of quarter sessions. If the defendant asked for a jury trial, a jury was impaneled from among the qualified citizens who were assembled in the courtroom. Usually the jurors heard evidence and reached a verdict on the spot. For example, "Ellen, a negress," was charged August 23, 1795, by her mistress, Maria Catherine Seneschal, with absconding from her service and stealing a shift and handkerchiefs, worth $118. At the September mayor's court a jury was sworn in. It found Ellen guilty of robbery, and she was sentenced to one year in prison, plus a fine of $118 and costs, which included the fees of the alderman, mayor, clerk, and the jury (a reason poor people seldom asked for a jury trial).[35]

Most disciplinary cases involving servants never went to court. Dozens of men and women were placed on the trial docket of the mayor's court by justices of the peace, charged with "absconding from the

34 Billy G. Smith, *The "Lower Sort": Philadelphia's Laboring People, 1750–1800* (Ithaca, N.Y., 1990), 140–2; Sharon V. Salinger, "Colonial Labor in Transition: The Decline of Indentured Servitude in Late Eighteenth-Century Philadelphia," *Labor History,* 22 (Spring 1981), 178–81; Richard B. Morris, "Labor Controls in Maryland in the Nineteenth Century," *Journal of Southern History,* 14 (Aug. 1948), 385–400.

35 G. S. Rowe and Billy G. Smith, "The Prisoners for Trial Docket for Philadelphia County, 1795," *Pennsylvania History,* 53 (Oct. 1986), 315; Mayor's Court of the City of Philadelphia, Appearance Docket, September Session, 1795, 392, Philadelphia City Archives, RG 20.2. On role of the mayor and courts, see Kenneth Roberts and Anna M. Roberts, *Moreau de St. Méry's American Journal [1793–1798]* (Garden City, N.Y., 1947), 359; G. S. Rowe, "Black Offenders, Criminal Courts, and Philadelphia Society in the Late Eighteenth Century," *Journal of Social History,* 22 (Summer 1981), 687–712; G. S. Rowe, "Women's Crime and Criminal Administration in Philadelphia, 1763–1790," *Pennsylvania Magazine of History and Biography,* 109 (June 1985), 335–68; Herbert William Keith Fitzroy, "Punishment of Crime in Provincial Pennsylvania," *Pennsylvania Magazine of History and Biography,* 60 (July 1936), 242–69.

service" of their masters. Others were accused of threatening, assaulting, or simply disobeying masters. Catherine Marks was held in
August, 1795, for "disorderly and outrageous behavior." Most such
individuals were committed to the penitentiary for "due course of
law." A committee of the prison board of inspectors, evidently
troubled by loose application of that term, asked the state's chief
justice, Thomas McKean, to define "the true construction of 'due
course of law,' in mittimus's [warrants of commitment to prison]
against disorderly servants." The justice answered that the servant
could be committed by a magistrate for no more than thirty days, and,
if recommitted, could be released by habeas corpus (though the judge
added that "if the Magistrate was waited on he would release them
without the trouble of Expense of a Habeas Corpus").[36] Quite often
offending servants were discharged into the custody of the master or
mistress after ten days or two weeks in jail, by the same justice of the
peace that had sent them to prison initially.

Unfortunately the trial dockets and prison records of Philadelphia do
not allow an unequivocal answer to whether or not wage workers who
were not bound by indentures were among those incarcerated for
"absconding." When the individuals brought before the mayor were
slaves, apprentices, or seamen, the records specify their status clearly, just
as African origins or descent were always noted. The trial dockets explicitly identified Louise Beutter and "John Walker, a negroe," among others,
as indentured. No doubt is left by the case of John McLean. He was
bound to Isaac Morton's service for eighteen months in 1795, but ran
away after ten days, at or about the same time that another of Morton's
indentured servants, Alice Cassady, also escaped. Both were brought
before magistrates. Cassady was sentenced to thirty days at hard labor for
vagrancy, then claimed by her master ten days before the end of the
sentence. McLean had two years added to his term of service for Morton,
but he ran away again and was subsequently held in the penitentiary for
more than five months before Morton took him out.[37]

In other instances, although those who were incarcerated were
adults, their legal status was not clear; most of them were clearly not
children. Joseph Butcher was charged with absconding from his master's service for upwards of four weeks; Charles Keopping was held six
weeks before being released to the master whom he was charged with
assaulting and deserting; and James Sutter was held for five days

36 Rowe and Smith, 316; "Report of the Committee to wait on the Chief Justice,"
    appended to first page of Philadelphia County Prison, Prisoners for Trial Docket,
    March 1790 to December 1797 (Philadelphia Archives, RG 38.39).
37 Mayor's Court Docket, 1790–1797, 232, 242, 399; Philadelphia Prison Vagrants
    Docket, May 31, 1790 to Dec. 29, 1797. Inspectors of the Jail and Penitentiary
    House, County Prison (RG 38), 308.

accused of "having frequently absconded from his Master Abraham Morrow," yet no mention of indentures appears in the records of these cases. Perhaps "indentured" was simply assumed by the clerk when he wrote the word "servant." Perhaps not.

In those few instances where servants were formally indicted before a trial court, the accusations specified were theft, disorder, and assault, with no mention of the words "absconded . . . and . . . ," which had, however, appeared on the mayor's trial docket. It is evident that many people charged were household workers, and the French writer Moreau de St. Méry, who devoted close attention to the role of magistrates in forcing servants to work, wrote in 1795 that the difficulty of employing white household workers in Philadelphia meant that "they are almost all indentured servants." Moreover, the gradual emancipation act of 1780 and the recent influx of white refugees from Saint Domingue accompanied by their slaves had led to a major increase in long-term indentures of black servants.[38]

To complicate matters for the historian, there was more than one way to enforce performance of labor contracts through the jail. The vagrancy dockets kept by twelve inspectors of the county prison were replete with names of servants incarcerated for disobeying or absconding from their masters. Commitments for vagrancy were made by justices of the peace, usually for one month, and they often specified either hard labor or solitary confinement. President George Washington had two of his servants, Wilhelmina Tyser and Martin Cline, imprisoned as vagrants for misbehavior. Because masters had to pay the costs of confinement, they often had their servants released before the term was finished (though McLean's master kept him there for more than five months). More than one person was bounced back and forth between vagrancy charges and the mayor's court, as McLean and Cassady had been. In either case the accused was kept, by order of a justice of the peace, in the penitentiary, which also served as the prison for most of the state's convicts. Thus in 1795 the 285 prisoners, whom a visiting investigator found "kept in awe" by a small staff of five men, included only 90 people who had been convicted by formal trials. The other 195 had been committed by magistrates, for "due course of law" or for vagrancy.[39]

38 Prisoners for Trial Docket, 1790–1797, 225, 291, 295; Rowe and Smith; Roberts and Roberts, 293–6. The quotation is on p. 293.
39 Vagrants Docket, May 31, 1790 to Dec. 29, 1797; Smith, "Lower Sort," 24; François Alexandre Frédéric, duc de La Rochefoucault-Liancourt, On the Prisons of Philadelphia (Philadelphia, 1796), 33, 34; Caleb Lownes, An Account of the Alteration and Present State of the Penal Laws of Pennsylvania, also, an Account of the Gaol and Penitentiary House of Philadelphia (Boston, 1799).

If incarceration for absconding and for vagrancy made city officials
instruments for the enforcement of the personal subordination of
some workers to their own particular masters in the Philadelphia of
the 1790s, poor relief provided another. The practice of consigning
people from the poor rolls to long-term indentures with individuals
who would purchase them had a long history. It is not surprising to
find in the records of the Philadelphia almshouse for July 7, 1800, the
entry: "Bound Mary Brown, a Black child to Matthew Carey of this
City, Printer, to serve him twelve years and six months as per indenture
of this date." A week later William Barton, who had been two years in
the almshouse, was bound to work fifteen years for a weaver in Montgomery County.[40]

It was from the poor rolls that Philadelphia drew the labor force
for its first postrevolutionary experiments with textile factories.
The Pennsylvania Society for the Encouragement of Manufactures
and Useful Arts, which was capitalized by private subscription in
1787, initially engaged women who had applied for winter relief to
spin flax in their homes, and it later established a manufactory
where women were taught to run spinning jennies. One of the
subscribers was John Nicholson, the master who sent Catherine
Marks to jail for two days for "disorderly & outrageous behavior."
The new factory burned down under suspicious circumstances in
1790, only to be replaced by a more ambitious enterprise. A manufacturing committee of the Guardians of the Poor solicited funds
from "patriotic individuals," who could obtain the "profits or interest on the capital" by putting the county's resident paupers to work
hackling flax and spinning in nearby Manayunk. The paupers
received no pay unless they exceeded production quotas, which
were regularly adjusted to meet market conditions, while women
on outdoor relief spun at home on a piecework basis. Artisan
weavers and stockingers were hired for wages and provided board
in the almshouse, though they often rebelled at the stigma that
residence entailed.[41]

In the Philadelphia region, as was often the case in continental
Europe, the first women in textile factories were paupers, toiling
under the supervision of almshouse guards (or nuns in Catholic
countries), and subject to punishment if they "eloped" from their
confinement. The connection between early manufacturing enterprises and the poorhouse helps us understand the antipathy felt by
many working people toward factories in the early nineteenth cen-

40 Billy G. Smith and Cynthia Shelton, "The Daily Occurrence Docket of the Philadelphia Almshouse: Selected Entries, 1800," *Pennsylvania History,* 52 (April 1985), 96,
   101.
41 Shelton, 37–46; Rowe and Smith, 316.

tury.[42] As Cynthia J. Shelton has demonstrated in her excellent
history of Manayunk, after 1811, even though the Guardians of the
Poor still put out flax for spinning by indigent women, the poorhouse could not compete with the small, mechanized spinning
mills that had sprung up in the region employing wage labor, or
with the immigrant handloom weavers. The number of people
applying for relief spiraled upward steadily through the 1810s and
1820s, generating the controversy over outdoor relief that will be
discussed in the next chapter, but factory production had moved
decisively out of the almshouse.

Free Labor in the Shadow of Slavery

In contrast to England, where specific enforcement of contracts was
reinforced by the master-and-servant law of 1823, therefore, indentured servitude and confined pauper labor in the United States were
eroded from two directions: by the competitive supremacy of wage
labor in industry and by the revulsion against direct, personal subordination of worker to master that fed – and in turn fed upon – the
Jeffersonian upheaval in politics. As long as chattel slavery (the most
draconic form of specific enforcement) flourished, however, indentured servitude also maintained a desultory existence.

Even in England, as Daphne Simon has shown, criminal sanctions against workers who quit were levied mostly in agriculture and
in the more backward sectors of mining and manufacturing, and
not in such technologically advanced sectors as textile factories,
which relied for discipline, like their American counterparts, on
monetary sanctions, dismissals, and blacklists. After the War of
1812, migrants from Britain and especially from Germany, who
continued to be marketed in significant numbers in the port of
Philadelphia, were virtually all sold to *rural* employers – for labor in
the fields, within households, or on construction projects. Their
status was recognized by reforms adopted by the state legislature by
1818, requiring schooling for servants' children and inhibiting the
separation of families and the sale of servants outside of the state.
Although the number of incarcerations for "absconding" in Philadelphia declined after 1800, it rose again during 1819 and 1820. As
late as 1833 the trial dockets revealed three men, all with Irish

42 See Michelle Perrot, "The Three Ages of Industrial Discipline in Nineteenth-Century
France," in John M. Merriman, ed., *Consciousness and Class Experience in Nineteenth-Century Europe* (New York, 1979), 149–68; Fernand Braudel, *Civilization and Capitalism,
15th–18th Century* (3 vols., translated by Sian Reynolds, New York, 1981–4), vol. 2,
297–342; Nell Kull, ed., "'I Never Can Be Happy In There Among So Many Mountains':
The Letters of Sally Rice," *Vermont History,* 38 (Winter 1970), 49–57.

names, charged with absconding from their masters in the months of July and August alone.[43]

Next door in Maryland, where Richard B. Morris found "white absentee employees [on occasion] jailed without specifying whether they were apprentices, ordinary indentured servants, or hired hands," specific enforcement continued to flourish in the countryside. Maryland's large population of free African Americans was enmeshed in long-term labor contracts, apprenticeships, sales for jail fees as vagrants, and agreements made by slaves to long indentures as the price of manumission. In 1854 the legislature explicitly levied criminal sanctions against black workers who absconded from labor contracts.[44]

In the Middle West, the famous prohibition of slavery and involuntary servitude contained in the Northwest Ordinance of 1787 had been partially circumvented as early as 1803 by a law of what was then the Indiana Territory making indentures specifically enforceable in court and assignable by sale or testament. The law also authorized disobedient or lazy servants to be "corrected by stripes on order from a justice of the county." Two years later, masters were permitted to bring in slaves, provided they signed indentures within thirty days. In Indiana and Illinois, as in Pennsylvania, New York, and Maryland, the case law dealing with specific enforcement arose largely out of disputes involving the indenture of former slaves. One such case in Indiana produced a resounding affirmation of a wage worker's freedom to quit. But next door in Illinois courts continued to enforce indentures with criminal sanctions until about 1850.[45]

In the northern cities the steady disappearance of journeymen residing within the households of employing artisans, the substitution of day-to-day money wages for board and services provided by the master's wife ("found"), and the large influx of immigrant journeymen after 1790 had undermined the eighteenth-century reliance of Philadelphia's artisans on indentured whites and of New York's ar-

43 Simon, "Master and Servant"; Cheesman A. Herrick, *White Servitude in Pennsylvania: Indentured and Redemption Labor in Colony and Commonwealth* (Philadelphia, 1926), 263–4; Philadelphia Prison, Prisoners for Trial Docket, Oct. 21, 1831, to Jan. 28, 1834 (Philadelphia Archives, RG 38.38), 515, 537. Sharon V. Salinger's otherwise excellent study of indentured servitude, *"To Serve Well and Faithfully,"* leaves the impression that the trade had virtually ended by 1803 and that only a few Germans trickled in thereafter.

44 Morris, "Labor Controls in Maryland," 385–400; Barbara Jeanne Fields, *Slavery and Freedom on the Middle Ground: Maryland during the Nineteenth Century* (New Haven, Conn., 1985), 67–82.

45 Howard D. Hamilton, "The Legislative and Judicial History of the Thirteenth Amendment," *National Bar Journal*, 9 (March 1951), 26–134; David Brion Davis, "The Significance of Excluding Slavery from the Old Northwest," *Indiana Magazine of History*, 84 (March 1988), 75–89; Helen T. Catterall, *Judicial Cases Concerning American Slavery and the Negro* (5 vols., Washington, D.C., 1936), vol. 4.

tisans on black slaves. In New York City, where the owning of slaves had been remarkably equally distributed throughout the white population before the Revolution, most slaves of 1800 were found in households of the wealthy, and bondspeople still employed by artisans had declined to only 18 percent of the total. White artisans, laborers, and household workers alike vociferously objected to being called "servants" and to physical punishments, which they considered badges of servitude.[46]

Both chattel slavery in its New York and New Jersey agricultural strongholds and indentured servitude on Pennsylvania and Maryland farms were plagued with runaways and with (often successful) efforts of bondspeople to negotiate better terms with their owners. Shane White's study of the decline of slavery in New York has produced evidence of many black slaves negotiating their way to freedom through long-term indentures, especially after the enactment of the gradual manumission law of 1799. Subsequently, a number of those men and women challenged those indentures in court, often with the aid of antislavery societies. A prestigious counsel's argument of 1812 in Pennsylvania unequivocally excluded wage earners from specific enforcement by confining the use of the term "servant" in the state's law to "imported servants and people of colour, bound to serve to the age of twenty-eight" (in compliance with the emancipation act of 1780). Simultaneously, popular antipathy toward bondage for white people created difficulties for owners who sought to enforce the terms of indentures.[47]

In Pennsylvania the electoral victory of the state's Democratic-Republicans in 1799 opened two tumultuous decades of public controversy over democratization of government, selection of judicial officials, and the place of common law in the judicial system. In 1810 the legislature prohibited the citation in court of any court decisions or legal commentaries produced in England after July 4, 1776, and by 1822 the revolutionary émigré John Binns was to be found among the magistrates of Philadelphia. Although master-and-servant law never figured prominently in the state's debates over the legacy of British common law, it is evident that incarcerations of servants for absconding from their masters had virtually disappeared from the city's trial dockets by 1801, then made a resurgence after 1816, only to dwindle to occasional cases by the

46 Shane White, *Somewhat More Independent: The End of Slavery in New York City, 1770–1810* (Athens, Ga., 1991), 27–55. On found labor see Blackmar, 57–9, 62. On objections to "servants," see Matthews, 233–4; Alfred F. Young, "The Mechanics and the Jeffersonians: New York, 1789–1801," *Labor History,* 5 (Fall 1964), 247–76.
47 White, 47–50, 107–48; Catterall, 4, 256–318, 355–402. The quotation is from *Ex parte Meason*, 5 Binney 167, in Catterall, 4, 271.

1830s. All the while the numbers of men and women picked up by night watchmen or brought before magistrates by residents and charged with vagrancy, disorderly conduct, lewd conduct, and prostitution grew. In 1819 city authorities appear to have launched a campaign against idleness and vice. Many disobedient or absconding indentured servants, clearly identified as such, were locked up in the dragnet, though most were quickly released again to their masters. Nevertheless, they were far outnumbered by those confined for thirty days as "strolling vagrants," idle drunkards, or homeless.[48]

Institutionalized forms of social discipline predicated upon wage labor were decisively displacing the personal subordination of servant to master, except where that subordination appeared in its most extreme form: chattel slavery. Philadelphia's temperance pamphleteer James W. Alexander lamented, "Insubordination, radicalism, and a false and impracticable theory of equal rights, have destroyed the gentle authority which used to exist."[49] Even indentures of apprentices, he said, had become but "a mere formality." The memoirs of ship carpenter Frank Harley lend a more positive evaluation to the same phenomenon and suggest that hostility to indentures of any kind was not uncommon among artisans of the 1830s. When Harley was hired by "Boss Sneeded" in a New York ship yard, it was the boss who said: "I don't want any binding indentures, and all that sort of thing. When I don't like you, or you don't like me, we'll quit and separate. Master and man, or man and wife had always better cut a drift when they get to quarreling."[50]

The embattled persistence of indentured servitude is revealed by the experiences of Ludwig Gall – ironically, a German follower of Fourier who came to Pennsylvania in 1819 in search of a site for a phalanstery. Gall brought twelve servants with him. When they arrived in Philadelphia, Gall recorded:

48 Sylvester K. Stevens, *Pennsylvania: Birthplace of a Nation* (New York, 1964), 168–71; John Milton Goodenow, *Historical Sketches of the Principles and Maxims of American Jurisprudence, in Contrast with the Doctrines of English Common Law on the Subject of Crimes and Punishments* (Steubenville, Ohio, 1819), 424n; Perry Miller, ed., *Legal Mind in America: From Independence to the Civil War* (Garden City, N.Y., 1962); Philadelphia Prisoners for Trial Docket, March 17, 1796, to March 5, 1802 (RG 38.38); Prisoners for Trial Docket, Feb. 1, 1819, to March 2, 1821 (RG 38.38); Prison Vagrant Docket, June 1, 1817, to July 12, 1822; Philadelphia Society for Alleviating the Miseries of Public Prisons, *A Statistical View of the Operation of the Penal Code of Pennsylvania* (Philadelphia, 1819).

49 Charles Quill [pseud.], *The Working-Man* (Philadelphia, 1839), 115. In 1837 the Pennsylvania Supreme Court also ruled that black people could be "free as the winds," and still be "unsafe depositories of popular power." *Hobbes et al.* v. *Fogg*, 6 Watts 553 at 558, in Catterall, 4, 289.

50 "Chips," *Fincher's Trades Review*, Jan. 27, 1866.

They had scarcely come ashore when they were greeted as countrymen by people who told them that contracts signed in Europe were not binding here; . . . that they were free as birds here; that they didn't have to pay for their passage, and nobody would think ill of them if they used the money instead to toast the health of their European masters. . . . The last scoundrel said: "Follow me, dear countrymen; don't let yourselves be wheedled away into the wilderness."[51]

Gall resorted to the threat of debtors' prison to make his "companions" repay their passage. He brought one defiant servant before a justice of the peace and had him incarcerated, only to discover that he (Gall) had to pay the prisoner's maintenance, and a late payment the second week set the man free. Although that servant seems to have enjoyed his stay with a "boisterous group" of three hundred debtors, vagrants, and other victims of that year's draconic arrests, who "formed their own little republic" in the Walnut Street prison, the other eleven were persuaded by the threat of jail to indenture themselves to Gall for three to four years in return for Gall's promise to pay them ten dollars a year.

Gall's troubles did not end there. His anxiety to rush the servants out of the city before they learned the ways of American life was well founded: Five men whom he had boarded apart from his family deserted him the day he left Philadelphia. The remaining servants made Gall cut short his westward journey in Harrisburg. Five days after his departure from Philadelphia, he wrote: "Two of my servants deserted me between Montjoie and here [Harrisburg]; and my choice was to continue the journey with hired help, whom I should have to pay $2 a day, or stay here perforce." He rented "a pretty country house" with thirty-six tillable acres, "precisely as much as the [one man and two women] who remained true to me can care for with two horses."

Alas, the remaining man did not "remain true" for long. He soon demanded a seat at the family table and good Sunday suit, and, on Gall's refusal, absconded. A neighborhood farmer captured the man and had him jailed by the justice of the peace. From prison the man spent six weeks negotiating the terms of his own release while Gall paid his maintenance. His prison had cards, whiskey, and in fact, growled Gall, "Methodists with a misplaced love of humanity supplied him and his fellows with an abundance of food and drink. . . . Indeed, everything was in vain. In the end I had to let the fellow go."

51 Frederic Trautman, "Pennsylvania Through a German's Eyes: The Travels of Ludwig Gall, 1819–1820," *Pennsylvania Magazine of History and Biography*, 105 (Jan. 1981), 40.

Just to rub it in, the "French-speaking Swiss immigrant" whom Gall hired in the servant's place threatened to drag Gall before a justice of the peace for asking him to feed the horses on Sunday (in violation of state Sabbath laws). Gall settled out of court, paying the hired man half the anticipated fine.[52]

The Chesapeake and Ohio Canal Company reproduced Gall's experiences on a larger scale when it brought some five hundred laborers from Ireland in 1829 only to have them depart for Baltimore or to nearby railroad construction where higher wages were available. The indentures had been for very short terms (six months or less) and applicants had flocked to sign up with the company's agents in Manchester, England, but no sooner were they in Maryland than they began to drift away. Prosecution of the runaways proved prohibitively costly to the company, and juries refused to convict the workers. Even a federal judge willing to enforce Maryland's 1715 statute against runaway servants acknowledged that bound wage labor was "opposed to the principles of our free institutions and . . . repugnant to our feelings." Incessant expansion and contraction of the labor force and the chronic inability of labor contractors to meet their payrolls made the canal the scene of ten major conflicts between 1834 and 1840, and troops often patrolled the work camps. Nevertheless, no worker faced imprisonment for breach of contract, as they would have risked in England.[53]

The repugnance felt by Maryland's federal judge had been written into law by the Indiana Supreme Court in an 1821 ruling, *The case of Mary Clark, a woman of color.* The case was brought by a free black woman in a free state, whose master made the familiar claim that she had bound herself voluntarily in 1816 "to serve him as an indented servant and house-maid for 20 years." When her suit for habeas corpus was denied by a lower court, Clark appealed to the state supreme court, which set her free with the resounding declaration that no one but apprentices, soldiers, and sailors could be subjected to criminal prosecution for deserting a job in violation of a contract. Because a contract for service "must be performed under the eye of the master" and might "require a number of years," enforcement of such performance by law "would produce a state of servitude as degrading and demoralizing in its consequences, as a state of absolute slavery."[54]

Although legal commentaries soon began to quote *The case of Mary Clark,* it did not appeared frequently as a cited precedent until after

52 Ibid. The quotations are on pp. 41n, 57n, 55, 60, and 62–3.
53 Steinfeld, *Invention,* 166–8, 246–7. The quotation from Judge Cranch is on p. 268. On the strikes, see Peter Way, "Shovel and Shamrock: Irish Workers and Labor Violence in the Digging of the Chesapeake and Ohio Canal," *Labor History,* 30 (Fall 1989), 489–517.
54 *The case of Mary Clark, a woman of color.* 1 Blackford 122 (Ind., 1821) at 124–5.

the Civil War. In fact, we have noted that indentures were specifically enforced in Pennsylvania, Maryland, and Illinois many years after the Indiana decision. What the Indiana case did reveal, however, is that by the second quarter of the nineteenth century the paradigm for judicial consideration of labor was being recast to suit the new economic realities: It recognized workers, who were free to quit and whom employers could dismiss at will, and it recognized slaves, who were bound to servitude for life, as were their offspring. It was, therefore, the overthrow of slavery itself that produced the decisive final round of struggle against specific enforcement of labor contracts.

After the Thirteenth Amendment had prohibited slavery or involuntary servitude throughout the land, the former Confederate States adopted Black Codes – labor codes applying specifically to African Americans, whose central feature was the imposition of criminal prosecution for those who failed to sign one-year labor contracts, or who left a job after they had signed such a contract. The codes evoked a vigorous reaction, first from black southerners and then from the federal Congress. "I hope soon to be called a citizen of the U.S. and have the rights of a citizen," a black soldier from South Carolina had written in 1866. "I am opposed myself to working under a contract. I am as much at liberty to hire a White man to work as he to hire me, I expect to stay in the South after I am mustered out of service, but not to hire myself to a planter."[55]

Senator Henry Wilson of Massachusetts charged that the codes made "the freedmen servants . . . and the persons for whom they labor . . . their masters, [and] the relation between them shall be master and servant." He supported the 1866 Civil Rights Act, and subsequently the Fourteenth Amendment to the Constitution, both of which nullified contractual requirements of the Black Codes and put in their place principles of "freedom of contract" to regulate both economic and family life throughout the United States. Even Senator Edgar Cowen of Pennsylvania, who opposed the remedial federal legislation, argued that if a southern legislature "declared that a contract for the performance of labor can be specifically performed, . . . such a law is clearly void." When Abram Hewitt told the British parliament during the same year that such a master-and-servant law as England had would be both politically impossible and "very undesireable" in the United States, he spoke for both political parties.[56] The promise

55 Melton R. Linton to *South Carolina Leader*, March 31, 1866, quoted in Gerald D. Jaynes, *Branches without Roots: Genesis of the Black Working Class in the American South, 1862–1882* (New York, 1986), 73.
56 The Wilson and Cowen quotations are from Lee S. VanderVelde, "The Labor Vision of the Thirteenth Amendment," *University of Pennsylvania Law Review*, 138 (Dec. 1989), 489. On Hewitt, see this chapter, n. 28.

sought by the black soldier, of equal application of the principle of employment at will, had become the law of the land. Its practical significance for the daily lives of southern rural workers provides an especially dramatic illustration of the dialectic of democracy and the law of wage labor, and will receive close attention in the final chapter.

The demise of master-and-servant law coincided with the gradual abolition of imprisonment for debt and of distress suits by landlords against their tenants. In both cases political mobilizations and individual acts of defiance by working people helped spur state legislatures into action, but the shape of the laws that replaced the hated practices was determined by new propertied interests. Debtors' prison was a very real menace to the urban poor of the early nineteenth century. Defaulting debtors in Pennsylvania had to spend at least thirty days in jail, with their keep paid by the creditor. After that debtors could sue for relief, even if they had not yet paid what they owed.

Peter Coleman has calculated that the courts of Philadelphia received an average of seven hundred and fifty such petitions each year between 1822 and 1830, most of them for petty claims against poor artisans and laborers – claims that often ran to as little as sixty cents, and in one famous case of 1830, two cents. The rapid growth of the wage-earning population stimulated not only demands for abolition of debtors' prison, but also powerful opposition to those demands, especially from the vast network of petty creditors with whom working people dealt. Consequently, long after the U.S. Supreme Court had sanctioned state bankruptcy laws and the abolition of imprisonment for debt, the practice continued vigorously in the industrializing regions. By that time, however, more than one creditor agreed with Ludwig Gall that to improve their own bargaining position, debtors often used partisan justices of the peace and the creditors' obligation to pay their board in prison. Pennsylvania abolished debt imprisonment in 1842, and Massachusetts's Know-Nothing–dominated legislature followed suit in 1857. The new state bankruptcy laws took years to enact because they were painstakingly fashioned around the difficult problems of balancing the claims of various creditors and securing at least partial repayment through the reclaiming of consumer goods and garnishment of wages.[57]

Under the common law doctrine of distress, landlords were entitled to seize tenants' personal property for nonpayment of rent. When, for example, Ann Adams of Philadelphia, who was about to give birth to

---

57 Peter J. Coleman, *Debtors and Creditors in America: Insolvency, Imprisonment for Debt, and Bankruptcy, 1607–1900* (Madison, Wis., 1974), 147–54. For an argument minimizing the significance of debt imprisonment, see Edwin T. Randall, "Imprisonment for Debt in America: Fact or Fiction," *Mississippi Valley Historical Review,* 39 (June 1952), 89–102.

her second child in 1803, was deserted by her husband, the landlord seized all her possessions in lieu of rent, forcing her to move into the almshouse. The practice generated fierce controversies in New York City, where popular politicians helped tenants bring charges of assault and battery against landlords who had broken in and seized belongings, and the Anti-Rent War of upstate farmers against the patroons' estates evoked vigorous political campaigns in the city against landlords' powers, encouraged by the spellbinding oratory of Democrat Mike Walsh. Last but hardly least, manufacturers protested that materials and tools they had let to outworkers were seized by landlords through distress claims. A state law of 1846 abolished landlords' rights of distress. In its place the law made eviction orders easier to obtain in court and reduced the required notice for eviction to one month. The reform accelerated landlords' actions against urban tenants, but also against farm tenants, who had been accustomed to leases of six months or a year, based on the seasons of farming.[58]

In each case, therefore, physical or criminal sanctions were replaced by monetary ones, and whatever remained of the reciprocal obligations the master, creditor, or dwelling owner had owed the worker died also. Inequality and coercive power that had rested, in Cornelius Blatchly's familiar words, on "ancient usurpation, tyranny, and conquest" was replaced by that of the "free market."[59] The triumphant legal principle was the one repeated by the Tennessee Supreme Court in 1884: "Either party may terminate the service, for any cause, good or bad, or without cause, and the other cannot complain in law."[60]

Quitting and Getting Paid

In practice and in law the relationship between worker and employer had become one in which the use of one person's ability to work was purchased by another for money. Monetary sanctions also became the instrument for enforcing discipline on the job and for holding workers to

58 Billy G. Smith and Cynthia Shelton, "The Daily Occurrence Docket of the Philadelphia Almshouse: Selected Entries, 1800–1804," *Pennsylvania History,* 52 (July 1985), 198; Blackmar, 217–25. On Walsh, see Wilentz, 327–35.

59 Cornelius C. Blatchly, *Some Causes of Popular Poverty, Arising from the Enriching Nature of Interest, Rents, Duties, Inheritances, and Church Establishments. Investigated in Their Principles and Consequences* (Philadelphia, 1817), 198, quoted in David Harris, *Socialist Origins in the United States: American Forerunners of Marx, 1817–1842* (Assen, Netherlands, 1966), 13. Another component of the decline of traditional subordination was the outlawing of flogging at sea in the 1830s. For an eloquent defense of flogging, see Robert S. Forbes, *An Appeal to Merchants and Ship Owners on the Subject of Seamen* (Boston, 1854).

60 *Payne* v. *The Western Atlantic Railroad Company,* 81 Tenn. 507 at 517. The case is condensed in Matthew W. Finkin, Alvin L. Goldman, and Clyde W. Summers, *Legal Protection for the Individual Employee* (St. Paul, Minn., 1989), 10–14. It involved a railroad manager who dismissed workers that traded at a store banned by company rules.

the terms of their contracts. Employers in agriculture and in industry as well as the legal profession elaborated new monetary sanctions during the decades when indentured servitude was disintegrating.

It is noteworthy that most of the cases involving breach of labor contract by workers that came before the courts between the 1820s and the 1850s concerned farm laborers.[61] They were the classic "servants" to whom the English law had primarily been addressed, hired on long-term (usually annual) agreements, boarded in the household of the farmer, and pursuing such tasks as were assigned to them with the varying seasons. The man who advised Gall's servants against being "wheedled into the wilderness" knew well that virtually all redemptioners who arrived in Philadelphia by 1819 were immediately dispatched westward to farms, where they had provided the labor force for a century past.[62] Quite different was the practice in eighteenth-century New England, where most "hired hands" were sons or daughters of neighboring freeholders, and expected one day to come into farms of their own; meanwhile, they were integrated into the life of the towns by bonds of kinship. By the 1850s, however, enough young people had migrated west or to urban life that citizens became older and laborers became aliens. The Middlesex Society of Husbandmen and Manufacturers lamented in 1851, "The sons of our farmers are looked for in vain upon the old homesteads; and in their places we find *foreigners* assisting the *father* in the ordinary business of the farm."[63]

In the newer farming regions from Ohio westward to Iowa, the number of laborers hired for seasonal work or for particular tasks (like breaking ground and digging wells) swelled steadily, many of them wintered in towns, and those who resided in farmers' households found their work intensified (for example, by providing indoor work or deducting pay for rainy days) and their conduct increasingly sub-

61 See Steinfeld, *Invention;* Christopher L. Tomlins, "The Ties that Bind: Master and Servant in Massachusetts, 1800–1850," *Labor History,* 30 (Spring 1989), 193–227; Finkin, Goldman, and Summers, 1–15; Wythe Holt, "Recovery by the Worker Who Quits: A Comparison of the Mainstream, Legal Realist, and Critical Legal Studies Approaches to a Problem of Nineteenth Century Contract Law," *Wisconsin Law Review,* 4 (1986), 677–732.
62 Salinger, *"To Serve Well and Faithfully";* Trautman; Marcus Lee Hansen, *The Atlantic Migration, 1607–1860: A History of the Continuing Settlement of the United States* (New York, 1961), 50–5, 103–5; Frances Wright, *Views of Society and Manners in America,* edited by Paul R. Baker (Cambridge, Mass., 1963), 240–3.
63 Richard S. Dunn, "Servants and Slaves: The Recruitment and Employment of Labor," in Jack P. Greene and J. R. Pole., eds., *Colonial British America: Essays in the History of the Early Modern Era* (Baltimore, 1984),183–8; Middlesex Society of Husbandmen and Manufacturers, *Transactions,* 1851 (Lowell, Mass., 1851), 24. See also Hal S. Barron, *Those Who Stayed Behind: Rural Society in Nineteenth-Century New England* (New York, 1984); Harold F. Wilson, *The Hill Country of Northern New England: Its Social and Economic History, 1790–1930* (New York, 1936); LaWanda F. Cox, "The American Agricultural Wage Earner, 1865–1900," *Agricultural History,* 22 (April 1948), 95–114.

ject to evangelical discipline. By the 1870s more than ten thousand men worked the fields of the Iowa-Minnesota-Wisconsin region as day laborers. During that decade and the next, however, the combined impact of falling prices for agricultural staples and rapid mechanization of wheat farming drove smallholders to intensify their own work, while the wage labor of Germans, Norwegians, and Swedes became increasingly concentrated on large units.[64]

The influential Massachusetts Supreme Judicial Court decision of 1824, *Stark* v. *Parker*, established the basis on which the legal status of these workers was erected until the employment of day workers made it obsolete in many regions. Although neither the court nor the farmer's attorney in this case charged the absconding laborer with a criminal offense, the justices ruled his claim to wages corresponding to the months he had actually worked a "monstrous absurdity" and especially dangerous in "this commonwealth . . . where the important business of husbandry leads to multiplied engagements of precisely this description." Only "upon the performance of his contract, and as the reward of fidelity" was "the labourer worthy of his hire," that is, legally entitled to payment for any of the work done. The court explained, "Nothing can be more unreasonable than that a man, who deliberately and wantonly violates an engagement, should be permitted to seek in a court of justice an indemnity from the consequences of his voluntary act."[65]

The converse of the workers' freedom to quit at the cost only of lost wages was that the employer owed him or her nothing but wages for work properly performed. Court rulings and prestigious commentaries on the common law agreed that the employer had no obligation to retain or nurse an incapacitated farm laborer, and that no legal distinction existed between one type of hired worker and another. In the words of Connecticut's supreme court: A hired servant is a hired servant, "whether that servant is employed in husbandry, in manufacturing business, or in any other manner."[66]

---

64 David E. Schob, *Hired Hands and Plowboys: Farm Labor in the Midwest, 1815–60* (Urbana, Ill., 1975), 111–48, 222–57; Richard Mahon, "Wage Labor and Seasonal Migration in the Wheat Belt of the Upper Mississippi Valley, 1860–1875" (unpublished paper presented to the Chicago Area Labor History Group, Dec. 9, 1988, cited by permission of author); Cox, 105–6, 114.

65 19 Mass. (2 Pick.) 267, at 273, 275, 276. This case appears as the centerpiece of most historical discussions of employment at will. The opposing precedent of New Hampshire courts in *Britten* v. *Turner*, 6 New Hampshire 481 (1834), was seldom followed by any courts, according to Holt, "Recovery," 682–9. For the contrary argument that the New Hampshire ruling was widely favored by courts and commentaries from the 1840s onward, see Peter Karsten, "'Bottomed on Justice': A Reappraisal of Critical Legal Studies Scholarship Concerning Breaches of Labor Contracts by Quitting or Firing in Britain and the U.S., 1630–1880," *American Journal of Legal History*, 34 (1990), 233–6.

66 Steinfeld, *Invention*, 147–72; *Matthews* v. *Terry*, 10 Conn. 455, 458–9 (1835).

Long term contracts were signed and enforced in industry, as well as on the farm. The pattern of agreements to work for a full year that prevailed in Lowell was common in the textile mills of northern New England during the 1830s and 1840s, and it provoked appeals to the state legislature to "Stay the Hands of our persecutors," when operatives faced wage cuts during the course of the contract, and blacklisting if they quit.[67] When labor was in short supply, however, workers who had quit in violation of their contracts were readily rehired, even at the Hamilton Company in Lowell. A worker in Waltham had written in the 1820s that fellow workers often took "French leave" on payday, "without fear of being pursued, or advertised as a runaway." Twelve-month contracts had long since proved to be futile in the Blackstone Valley, where they were signed in April, but where workers in fact came and went throughout the year. Samuel Slater had despaired of enforcing annual contracts as early as the 1790s. "Probably the Common Law [enforcing entire contracts] is binding," he wrote, "but I think the law of Equity and Justice is not."[68]

The most common practice in factories by the eve of the Civil War, therefore, was to require two or sometimes four weeks' notice of quitting (except for people hired by the day), and to withhold pay for two weeks as a means of enforcing that rule. When workers sued for the money denied them for failure to give the required notice, juries tended to look favorably on their claims. Appeals courts did not. Even when judges began to relax their application of the "entire contract" doctrine of *Stark* v. *Parker,* as they did in many northern states by the 1850s, they upheld enforcement of rules of notification, leaving up to juries only the question of determining whether the rule had been adequately explained to the worker who quit. The most important practical consequence of such withholding of pay was evident in the high level of absenteeism after payday and in the timing of strikes. Strike statistics collected by the federal government after 1881 revealed a strong tendency for workers to begin their strikes on the first or fifteenth day of the month, or on the Monday after they had received their pay.[69]

67 "Petition of Ruth Hancock et al., in relation to the employment of operatives in factories." Unpassed Legislation Files, House of Representatives 1863, #1215/4. Massachusetts Archives. I am indebted to Paul Foos for this document.
68 David A. Zonderman, *Aspirations and Anxieties: New England Workers and the Mechanized Factory System, 1815–1850* (New York, 1992), 155; Prude, 150–3. The quotation from Slater is in Prude, 45. By midcentury Republican judges in the Midwest had begun to apply the doctrine of *quantum meruit* to claims of farm laborers, awarding them payment for the time they had actually worked. Karsten, 237–47.
69 Evidence for this argument is from Karsten, though I interpret that evidence differently than he does. On strike patterns, see David Montgomery, "Strikes in Nineteenth-Century America," *Social Science History,* 4 (Feb. 1980), 81–104.

Citizenship and the Terms of Employment

An influential article by Christopher Tomlins contends, in contrast to what I have argued here, that, rather than eliminating master-and-servant law, antebellum judicial decisions infused the whole developing law of wage labor with its principles.[70] Tomlins has in mind not criminal sanctions for quitting work, which survived only for slaves, sailors, military personnel, and (rather ineffectively) apprentices, but rather the legally sanctioned authority of the employer over the worker on the job. They are two quite different things – as the striking Australian coal miners and sheep shearers who were imprisoned for deserting their masters in the 1890s, Belgians obliged by the police to have their *livrets* signed off by employers before leaving a job, or Russians needing clearance of their internal passports and workbooks to move, were all very well aware.[71] Historians who portray only the rise of new hierarchies in the transition from traditional to industrial society find no place in their schema for workers' abiding hatred of the old regime. Conversely, those who favor a paradigm of "modernization," or some other present-day version of the progress from status to contract are constrained to interpret workers' protests *only* as evidence of cultural baggage carried over from an earlier era.

The new exploitation and discipline of industrial society were sanctioned and strengthened by court rulings predicated on freedom of contract, just as Tomlins contends. "Contracts of hiring are generally made verbally," a legal commentator of 1886 recognized, "but few words are used. The rest is left to the custom of the trade, and the parties are bound by it."[72] Courts in Massachusetts, Pennsylvania, and New York decided during the 1870s and 1880s that rules posted by a company became part of the contract between employer and employee. Even if the rules were not explicit, decided a New York court of appeals, workers "entered into the contract with the knowledge of the established usages of the employment." Usages could even overrule acts of the legislature: Despite the fact that the state's law had declared eight hours a day's work in 1867, a scowman was bound by the custom of the docks, which was ten hours.[73]

Factory regulations, sometimes posted, more often simply understood, required workers to be at their machines from first whistle to

70 Tomlins, "Ties That Bind."
71 Van der Linden and Rojahn, 27–8, 588; Reginald E. Zelnik, *Labor and Society in Tsarist Russia: The Factory Workers of St. Petersburg* (Stanford, Cal., 1971), 33–4, 125–9, 141, 358–9.
72 Henry A. Haigh, *A Plain Statement of the Laws Relating to Labor* (Detroit, 1886), 2, quoted in Amy Dru Stanley, "Contract Rights," 57.
73 *McCarthy* v. *Mayor, Aldermen and Commonality of the City of New York*, 96 N.Y. 1, 7 (1884), quoted in Stanley, "Contract Rights," 62.

last, to abstain from conversation, to complete assigned tasks and quotas of output, to give two weeks' notice or more of intention to quit, to refrain from joining unions, and to act with deference and obedience toward "superiors." Such rules were often flouted, to be sure, but the employers' sanctions of dismissal, humiliation, fines, blacklists, and evictions from company-owned housing were reinforced by the workers' own need for income and the self-imposed pace, known as a "piece-work gait." Conversely, customs and usages of the trade that ran counter to an employer's rules or practices enjoyed no legal sanction. They were often defended by the workers' own collective action and enshrined in trade union rules. Union enforcement of those rules, however, could and did bring their members before the courts charged with conspiracy to injure an employer or to obstruct commerce. Unions that fined an employer for violations of union rules were guilty of extortion.[74]

One of the most important components of Tomlins's thesis is that employer-made rules gained legal authority not through enactments by popularly elected legislatures, but through judicial decisions and commentaries on the common law. The legal profession, which had carefully cultivated its own professional expertise and exclusiveness since the 1750s, formulated the arguments, wrote the volumes of legal commentary, and handed down the decisions through which the authority of the master and the obligations of the servant were read into the developing law of employment in the United States. In striking contrast to the contemporary development of slave codes, state legislatures had little to say about the rights and duties of wage earners before the Civil War, except to require in a few states that working children attend school part of the year and that hours of labor be limited to ten per day in the absence of any contract to the contrary. Even in those cases, enforcement of the laws was left up to the offended party personally, who would need to bring charges in court. The law of "free labor" was judge-made law.

Many Jeffersonian Republicans, both prominent and plebeian, denounced the whole apparatus of the common law. That law claimed its basis in peaceable popular acquiescence to reasonable and ancient rules, which had been rendered certain and consistent with each other through the learned discourse of the legal profession itself. "The lawyers could hardly conduct a suit without appealing to the Common Law," wrote John Adams, "but in the very act laid themselves

74 On company rules and union rules, see Montgomery, *Fall*, 9–44, 148–70, 203–13. *Conseils de prud'hommes* in France did give legal sanction to customs of the trade that ran counter to employers' rules. Alain Cottereau, "Justice et injustice ordinaire sur les lieux de travail d'après les audiences prud'homales (1806–1866)," *Le Mouvement Social*, 141 (Oct.–Dec. 1987), 25–60.

open to the charge of subversion; thus, they were invariably certain to inflame the emotions of democratic juries, and see their cases decided by chauvinistic passions, which ignorant judges could not control."[75] Adams's remedy was to perfect the training of lawyers and judges and to encourage such learned commentaries as those produced by Chancellor James Kent and Tapping Reeve in the opening decades of the nineteenth century.

The refugee Irish revolutionary William Sampson demanded that American law free itself from "the degrading paths of Norman subtleties" and "models of Saxon barbarity," and base itself exclusively on "natural reason, universal justice, and present convenience." Even the common law's vocabulary – reeking of master and servant, baron and femme – was an offense against republican America. As Benjamin Rush had asked, "Do not men use Latin and Greek as scuttlefish emit their ink, on purpose to conceal themselves from an intercourse with the common people?" The roots of the ancient law lay in "the monarchy, the hierarchy, and the privileged orders," all of which America had overthrown after 1776. Codification could cleanse the laws of "the loathsome shades of feudalism," argued his colleague John Milton Goodenow. Only then, Sampson insisted, "The law will govern the decisions of judges, and not the decisions the law."[76]

Without a doubt the common law provided the legal discourse within which the respective rights of employer and worker were defined. The decisive role of a self-regulating legal profession with a mysterious language all its own in sanctioning employers' authority and even overruling legislation desired by workers and adopted by their elected representatives helps us understand workers' antipathy toward the legal profession itself, and the famous prohibition of the Knights of Labor against lawyers as members of the order.[77]

Nevertheless, one cannot conclude that employers' authority in the workplace was created by legal discourse. Employers in continental Europe wielded similar authority over their employees and enjoyed

75 Quoted in Miller, 17.
76 William Sampson, "Anniversary Discourse," in Miller, 121–34 (the quotations are on pp. 125, 132); Rush to John Adams, July 21, 1789, quoted in Kerber, 218; Goodenow. On Sampson, see Walter J. Walsh, "Redefining Radicalism: A Historical Perspective," *The George Washington Law Review,* 59 (March 1991), 636–82.
77 So numerous were lawyers among the elected legislators, however, and so frequently did labor activists themselves study law, that General Master Workman Powderly allowed a grudging exception to the ban. He ruled at the General Assembly of 1880, "A law student is not eligible to membership; but if a member becomes a lawyer after becoming a member, it does not interfere with his membership, provided he is true to the cause, and the L.A. of which he is a member must be the judge of that." Knights of Labor, *Record of the Proceedings of the Fourth Regular Session of the General Assembly, Held at Pittsburgh, Pa., Sept. 7–11, 1880* (n.p., n.d.), 263.

the legal sanctions of the state without calling upon any tradition of common law. Moreover, although as Perry Miller wrote, the leading Whig lawyers, who infused the spirit of master and servant into American common law, "held the word 'codification' to be obscene," the fact remains that the most eminent advocates of codification like Sampson and Goodenow rarely mentioned master-and-servant law in their critiques. They denounced the law's legacy of primogeniture, established religion, and conspiracy doctrines. Goodenow's long critique of common law includes but three examples of archaic and unjust prosecution under the common law of deeds against which there was no statutory prohibition: one charge of sodomy, one of engrossing, and one of "selling unwholesome provisions."[78]

When William Sampson defended the shoemakers of New York, who had been charged in 1809 with forming "an unlawful club and combination" to extort money from their employers and exclude from employment other workmen who did not adhere to their organization's rules, he delivered a lengthy argument in support of his unsuccessful motion to quash the indictment on the grounds that the action of the journeymen was no crime. In the course of his presentation Sampson excoriated the British legacy of hunting down absconding laborers, incarcerating them, and punishing persons who harbored them. A legal code that classified the "lower orders" as "servants, labourers, artificers, and beggars," he thundered, "is surely not American!" Nevertheless, the main thrust of his brief was that eighteenth-century conspiracy indictments of combinations of workers in England had been based not on common law but on the fourteenth-century statutes of laborers and artificers. Those statutes, he claimed, were not only alien to the spirit of a republic where "no man is subject, and no man lord and master," but also "were never in force in the United States of America, not when they were colonies, and certainly not since." Although Sampson never passed up an opportunity to express his contempt for lawyers who invoked "the spirit of departed fools," this, his most famous denunciation of master-and-servant law linked it explicitly to archaic English statutes.[79]

The intellectual hero of advocates of codification was Jeremy Bentham, also an ardent foe of archaic laws, but the stern advocate of a rigidly disciplined industrial state. His proposed code would have emancipated market activities from the traditional common law principle that "private right shall be subject and subservient to

78 Miller, 135; Goodenow, 392–3, appendix.
79 John R. Commons, et al., *Documentary History of American Industrial Society* (10 vols., Cleveland, Ohio, 1910–11) vol. 3, 252, 257, 261, 278.

the public good." The law against engrossing (cornering the market on necessities of life), which Goodenow had criticized, was just such a provision. That legacy of the common law was even summoned up (unsuccessfully) by a lawyer from Youngstown, who sought to pros- ecute Andrew Carnegie during the Homestead lockout.[80] In short, the common law provided the form in which legal discussions of master and servant were cast in nineteenth-century American courts, but the employers' awesome power would have existed whatever the discourse with which it was sanctioned.

What was most important for workers in the republican critique of the common law was the challenge to conspiracy judgments. The 1806 trial of Philadelphia's shoemakers for "deceitfully designing and intending to form and unite themselves into a club and combination, and to make and ordain unlawful and arbitrary bye laws, rules and orders amongst themselves, and thereby to govern themselves and other artificers," occurred in the midst of that state's intense agitation over codification. Foes of the common law like Sampson and Caesar Rodney came forward to defend indicted journeymen in that trial, or in its sequels in New York and Pittsburgh. Philadelphia's shoemakers, in turn, published their position in the Democratic-Republican paper, *Aurora*. The constitution of the state guaranteed citizens "a right in a peaceful manner to assemble together for the common good," they proclaimed, and "for fifteen years and upwards we have assembled together in a peaceable manner . . . to promote the happiness of the individuals of which our little community is composed."[81]

Goodenow pointed to early conspiracy charges based on common law against Lollardism, witchcraft, and heresy, and concluded, "How absurd, then, in a free government to leave to any body of men, wise as Solomon and honest as Job, to say what should or should not constitute a crime after the facts had been committed; and how impolitic would it be to intrust [*sic*] this power of *declaring* the law in those who were to try the supposed offenders."[82] Delegates to a New England workingmen's convention in 1833, pointing to the incarcera- tion of carpet weavers at Thompsonville, Connecticut, on charges of conspiracy to injure their employer, summed up the violation of Jeffersonian Republicanism involved in the court's action: "The use of the common jail in enforcing the regulations of a factory, made without the consent of those employed, is an alarming abuse of power,

80 See the highly critical treatment of Bentham throughout E. P. Thompson, *Making*. On the legal appeal to common law against Carnegie, see Krause, 341.
81 Commons, *Documentary History*, vol. 3, 66; John R. Commons, *et al.*, *History of Labour in the United States* (4 vols., New York, 1918–35), vol. 1, 141.
82 Goodenow, 42.

which ought to be resisted."[83] They concurred that master-and-servant law had been revived under a new disguise.

In the immediate aftermath of the Civil War a new wave of conspiracy prosecutions came before state courts. Some cases involved employers' associations establishing price scales for their members; others concerned trade unions pledging their adherents not to accept employment at less than union wage rates. In yet another type of case, the owners of waterfront taverns of Boston were brought before the bar for vowing not to permit seamen to be hired from their premises for less than eighteen dollars a month for the Atlantic Ocean or twenty dollars for more distant waters. Where such actions did not appear to involve coercion of individuals who had not joined the associations, courts of the 1860s were rather tolerant of them. Judges set their faces sternly, however, against trade union actions to obstruct the work of strikebreakers and to prevent the hiring or apprenticing of nonmembers or of people who would work below union scale, and prohibited such actions with increasing frequency during the next two decades. Wrote the Supreme Judicial Court of Massachusetts, such acts "establish a tyranny of irresponsible persons over labor and mechanical business, which would be extremely injurious to both."[84]

From the vantage point of workers, however, the true "tyranny of irresponsible persons" was that exercised by the very owners of large enterprises who celebrated the free market:

> He stood before the workingmen
>   As ruler of the mills;
> Who lived among the "upper ten"
>   And sneered at labor's ills,
> And bid them come to meet him in
>   His office one by one,
> To sign a new "agreement;" "then"
>   He said, "the mills will run."[85]

To men like Michael McGovern, the "Puddler Poet" who penned those lines, the precious legacy of the Jeffersonian doctrine lay in the sanction it offered to the collective initiatives of working people trying

---

83 Commons, *History*, vol. 1, 314.

84 *John Carew* v. *Alexander Rutherford and others*. 101 Mass. 1 (1870), at 15. See also *Master Stevedores' Association* v. *Peter H. Walsh*, 2 Daly 1 (1867); *Samuel Walker and others* v. *Michael Cronin*, 107 Mass. 555 (1870); *State* v. *Donaldson et al.*, 3 Vroom 151 (1867); [anon.,] "Law and Labor," *Galaxy*, 6 (Oct. 1868), 566–7. For discussions of later conspiracy cases and their impact on the labor movement, see Forbath; Victoria Hattam, "Economic Visions and Political Strategies: American Labor and the State, 1865–1896," *Studies in American Political Development*, vol. 4, edited by Karen Orren and Stephen Skowronek (New Haven, Conn., 1990), 82–129.

85 Michael McGovern, "Squeezing His Lemons," in *Labor Lyrics, and other Poems* (Youngstown, Ohio, 1899), 6.

to regulate economic life for the common welfare, and in the access it offered to the use of government to further this goal. Treasured though the ability to quit a job was to any worker, everyday experience mocked the notion that the search for work was guided by free choice. "An empty stomach can make no contracts," wrote labor reformer George McNeill. Workers, who "must sell to-day's labor to-day, or never . . . *assent* but they do not *consent,* they submit but they do not agree." The lesson to be learned from this experience was clearly stated in 1867 by the National Labor Union: "Until capital and labor become organized into a system of mutual co-operation, the working-men must protect themselves by means of co-operation with one another."[86] As long as socially organized production was directed in the interests of individual profit, they believed, industrialization would fail to fulfill even its promise of material well-being.

"We prate religion," wrote Alexander Troup of New Haven. "We indulge in morbid sentimentalism over 'happy homes,' we spread ourselves in eagle flights of oratory over our American institutions and the liberty and equality we enjoy under the law, while at the same time we are manufacturing paupers to an extent which places it among our leading industries."[87]

To the courts, however, the basic principles of the republic required defense of individual initiative in economic life against both governmental and social interference. In 1837 the Massachusetts Supreme Court made this clear while reasserting that a farm laborer hired for six months who had quit at the end of five was entitled to no pay. The judges declared, "Laborers, and especially that most improvident part of them, sailors, may excite sympathy; but in a government of equal laws, they must be subject to the same rules and principles as the rest of the community; and a court of justice is almost the only place where sympathy should have no influence."[88] Forty years later, during the great strikes that swept the country in July 1877, the editors of the *Buffalo Express* voiced their sympathy for the suffering workers, as did those of many other journals. But their principles made them abjure that sympathy. "The right to hire men for what labor is offered in the market must be upheld against brute force, whatever shape it takes," they wrote, "and the railroad companies have the support of all law-abiding citizens in upholding it."[89]

86 George E. McNeill, *Argument on the Hours of Labor. Delivered before the Labor Committee of the Massachusetts Legislature* (New York, n.d.), 13, 17–8. *Address of the National Labor Congress to the Workingmen of the United States,* in Commons, *Documentary History,* vol. 9, 151.
87 *New Haven Daily Union,* Sept. 12, 1891.
88 *Olmstead v. Beale,* 36 Mass. (19 Pick.) 528, at 528–9.
89 *Buffalo Express,* July 27, 1877, 2.

During the next fifteen years state and federal courts vied with each other to underwrite the legal claims of property owners in a market economy against the collective initiatives of working people. Because coal miners led the country in strike activity, they were the most likely to face indictments and convictions for conspiracy, despite legislation in Pennsylvania and other states explicitly designed to prevent such charges. When the state of Tennessee passed a law allowing miners to select their own checkweighman (to weigh the coal they had dug), the state's chief justice ruled that a company was perfectly within its rights to "refuse to continue to work the mines," if it did not approve of the man the miners had chosen. A federal statute penalizing employers who threatened to fire workers if they voted was ruled unconstitutional. Most important of all, courts throughout the land outlawed a favorite weapon of the 1880s labor movement, the citywide boycott of the products of a company whose workers were on strike. "The Boycott Attacks Freedom," proclaimed the New Haven *Journal Courier* in 1886. "It is to the legitimate strike what rum is to the idler." A trial judge in Virginia agreed. If boycotts "can be perpetrated with impunity, by combinations of irresponsible cabals or cliques, there will be an end of government." The courts found a remedy for workers' interference with sales by updating common law doctrines of conspiracy to bar any interference with the "pecuniary interests" and "exchangeable value" of a company's business.[90]

In conclusion, democracy hastened the destruction of onerous forms of personal subordination to masters, landlords, and creditors that American working people had historically faced. The voting rights extended to white male wage earners in the early nineteenth century provided them with both liberty of action and political influence, which helped them eliminate master-and-servant laws, imprisonment for debt, and seizure of personal property for nonpayment of rent. During Reconstruction the same developments were repeated for southern black workers, though under much more fiercely contested circumstances.

The new law that replaced the old, however, was defined not by the daily needs of wage earners, but by the emerging requirements of wage contracts for labor, rental of urban housing, expanded circulation of commodities, and the promotion of economic innovation. The legal status of employers and employees was basically defined through common law by the legal profession rather than by elected legislators. Court rulings translated the private initiatives celebrated by Jeffersonian Republicanism into the doctrine of the "free market." That

90 Forbath, 83–94, 185; *Crump* v. *Commonwealth*, 84 Va. 927, 946 (1888), quoted in ibid., 84; Krause, 157–9; New Haven *Journal Courier*, April 12, 1886.

Was it really so free?

doctrine, in its turn, enshrined rules established by employers in the legal definition of the wage contract. It also justified severe restriction of the use working people could make of their democratic rights and powers through their own collective initiatives or through governmental action. Moreover, the advocates of the free market used both governmental coercion and their own wealth to regulate the personal as well as the collective behavior of working people. That effort, and the controversies it aroused, will be the subject of the next chapter.

2

Policing People for the Free Market

The term "market" has many meanings and many more connotations, which are often jumbled together in order to impart some desired ideological message or other. The "propensity to truck, barter, and exchange one thing for another," which Adam Smith believed arose from man's "almost constant occasion for the help of his brethren" and distinguished humans from all other species of animals, has been variously identified with a village fair, the Chicago grain exchange, and the morning shape-up outside the gates of a packinghouse. As Barbara J. Fields has noted, to describe people as "market-oriented" carries about as much information as to say that they were "clothes-wearing."[1]

Specifying what we mean by market activity has especially important bearing on the question of human liberty. On one level we may note that so-called free-market economies have coexisted at various times with governments as libertarian as that of contemporary Sweden and as oppressive as that of Pinochet's Chile. The creation of such an economy has always entailed forceful governmental suppression of its foes. In the United States it involved civil war. On another level, the range of personal behavior tolerated or even encouraged by marketing has varied radically from one context to another. The marketplaces of early modern Europe, where men and women haggled over wares they usually could hold in their hands, were notorious theaters of license and subversion. The ostensibly impersonal relationships of commodity exchange made famous by Adam Smith imposed a firm behavioral discipline on buyers and sellers alike. Both the hiring and the use of wage labor brought with them strict regulation of the personal conduct of working people, on and off the job. E. P. Thompson described the psychological as well as the judicial imperatives of this regulation in a famous passage: "In all these ways – by the division of labour; the supervision of labour; fines; bells and clocks; money incentives; preachings and schoolings; the suppression of fairs and

---

1 Adam Smith, *An Inquiry into the Nature and Causes of the Wealth of Nations* (New York, 1937), 13, 14. Barbara Jeanne Fields, review of Steven Hahn, *Roots of Southern Populism*, in *International Labor and Working-Class History*, 28 (Fall 1985), 139.

sports – new labour habits were formed, and a new time-discipline was imposed."[2]

The connection between habits of work and systems of exchange and exploitation emerges clearly from Merritt Roe Smith's study of the Harpers Ferry Armory. "Every way considered," a newly arrived master armorer had observed in 1831, "there are customs and habits so interwoven with the very fibers of things as in some respects to be almost hopelessly remitless."[3] Because the armory belonged to the federal government, military officers appeared as its most articulate and influential utilitarian reformers, and political patronage supplied the dominant personalities of the enterprise. The same circumstances also generated, there and at the other federal armory in Springfield, Massachusetts, a uniquely rich record of the economic and cultural transformation then under way in privately owned firms as well, but ordinarily without leaving such thorough documentation for the benefit of historians.

The "very fibers of things" to which the new master armorer had referred consisted of a rather isolated rustic setting in which artisans' customs had been nurtured and sheltered, not only by the independence with which workmen plied their difficult trades, but also by the familial style of domination and exploitation exercised by the local gentry. Those gentry, in fact, give the impression that the systematic use of governmental power and patronage by eminent personalities for their own self-aggrandizement, which John Binns would have identified with "Old Corruption" (as radicals of his generation called the British monarchy), was still to be found in the new republic. Between 1807 and 1828 a "junto" of four intermarried families had dominated every aspect of life at Harpers Ferry. Their agents controlled all purchases of wood, coal, and iron for the works. The husband of the armory superintendent's adopted daughter owned the land on which the town was built and the ferry rights that gave access to it. Master armorers and inside contractors were appointed only with the junto's patronage. The owner of the dry goods store was married to the daughter of the local congressman, and all members of the junto were on familiar terms with established leaders of Virginia politics, as well as with Henry Clay and President John Quincy Adams. No candidate could hope to carry local elections without their blessing.

While rents, interest, fees, and monopoly profits flowed to the junto from a multitude of sources, the high rents and store prices charged

2 Thompson, "Time, Work Discipline," 90. On early modern markets, see Braudel, vol. 3, 25–113.
3 Benjamin Moore to Major Rufus L. Baker, May 5, 1831, quoted in Merritt Roe Smith, *Harpers Ferry Armory and the New Technology: The Challenge of Change* (Ithaca, N.Y., 1977), 279.

the workers were offset by lax piece rates, which allowed the men relatively high earnings. Steady drinking on the job provoked no punishment, as the armory's superintendent owned the distillery and tavern. Within the shops, one protesting officer reported, "workmen came and went at any hour they pleased, the machinery being in operation whether there were 50 or 10 at work." Moreover, he noted, popular activities dissolved the boundary between workshop and community:

> The shops were made places of business. *I* have seen four farmers at one time in one shop with paper and pencil in hand, surrounded by more than a dozen workmen, who were giving orders as to the number and weight of hogs they were to receive at killing time. All debts were done for in the Shops, . . . and arrangements of all kinds, whether for politics, pleasure or business were concluded there.[4]

The work practices of Harpers Ferry cannot be explained simply by its isolated, southern location. Routine and incorrigible drinking and reading, even in the presence of military inspectors, and defiance of posted rules were also evident in Springfield. Superintendent Lee of the Massachusetts armory was especially embarrassed by the response of his workmen to the dismissal of two of their number for wrestling in the shop in 1815 because his counterpart from Harpers Ferry was visiting at the time and witnessed the episode. Custom in the works required that anyone leaving its employ had to stand drinks for everyone else around the flagstaff ("liberty pole") before departing. The artisans vehemently debated a proposition to cut down the flagstaff in mourning for the death of liberty to wrestle.[5]

The attack on the junto's regime and on the artisans' customs was led by Col. George Bomford, chief of ordnance of the United States, who sought less expensive and more uniform weapons for the army, and who also enjoyed good political connections – in his case with Andrew Jackson and the Democrats of Pennsylvania. His efforts were supported by producers of wood and coal in western Virginia, who were eager to participate in competitive bidding for armory supplies, and by state politicians, who had attached their fortunes to Jackson's successful presidential campaign. The new president's spoils system quickly swept the junto out of control of the armory and opened the way to a protracted assault on local work practices and customs, which the artisans and their plebeian neighbors now defended by themselves.

4 Lieutenant John Symington to Maynadier, July 12, 1849, quoted in ibid., 270. Cf. the discussion of incorrigible drinking and reading at the Springfield armory, in Zonderman, 54, 145–8.
5 Zonderman, 54, 145–8, 159.

The new superintendent posted rules forbidding loitering, gambling, and drinking on the armory's premises, and he imposed stringent standards of inspection, which cut into piecework earnings. Armorers' protests against the new regime reached a bloody climax when one of them, Ebenezer Cox, drew a gun and killed the new superintendent. Though Cox's execution endowed local folk legends with a hero, and a popular Whig congressman from the Springfield district made himself a public champion of all the nation's armory workers against military despotism, the utilitarian campaign from Washington did not let up. In 1841 the hated rules were posted again, this time reinforced by a clock to set the boundaries of the working day. The entire work force went on strike and dispatched a delegation by riverboat to plead with President John Tyler against regulations that converted them into "mere machines of labor."

The workers' flamboyant exercise of their citizenship proved futile. Congress passed – and the president signed – a law establishing military superintendents at all arsenals. The posted rules grew in number, inside contractors slashed piece rates and refined the division of labor, and new machinery, at times tended by boys, reduced the works' reliance on the armorers' manual skills. As the report of an inspecting colonel summed up the situation: "We say to the Armorers – here are our Regulations; if you will not abide by them – go elsewhere – for we know that as many good or better workmen can be had at any moment. They answer – no, we will not leave the armory. We insist on working for the United States and will fix our own terms! ! !"[6]

The Harpers Ferry confrontation was unusual in two respects: The artisans were employees of the government, and the direct initiators of the new work regime were military officers seeking cheaper and better weapons rather than private employers facing competitive pressures. Nevertheless, the army officers championed an unrestricted market for both labor and materials, their efforts were supported politically by men who wished to supply the armory through competitive markets, and the new regulations and time clocks were no different from those of a privately owned Lowell textile mill or Philadelphia glass works.

The formation of mechanisms for disciplining the behavior of working people to replace the disintegrating personal subordination and task orientation of a deferential society entailed the creation of new types of business enterprise, new styles of government, and new roles for private associations, instituted to reform the social order. The failure of early experiments, like the manufacturing village estab-

6 Colonel George Talcott to Spencer, May 17, 1842, quoted in Smith, *Harpers Ferry*, 274–5.

lished outside of Philadelphia at the falls of the Schuylkill in 1794, helped point the way to more successful ventures that followed. As Cynthia Shelton has shown, the complex at Manayunk included a three-hundred-acre town with a glass works, spinning mill, stocking manufactory, stone quarries, river boats, and shops to build textile machinery and steam engines, all created by the wealthy speculator John Nicholson. Several talented British mechanics were contracted to recruit and direct the work of stockingers, glassblowers, machine builders, and other artisans, as Nicholson (who, it will be recalled, had also been involved in the employment of paupers by the Pennsylvania Society for the Encouragement of Manufactures and Useful Arts) attempted to supply his own mercantile activities with a broad assortment of wares.[7]

By 1797 the works had failed, and three years later Nicholson died in debtors' prison, owing $12 million. In Manayunk his capital had financed a cluster of homes, roads, water transportation, furnaces, and trip-hammers, while the work was performed in what Karl Marx called the "manufacture" stage of capitalism: Artisans worked in the "old handicraft-like way," but with "a systematic division of labour," and supervision. During its three years of operation Nicholson's works was plagued with absenteeism, desertion, and the customary insistence of artisans on doing the job their way. More noteworthy, however, was the prevalance of collective binges, work stoppages, and desertions. That collective action, Shelton argues, represented more than simply a persistence of old work habits. Again and again Nicholson and his agents were unable to pay their workers on time. Outside workers responded by leaving en masse, and workshop artisans, who were offered articles they had made, or even books, to sell as best they could, converted their personal mastery over their own working time into the stuff of group rebellion. Finally, the glassblowers brought down the firm by refusing to work altogether unless paid in cash.[8]

The next four decades saw the creation of a much more effective context for the enforcement of what Thompson called "time-discipline" inside privately owned manufacturing enterprises as well as in federal arsenals. New enterprises that sprang up, especially after the War of 1812, turned out a single product, or cluster of related products, rather than attempting to expand mercantile speculation by organizing the production of a random assortment of wares or turning a profit off of the local poorhouse. Even the mills established by the Boston Associates at Lowell, with thousands of employees, geared

7 Shelton, 1–10. On Nicholson and pauper employment, see this volume, Chapter 1.
8 Ibid., 1–25; Karl Marx, *Capital: A Critique of Political Economy* (3 vols., Chicago, 1906), vol. 1, 370.

their machinery toward the fabrication of yarn and cloth only. Although many firms generated extra income by selling supplies to their workers' families, renting homes, and dispensing some of the hay, coal, and oil they had purchased to local residents, the successful manufacturer of the mid–nineteenth century respected a new division of labor among entrepreneurs. What Fernand Braudel said of England applied as well across the Atlantic:

> Hitherto . . . the rule had been the indivisibility of the chief commercial functions – a businessman could be a jack of all trades: merchant, banker, insurer, ship-owner, industrialist. . . . [The new industrialists] had broken one by one the ties between pre-industry and merchant capitalism. . . . The talents they claimed to possess, the tasks they set themselves, were those of being conversant with new techniques, able to handle their foremen and workers and lastly having an expert knowledge of the market so as to be able to direct output themselves, changing course wherever necessary.[9]

Legislators and jurists encouraged the new enterprises with subsidies and with a framework of laws hospitable to their activities. As Ray Gunn has argued, the state of New York dispensed "bounties, subsidies, grants, stock ownership, and loans" in aid of agriculture, manufacturing, banking, and transportation, to the tune of $6.5 million between 1785 and 1826, and $12 million during the next twenty years, when it also poured another $50 million into canals and other transportation facilities. It also exempted specific manufacturers from taxes and other civic responsibilities: Among other things, the state passed a law in 1817 exempting the employees of woolen, cotton, or linen factories from jury and militia duty. During the 1840s, as we shall see, the state legislature contracted its contributions to specific enterprises quite abruptly, and concentrated its attention on enacting general legislation to facilitate the accumulation and investment of capital by private individuals and groups. That process was soon duplicated in other industrializing states, though the period of Civil War and Reconstruction produced a temporary resurgence of subsidies, from the federal government as well as from the states.[10]

Beginning in the early years of the century and with rapidly increasing clarity and uniformity after 1820, the courts declined to scrutinize

9 Braudel, vol. 3, 596–7. For examples of the new type of manufacturers, see Philip Scranton, *Proprietary Capitalism: The Textile Manufacture at Philadelphia, 1800–1825* (New York, 1983), 75–134; John W. Ingham, *Making Iron and Steel: Independent Mills in Pittsburgh, 1820–1920* (Columbus, Ohio, 1991).
10 Gunn, 81–114, 235. The quotation is on p. 100. See also Morton J. Horowitz, *The Transformation of American Law, 1780–1860* (Cambridge, Mass., 1977).

the content of business contracts and repudiated their historic concern for just prices and equal exchanges. The decision of New York's Court for the Correction of Errors in *Seymour* v. *Delancey* (1824) was of special importance for the judge's refusal to determine whether any bargain was "a beneficial one or not." What mattered was only that both parties knowingly and willingly agreed to it. The effect of such decisions, wrote James Willard Hurst, was "the release of individual creative energy" in directing the development of the economy. As far as the courts were concerned, the doctrine of "employment at will," which defined relations between employer and employee, was but one constituent element of a general doctrine of contracts, which did and should define human relationships.[11]

Underwritten by legislation and by new rulings at common law (including most emphatically those that upheld the employer's authority within the workplace) entrepreneurs were best able to induce new labor habits and a new time discipline through rules, sanctions, and pay systems imposed in the workplace itself. In contrast to the factory, however, in the antebellum city, the work rules of a single enterprise had about as much impact on plebeian customs as King Canute's voice had on the tides. The dense concentration of wage earners in New York, Philadelphia, and other cities nurtured social networks and organizations that not only defended embattled customs, but also transformed them into codes of mutualism and denied employers their desired access to other, more pliable workers who would have submitted to the new regulations.

Moreover, those customs and codes were defended as "popular liberties" against utilitarian and evangelical reformers, both by professional and clerical leaders of immigrant communities and by politicians soliciting working people's votes. New York's leader of the Subterranean Democracy, Mike Walsh, denounced the "gloomy, churlish, money-worshipping" spirit that prohibited or discountenanced "ballad singing, street dancing, tumbling, [and] public games, so that Fourth of July and election sports alone remain."[12] In 1845 he added, "No man devoid of all other means of support but that which his labor affords him can be a freeman, under the present state of society."[13]

In short, policing people for the needs of a capitalist market system required a restructuring of government. The capacity of government to enforce rules and to administer such public services as fire protec-

11 *Seymour* v. *Delancey*, 1824, 3 Cowens, 445 at 533. James Willard Hurst, *Law and the Conditions of Freedom in the Nineteenth Century United States* (Madison, Wis., 1956), 111; Gunn, 133–5.
12 Herbert G. Gutman, *Work, Culture, and Society in Industrializing America: Essays in Working-Class and Social History* (New York, 1976), 56.
13 *Subterranean*, Sept. 13, 1845, quoted in Wilentz, 332.

tion, sanitary regulation, and public schooling was increased substantially, while municipal protection of the living standards of the poor was abandoned, and most poor relief was taken over by private agencies. The repressive agencies of city and state government were professionalized and strengthened, while, in Ray Gunn's words, "the economy was effectively insulated from democratic control."[14]

During the last quarter of a century social historians have lavished attention on the efforts of evangelical churches, tract societies, moral reform agencies, temperance organizations, charities, and promoters of common schools to reshape the intractable and ominous daily life of the city. Other historians have scrutinized the reconstruction of state and local government during the same years. The two subjects need to be considered together if we are to understand how nineteenth-century efforts to police working people to suit the emerging market economy both replaced older forms of personal subordination and collided with popular aspirations for democratic government.

The intensity and persistence of that conflict suggests that the struggles of working people to preserve and even extend democratic control reveal a contrary current in urban life that often enjoyed some success. The expanded electorate exercised noteworthy influence over state legislatures, city governments, and political parties, and the freedom of association, which for workers was the most precious part of the Jeffersonian legacy, preserved political space for a variety of popular organizations with different ideals from those of the bourgeois reformers. To clarify the nature of this conflict, four aspects of the restructuring of power in the polity will be examined: the substitution of professional for private prosecution in criminal offenses, the simultaneous expansion of vagrancy law and privatization of poor relief, the reform of military service, and the regulation of the housing in which working people lived.

The Definition and Prosecution of Crime

"Experience convinced me," wrote Ludwig Gall in his litany of complaints about Pennsylvania in 1819–20, "that under the highly praised rule of law the principle obtains that where there is no plaintiff, there is no judge; and the law, the final authority in a republic, may be broken without punishment, if no individual brings charges."[15]

In Pennsylvania most criminal charges were then pressed before aldermen or a mayor's court by the offended party in person. John Binns, "the indefatigable conspirator" for Jacobin causes in England

14 Gunn, 2. Gunn's exclusive emphasis on the shrinking of state government's authority leads him to neglect government's growing coercive capacity.
15 Trautman, 64.

and Ireland who had fled to the United States in 1801 and immediately joined the Jeffersonian party, was appointed an alderman by the
governor in 1822. In his *Recollections* and in *Binns' Justice, or Magistrate's
Daily Companion,* which he published in 1840 (and which still appears
in revised editions to this day), Binns left us a valuable record of the
work of a Philadelphia magistrate and his relationship to plebeian
citizens. Binns heard cases involving all crimes but murder, sending
the more serious charges to grand juries and judging lesser cases in
person. He also licensed taverns, intervened personally in street
fights, summoning bystanders to his aid, and routinely charged bakers
with violating the assize of bread (only to be frustrated, he wrote,
because in Federalist Philadelphia, "The bakers always voted the *right*
ticket"). Because the fees paid him by prosecutors or convicted defendants constituted his income, Binns carefully located his office where
he best expected to do a "very large business." But he admonished his
fellow aldermen to rule "in a spirit of mildness, humanity, and a sense
of justice," because, he explained, "the mass of what is called criminal
law is concocted and enacted to protect the property of the wealthy
against the wants as much as the vices of the poor, the suffering, and
the ignorant."[16]

A large proportion of the charges of theft or assault and battery
were brought by women (against neighbors, husbands, and household servants) and by disfranchised African Americans. One unsym-
pathetic alderman described the typical prosecutor as one of "a class
that think all personal redress lie[s] in an appeal to the magistrate,
and a trifling quarrel in a neighborhood frequently leads to . . . a foot
race to see which shall first enter complaint before a magistrate." Allen
Steinberg's history of the Philadelphia judicial system depicts an alderman's "typical day" in 1848 as including six assault and battery cases,
three cases involving larceny, three breaches of city ordinances, one
fast driving charge, and one of throwing firecrackers onto the stage of
the Arch Street theater. In addition, during that imaginary day the
magistrate committed three boys to the house of refuge, issued two
landlords' warrants of eviction, two private notices and eight summon-
ses, had one man examined for life insurance and another operated
on for ophthalmia, and conducted one marriage ceremony.[17]

Aldermen were partisan figures, and none more so than Binns
himself. They mobilized voters for their parties while dispensing

16 Binns, *Recollections,* 299–300, 298, 292. The description of Binns is from Thompson,
   Making, 174.
17 Allen Steinberg, *The Transformation of Criminal Justice: Philadelphia, 1800–1880*
   (Chapel Hill, N.C., 1989), 26. The quotation is from ibid., 52. See also S. J. Kleinberg, *The Shadow of the Mills: Working-Class Families in Pittsburgh, 1870–1907* (Pittsburgh, Pa., 1989), 277–82.

justice in the neighborhoods where they practiced. Their encounters with the expanding electorate helped make the fee-for-service legal system more accessible to propertyless urban men and women than courts had been in colonial cities, and indeed more accessible than they would become after the professionalization of police and prosecutors during the middle decades of the nineteenth century. Binns was so outspoken as editor of the *Democratic Review* that a Federalist mob stormed his house after the election of 1824, and twenty years later the victory of the nativist American Republican party cost him his bench. A younger fellow Irishman, the cloth manufacturer Hugh Clark, was both alderman and leader of the Catholic faction of the Democratic party in the weaving suburb of Kensington. His prominence, and that of his tavern-owning brother, made their homes among the first of the thirty buildings burned by the armed Protestants from Philadelphia who marched against Kensington in May 1844.[18] Moreover, inexpensive urban newspapers kept criminal trials in the public eye by daily columns on happenings in the courts, and they used those cases to moralize about the decline of public virtue, about abusive landlords, creditors, and employers, and also about the dissolute lives of apprentice boys and servant girls who had succumbed to evil urban influences and entered "downward careers."[19] In a sense, private prosecution of criminal charges had become the poorer people's counterpart of civil cases among the propertied classes.

Despite the popular use of such courts, Binns also found much to denounce in the conduct of fellow magistrates, who "extort[ed] fees from those charged with crime." Neither magistrates nor trial judges were inclined to waive fees for prosecution, because the income of all court personnel was derived from them. Magistrates' fees added heavily to the punishment of vagrants and of disobedient or absconding servants who appeared before them. Moreover, the Philadelphia reformer and author of Gothic novels, George Lippard, described an ominous link between the poor and political skullduggery, which was provided by magistrates: "This mass of misery and starvation [in the slums of Moyamensing] affords a profitable harvest to a certain class of 'hangers on of the law' who skulk about the offices of aldermen, trade in licenses and do the

18 Binns, Recollections, 255–6, 292; David Montgomery, "The Shuttle and the Cross: Weavers and Artisans in the Kensington Riots of 1844," Journal of Social History, 5 (Spring 1972), 411–46.
19 Dan Schiller, *Objectivity and the News: The Public and the Rise of Commercial Journalism* (Philadelphia, 1981); Patricia Cline Cohen, "Unregulated Youth: Masculinity and Murder in the 1830s City," *Radical History Review*, 52 (Winter 1992), 33–52.

dirty work which prominent politicians do not care to do for themselves."[20]

Two years after he became an alderman, Binns was summoned on a
Sunday morning to the Walnut Street prison, where hungry and
abused inmates had risen in revolt and been put down by a company
of marines. Binns admired greatly the work of William Mullen, a
temperance advocate and activist of the workingmen's congresses and
the antislavery and land-reform movements who had used his position
as prison inspector to release hundreds of wrongly incarcerated
individuals. The poor, Mullen had charged, "may almost be called
bondsmen of certain depraved individuals upon whom they live in a
helpless state of dependence," who provided them with casual employment and paid them in "broken victuals ... poisonous liquor ... [and
a] night's straw upon which they are to sleep off its fumes."[21] Such
traditional, highly personal exploitation, Mullen argued, was ruthless-
ly reinforced by the fee-for-justice system. The determination to reform those archaic abuses led Mullen and magistrate William D.
Kelley eventually into the new Republican Party.

Benjamin Sewell, the Philadelphia street preacher, described as
commonplace evictions of residents of squalid dwellings who failed
to produce the nightly rent and received "a piece of printed paper
issued by that important dignitary, which belongs to, and is so
essential to a neighborhood like this, – I mean an Alderman. This
paper is served with a great deal of dignity by the Ward Constable,
and purports to be a notice to move within five days." A landlord
whipped a German neighbor of Sewell's mission house and then,
Sewell observed:

> trumped up a charge against him before a celebrated Alder-
> man not a mile off, who, being of that class of functionaries,
> (there are others like him,) who send all to jail if the *costs* are
> not paid, which are "*managed*" up to the amount of two dol-
> lars, made out a commitment for the unhappy man, and so

20 Binns, *Recollections*, 276; Fitzroy, "Punishment," 264; Rowe, "Women's Crime," 340;
   [George Lippard,] *Life and Adventures of Charles Anderson Chester, the Notorious Leader
   of the Philadelphia "Killers," Who Was Murdered, While Engaged in the Destruction of the
   California House, on Election Night, October 11, 1849* (Philadelphia, 1849), 29–30. In
   Frank Webb's 1857 novel of black life, *The Garies and Their Friends*, a venal lawyer
   enlisted an alderman and his hangers-on to start a race riot. Josephine Shaw Lowell
   charged in 1876 that some justices of the peace derived the bulk of their incomes
   from sentencing vagrants. Paul T. Ringenbach, *Tramps and Reformers, 1873–1916:
   The Discovery of Unemployment in New York* (Westport, Conn., 1973), 15.
21 Binns, 276–8. Mullen is quoted in Steinberg, 160. Caspar Sounder, on the other
   hand, described impoverished ragpickers as prominent litigants, "often encouraged
   by unscrupulous magistrates." Sounder, *The Mysteries and Miseries of Philadelphia*
   (Philadelphia, 1853), 17–18, quoted in Steinberg, 1.

poor Ereheart, for the first time in his life, was locked up in Moyamensing prison . . . [22]

Contrary to Mullen's and Sewell's criticism of private prosecution, however, the most systematic abuse of impoverished defendants by aldermen appears to have occurred in a growing number of cases in which the plaintiff was not an individual but the government. Offenses of disorderly conduct and vagrancy needed no indictment. The police charged men and women with those offenses before aldermen or juryless courts of special sessions (for a defendant to demand a jury would increase the fees considerably). In fact, the reform efforts of evangelists and utilitarians greatly increased the number of such prosecutions at the same time that they replaced private prosecution of crimes with charges brought by salaried government officials.

To be sure, police action against the disorderly and the destitute had long historic roots. During the eighteenth century city authorities had often rounded up people without legal settlement and expelled them before winter set in, in order to keep down the poor rolls. At the turn of the century vagrants were often brought before the magistrates for incarceration by the night watch or by city residents exercising their right to prosecute, and we have already noted the growing concern with urban poor and homeless in the 1810s. By the 1820s, however, the numbers of homeless poor in major cities had reached crisis proportions, and incarceration had replaced expulsion as the favored remedy. In 1822 New York's judges sentenced 450 boys and girls to prison for having no homes – usually for six months.[23] Philadelphia's magistrates sentenced 1,210 separate individuals in 1826. Priscilla Ferguson Clement has calculated that more "wandering poor" were imprisoned that year in proportion to Philadelphia's population than in any other year of the nineteenth century. Almost half those locked up in the 1820s had been women, and almost half were black. The population of white male vagrants fluctuated widely with the business cycle.[24]

The notorious charge, "drunk and disorderly," scourge of the early twentieth-century worker, had made its debut by the 1830s. In addition to the alderman's power to sentence an intoxicated person to twenty-four hours in jail and a fine roughly equal to two days of a

---

22 Rev. Benjamin T. Sewell, *Sorrow's Circuit, or Five Years' Experience in the Bedford Street Mission, Philadelphia* (Philadelphia, 1860), 324, 326.

23 Steinberg, 29; Blackmar, 170; Grace Abbott, *The Child and the State* (2 vols., Chicago, 1938), vol. 2, 348–9. On vagrants of the 1790s and 1810s, see this volume, Chapter 1.

24 Priscilla Ferguson Clement, "The Transformation of the Wandering Poor in Nineteenth-Century Philadelphia," in Eric H. Monkkonen, ed., *Walking to Work: Tramps in America, 1790–1935* (Lincoln, Neb., 1984), 59–66.

laborer's pay, disorderly drinkers who could not post $100 or $200 bond to keep the peace could be sentenced to an indefinite incarceration. That usually meant staying in jail until they were discharged by a prison inspector like William Mullen, or until someone greased the palm of the magistrate. Disorderly vagrants were confined an average of twenty-two days in 1854. Twenty-one percent of all arrests in Philadelphia in 1856 were on the drunk and disorderly charge, as 29 percent of all arrests in New York had been in 1846, when 4,241 persons had been so imprisoned in only three months.[25]

Uniformed police forces appeared in New York and Philadelphia in the 1840s, in deliberate imitation of Britain's "Peelers," but under the control of state-appointed commissioners rather than of the national government. Their appearance marked the culmination of a process that has been most carefully traced in New York. In the opening decade of the century an assortment of salaried constables, marshalls, and watchmen had first been added to the traditional array of municipal officeholders, who derived their incomes from the fees and forfeitures they collected. At the same time, the city ceased relying on individual residents to perform its housekeeping and began to employ its own work force for cleaning streets, eliminating public hazards, and keeping records of the population and its commercial activity. The size of the city watch grew from one member for every 663 residents in 1788 to one for every 388 in 1825 (428 watchmen in all).[26]

Even though the watch remained a ragtag force, distinguished primarily by wearing a leather hat, its growing size was accompanied by an even more important change in style of operation. As Paul Faler discerned in the case of Lynn, Massachusetts in the 1840s, the traditional emblem of authority, the constable's staff, was "cut . . . into pieces, and made billy clubs."[27] Jacob Hays, who was appointed high constable and captain of the watch, and who retained the posts, with some alteration of titles, until 1850, quickly earned a national reputation for a new style of police work. No longer did his watchmen and the magistrates rely on deference and persuasion (backed by the threat of a few hangings) to control crowds, as their predecessors had done. Hays preferred his forces to make direct physical contact with

25 Steinberg, 121–7,172–9; Blackmar, 181. John Peter Altgeld crusaded against corrupt plundering of "drunk and disorderlies" in Illinois in the 1880s. Altgeld, *Live Questions* (Chicago, 1890).

26 Gilje, 271–4; Hendrick Hartog, *Public Property and Private Power: The Corporation of the City of New York in American Law, 1730–1870* (Chapel Hill, N.C., 1983), 144.

27 Paul G. Faler, *Mechanics and Manufacturers in the Early Industrial Revolution: Lynn, Massachusetts, 1780–1860* (Albany, N.Y., 1981), 136.

miscreants, inflicting some pain even on those who were not arrested. Hays's methods anticipated the instructions given Milwaukee's police by their chief, William Beck, in 1863: "Never arrest a man until you have licked him in a fair fight first."[28]

The New York law of 1844, which authorized the city to establish a uniformed police force, was the first step in the creation of a professional municipal police, and one that would appear in cities all over the country during the next thirty years. At first glance the companies of patrolmen in their blue uniforms, directed from headquarters strategically situated throughout the city, appear to be a logical and indispensable element in a process of modernization of government. Two years earlier the New York legislature, overwhelmed by debts the state had accumulated as a result of the two previous decades of canal building and subsidies to business, had abruptly suspended virtually all canal work and instituted a state property tax, which was to serve as the basic source of state revenues for the rest of the century. Although the "stop and tax" policy had been introduced by the dominant Democratic Party in conformity with its faith in limited government, it enjoyed the articulate support of New York City's leading newspapers and bankers, and it was soon duplicated by other states throughout the North. The tax law represented, in Ray Gunn's words, "a landmark on the road to the modern conception of the state." The uniformed legions of municipal police were certainly another such landmark.[29]

A closer examination of the process through which the new police force came into being, however, suggests that the neighborhood, gender, workplace, and market relations nurtured by the growing city, and which the new force was intended to regulate, left their own indelible imprint on the police force itself. The local elections of 1844 had been carried handily in both New York and Philadelphia by the American Republican Party, which had mobilized its supporters in the name of defending the republic against what it depicted as the menacing political power of Catholic immigrants. No single element of the urban population had participated more ardently in the new party's mobilization than the mechanics (both masters and journeymen) of those handicrafts in which traditional work practices and social relations had suffered relatively little erosion from industrialization, and where the workers remained largely Protestants of American or British birth.[30]

Ship carpenters and caulkers belonged so clearly to this group that one can virtually map the country's strongholds of nativist politics

28 Gilje, 274–80; Sidney L. Harring, *Policing a Class Society: The Experience of American Cities, 1865–1915* (New Brunswick, N.J., 1983), 87.
29 Gunn, 161–9. The quotation is on p. 167.
30 Montgomery, "The Shuttle and the Cross."

during the 1840s and 1850s by locating the wooden ship yards. Frank
Harley's reminiscences of his youth in the trade suggest why: They
abound with stories of artisans who cherished their independence and
were prepared to preserve it through their artistry in shaping wood,
their readiness to move about in pursuit of good jobs, their immersion
in the trades' rituals and customs, their insistence on acting the equal
of any boss, and their certainty that the bosses would acknowledge
that status. Heavy drinking habits of individuals were the stuff of
legend, but even the character who "whistled" off a binge on a pile of
chips ultimately arose to perform a prodigious day's work. Not only
did employers continue to reside near their yards and their artisans
long after other manufacturers had moved to more exclusive residential neighborhoods, but, Harley contended, they also dealt honorably
with journeymen's strikes (in turn inducing their journeymen to
break "unreasonable" strikes), conceded the ten-hour day, and often
agreed when the workers depicted their unions as agencies of social
uplift and economic order.[31]

During the depression of 1837–43, temperance societies, like the
Washingtonians, recruited heavily among shipyard workers and their
wives. Evangelists like Philadelphia's James Alexander ("Charles Quill")
and Benjamin Sewell enjoyed a warm reception in their neighborhoods, as did social critics like George Lippard, who castigated the
corruption of justice caused, they believed, by alliances of magistrates
with politicians, as well as by attempts to hide from public view the
misdeeds of the rich and the subservience by office seekers to the
hierarchy of the Catholic church. They shared Quill's belief that the
true alternative to the barroom was the family sitting room, where an
artisan's family might gather round him at day's end in a well-kept
place they called their own. In fact, the gospel of domesticity assumed
its own distinctive character in Quill's preaching. "The English noble-
man, and those who ape his manners, may trample on these domestic
pleasures," he wrote, "but husband and wife, in our happier sphere,
are necessary to one another, and cannot be severed without loss and
anguish." Morover, Quill added, America's young people can marry
early, free from "that sullen, brooding prudence which is inculcated
by painful necessity on the peasantry of the old country."[32]

In New York, workers of this background found their political hero
in James Harper, whose printing of religious and temperance tracts
turned his firm into the largest publishing enterprise in the nation.

31 "Chips," *Fincher's Trades Review,* Jan. 20, Jan. 27, Feb. 10, March 3, 1866. See similar
   descriptions of the trade in McNeill, *Labor Movement.*
32 Quill, *Working-Man,* 24–5, 28. The subject of women in antebellum nativist movements still awaits its historian, but see Anna Ella Carroll, *The Great American Battle; Or,
   The Contest between Christianity and Political Romanism* (New York, 1856).

Well described by Sean Wilentz as "something of a parody of the dull, upright craft entrepreneur," Harper preached a simple gospel: "Observe carefully three rules and happiness will attend you: Trust in God, pay your bills, and keep your bowels open." But Fred Harley remembered him as the "benevolent old man" who first preached the gospel of the ten-hour day in Broadway Tabernacle to ship carpenters degraded by their own excessive toil during the 1830s.[33]

Harper was the mayor who first put <u>uniforms</u> on New York's police. He and his party had been swept into control of the city by the spring elections; they wasted little time going to work, enforcing Sunday closing of drinking places and dispatching Dr. John Griscom to make his famous survey of health hazards and sanitation in the housing of the poor. But the American Republican majority on the city council spurned the police law lately enacted by the Democrats in Albany and instead authorized the mayor to appoint 200 American citizens as salaried policemen, who were to wear blue coats with the letters "M.P." on the collar. The recruits refused to don the uniform, letting it be known that they were not liveried servants, but free Americans. George Wilkes's *Police Gazette* warned that subjecting the population to the combined force of venal aldermen and militarized police could produce a new despotism. An alert citizenry, informed about the way acquisitiveness bred crime and corrupt officials sheltered it, would most effectively provide the city's constables with the assistance they needed to deter criminals, he argued. Harper's scheme was quickly abandoned. The mayor's effort to enforce temperance and sanitation through traditional private prosecution and magistrates' courts, however, was also a pathetic failure.[34]

With the Democrats back in power the next year, however, the city council adopted the state's plan and <u>recruited eight hundred professional police, who conformed to quasi-military discipline and did put on uniforms and badges</u>. If a survey of 1855 is representative of the period as a whole, almost 60 percent of them were Irish. The great tailor's strike of 1850 provided an early test of the new force's martial skills. In one day's heavy fighting, police killed two German tailors (the first American workers ever to be killed in an urban strike) and badly wounded dozens of others.[35]

33 Wilentz, 318, 319; *Fincher's Trades Review,* Feb. 10, 1866.
34 John Bach McMaster, *A History of the People of the United States, From the Revolution to the Civil War* (8 vols., New York, 1910), vol. 7, 79–80; Wilentz, 317–23; John H. Griscom, *The Sanitary Condition of the Laboring Population of New York* (New York, 1845); Schiller, 133–4.
35 Wilentz, 322, 380–1; Elliott J. Gorn, "'Good-Bye Boys, I Die a True American': Homicide, Nativism, and Working-Class Culture in Antebellum New York City," *Journal of American History,* 74 (Sept. 1987), 399.

Three-fourths of the people arrested by the police in the routine course of their work, however, were charged with some kind of disorderly conduct. Moreover, the new role of the police was warmly and effectively endorsed by sponsors far more eminent and affluent than Harper's American Republicans had been. Incarceration of disorderly, homeless, and begging men and women was encouraged by developers of prestigious housing and shopping areas, who wished to insulate patrons from disturbance; by store owners, who also summoned city authorities to suppress the competition, cries, and horns of street vendors; and by moral reformers seeking to remove prostitutes and transvestites from the streets (in a word, to cleanse "the market" of its medieval attributes). The guiding force behind the quest for more orderly urban life in New York, however, was the Association for Improving the Condition of the Poor (AICP). Created in 1843 as the offspring of tract societies and Fourierism (called Associationism in the United States), the association attracted the talents of prominent intellectuals and the donations of many manufacturers, and it provided a model for urban reformers elsewhere in the nation. The AICP's early reports elaborated its goals: to create "new tastes, new desires, new activities and purposes" among the "respectable" poor, to secure its donors against "imposition" from unworthy solicitors of charity, and to draw "a line of distinction between the pauper and the independent laborer."[36]

Nevertheless, even the uniformed officers remained inextricably enmeshed in the very urban chaos they were supposed to police. Especially ominous to the reformers was the demimonde of saloons, brothels, fighting arenas, and gambling houses, whose centers of activity were located in working-class neighborhoods, and which spawned what Elliott Gorn has called "an intensely masculine world where status was distributed according to prowess and bravado." The deep group loyalties and belligerent gangs nurtured there often (but by no means always) followed ethnic lines, and they were incorporated into the mobilization of both the Democratic and the Know-Nothing parties. It was through this domain of "masculine bravado, group loyalty, and bold self-assertion" that men from working-class homes obtained the prominence and the wealth that made them influential political figures. "Butcher Bill" Poole, whose murder in a saloon gunfight brought a greater crowd to pay last respects than New York had turned out for the obsequies of Andrew Jackson or Henry Clay, had

---

36 1850 Report of the AICP, quoted in Bernstein, 181; Robert M. Hartley, quoted in ibid., 182. On efforts to suppress street activities, see Davis, *Parades*, 30, 107–8; Blackmar; George A. Chauncey, Jr., "Gay New York: Urban Culture and the Making of a Gay Male World, 1890–1940" (Ph.D. diss., Yale University, 1989).

pulled one hundred dollars in gold pieces from his pocket, for his (last) wager that he could whip any man in the room.[37]

Consequently, the AICP and other reformers appealed to the state legislature to sever all links between the city's police force and municipal politics. The Republican legislators responded by placing New York City's police, along with those of Brooklyn, Westchester County, and Staten Island, under a metropolitan service district headed by state appointees in 1857, as it did also with the region's fire and health departments and its new public parks. The immediate consequence was to make the city as dangerous as it was disorderly.[38]

Mayor Fernando Wood defied the new metropolitan commissioner, and his defiance was supported by the city council, local courts, and some eight hundred police officers. Another three hundred officers sided with the new force. A dozen policemen were wounded in a pitched battle between the two forces for control of a headquarters building before the appeals court proclaimed the legitimacy of the new metropolitans. A few days later on July 4, however, the largely Irish Dead Rabbit gang engaged in a gun battle with the new police, who in turn were reinforced by the nativist Bowery Boys. Hundreds of local residents, shooting and hurling rocks and bricks from rooftops, helped the Dead Rabbits rout the police and the Bowery Boys, leaving twelve people dead and about a hundred wounded at the day's end. It was only with the aid of two regiments of troops that the police had some success enforcing Sunday closing laws against liquor dealers the following day. One week later the police again needed army reinforcements to prevail in a daylong battle over Sunday closing with German immigrants in another part of the city. A massive funeral procession for a German worker who had been killed was joined by both Democratic and Republican politicians. As if in anticipation of the draft riots six years later, Democratic alderman William Wilson denounced the authors of the new legislation as "traitors to the United States," who "ought not to be obeyed." It was "the duty of the citizens in mass to resist them," he proclaimed.[39]

37 Gorn. The quotations are on p. 403. See also Lippard, "Charles A. Chester."
38 Eric H. Monkkonen, "From Cop History to Social History: The Significance of the Police in American History," *Journal of Social History*, 15 (Summer 1982), 583; Hartog, 237.
39 Paul O. Weinbaum, "Temperance, Politics, and the New York City Riots of 1857," *New-York Historical Society Quarterly*, 59 (July 1975), 246–70. A different version of the riots can be found in Joel T. Headley, *The Great Riots of New York, 1712–1873* (New York, 1873), 129–34. In Philadelphia, where Marshall John Keyser of the county force recruited heavily from nativist street gangs and fire companies, the Irish "Buffers" sang: "Go up and get John Keyser and all of his Police;/ Come up to the Market, and there you will see fun,/ To see the Buffers thump old Keyser,/ And make his puppies run." Steinberg, 151.

Philadelphia's consolidation act of 1853 had assigned one alderman to each of fifty police districts, empowered the city council to
elect them, put them on salary, and prohibited them from collecting
fees. The reform had been made possible by the triumph of Know-
Nothing candidates, following a decade of annual riots and a wave of
bloody street confrontations involving antagonistic Protestant and
Catholic street gangs and volunteer fire companies. The new mayor,
Robert T. Conrad, wasted no time dispatching the seven-hundred-
member police force against those he called "perverted immigrants."
Conrad's police sweeps against the "idle and vicious" were previews of
the dragnets ordered by Police Commissioner John A. Kennedy of
New York in 1860 and by Mayor Morton McMichael of Philadelphia in
1866.[40]

Throughout the remainder of the nineteenth century the number
of policemen in American cities grew more rapidly than the population (between 1882 and 1909 much more rapidly). Drink and
disorder continued to dominate the arrest lists. Nevertheless, some
important changes lay ahead. The discipline under fire demonstrated
by New York's police in the draft riots of 1863 persuaded business and
professional leaders throughout the land of the value of uniformed,
professional officers. Although budget crises of the 1870s led many
cities to reduce their forces, the pattern of growth resumed so rapidly
in the 1880s that Chicago's police increased over the decade from one
for every 1,033 residents to one for every 549, and Pittsburgh's grew
from one for every 1,958 residents to one for every 816. Simultaneously, the uniformed police took over tasks of reporting health
hazards, advising travelers, and lodging wanderers, that had formerly
been done by watchmen and magistrates. They also began to institute
their own surveillance of workers' political activities. Chicago's Haymarket Affair was followed by raids on scores of workers' clubs and
unions, and in New York uniformed policemen ostentatiously entered
Cooper Union when Terence Powderly was scheduled to speak, leading the general master workman to adjourn the meeting rather than
address Americans under the watchful eye of police.[41]

Correspondingly, the conduct of police became a prominent issue
in workers' political protests. Workingmen's parties from Lynn to
Milwaukee promised to halt the cracking of hickory clubs against
strikers' skulls and to dismiss obnoxious police chiefs. When Terence
Powderly was mayor of Scranton, Pennsylvania, he returned arrested

40 Steinberg, 147–9, 165–71, 172–9; Bernstein, 184.
41 Monkkonen, "Cop History to Social History," 578–85; Harring, *Policing*, 44–75 (the
   figures are on page 35); Paul Boyer, *Urban Masses and Moral Order in America,
   1820–1920* (Cambridge, Mass., 1978); Paul Avrich, *The Haymarket Tragedy* (Princeton, N.J., 1984); *New York World*, July 2, 4, 1886.

drunks to their families rather than locking them up. At the turn of
the century, mayors Samuel "Golden Rule" Jones of Toledo and Tom
Johnson of Cleveland enlarged on that policy, escorting drunks home
and releasing petty offenders on their own recognizance after inscrib-
ing their names on a Golden Rule book. By the 1910s fierce public
clashes between socialist mayors and state-appointed police chiefs
over the treatment of local workers had become commonplace.[42]

Over the course of a century a new machinery of "law enforcement"
had been created for America's cities. Magistrates paid by fees had
either been replaced by or incorporated into a system of criminal
justice that was based on the initiatives of salaried police, prosecutors,
and judges. The capacity of the state to govern had been greatly
increased where it mattered most: in the suppression of popular
behavior that disrupted the mastery of society by capitalist markets.
The control of elected local officials over the work and conduct of
police forces was denounced as a corrupting influence and replaced
by the authority of higher levels of government. The same upper-class
reformers who wished to strengthen government's capacity to rule,
however, also sought to reduce government's sphere of authority. That
effort involved ending municipal efforts to regulate the marketing of
necessities for the benefit of the poor, and transferring the administration of poor relief from public to private hands.

The Privatization of Poor Relief

There had never been a clear line of demarcation between public and
private charity in North America, and none can be drawn today.
Associations of private citizens have received state charters and public
funds to assist their benevolent activities, and public authorities have
delivered indigent men and women into the care of private individuals
and groups, ever since the founding of the republic. Moreover, the
history of poor relief is filled with plans and legislation that boldly
promised fundamental reforms in the treatment of the poor, but
which in practice turned out to change little or nothing. "Outdoor
relief," or government donations of money and supplies to impoverished individuals who were not institutionalized, was officially abolished several times by various industrial states during the course of the
nineteenth century, but it never went away.

Poor relief was also an arena of social and political activity in which
women were especially prominent, both as recipients and as donors.

42 Alan Dawley, *Class and Community: The Industrial Revolution in Lynn* (Cambridge,
   Mass., 1976); Fink, *Workingmen's Democracy;* Harring, *Policing,* 40, 181–90; Samuel A.
   Walker, "Terence V. Powderly, the Knights of Labor and the Temperance Issue,"
   Societas, 5 (Autumn 1975), 279–93.

Many women were to be found among the most prominent administrators and philosophers of poor relief, just as those who benefited and suffered most from its dispensation were disproportionately women from the poorest strata of society. For example, the Female Association of Philadelphia for the Relief of Women and Children in Reduced Circumstances, which was founded in the 1780s, raised most of its funds at religious services, aided by appeals from ministers. Its managers were women, as were those of other women's benevolent societies, but it reserved the post of treasurer for an unmarried woman so that no husband could lay claim to the money. In New York, societies headed by women successfully petitioned the city and state governments for funds to use in their work on behalf of aged women, orphans, and impoverished mothers during the early years of the nineteenth century.[43]

Gender profoundly shaped the everyday experience of class in the distribution of public charity, and public charity ranked among the most important instruments of class rule in the democratic polity. Nevertheless, the diversity of American society and its remarkable openness to self-organization prevented any single class, gender, or institution from securing monopoly control over benevolent activity, no matter how hard some tried. As early as the 1780s societies of German, Irish, French, and English immigrants, of tradesmen and mechanics, and of self-supporting religious denominations offered assistance to constituents they defined for themselves, and on terms they set.[44]

Every urban area had a public almshouse in 1800. The one in Philadelphia admitted destitute men, women, and children from the entire county, who were certified by Guardians of the Poor to show "deserving character" and to have paid taxes or rent in some town during the previous year. Many were seriously diseased or disabled, but all who were capable of work were kept constantly engaged in some task, such as weaving linen or unraveling discarded rope for use in caulking boats. Some inmates "eloped" from their confinement, only to be returned by city watchmen. Others had their expenses paid by an individual relative or master, or were bound out to indentures. As was noted in the previous chapter, in the 1790s inmates provided a major source of labor for societies for the promotion of manufactures, which operated in quest of private profit. Many entries in the daily docket revealed both protracted hardship and a view of "deserving character" which was less censorious than that taken by benevolent societies half a century later. For example:

> Admitted Sarah Ferguson of legal residence, has the venereal disease and don't appear to be more than seventeen or eighteen years of age. She says her parents came to this City, from Ireland when she was but a suckling Baby, that they never bound her out, or took any care of her education, that they have been dead three years and upwards, & that ever since, she has been a wanderer through the streets having no place wherewith to lay her head, by which means she has been exposed to every vile temptations being thus situated.[45]

The rapidly rising tide of urban poverty in the 1810s and 1820s provoked widespread controversy over the costs and purposes of poor relief. "Patrician confidence in urban benevolence faltered before the pressing demands of the poor during and after the War of 1812," writes Christine Stansell; "by 1817, it had all but collapsed."[46] Thousands of urban residents, who were dependent on the capricious wages of maritime, construction, and portage work routinely became supplicants for outdoor relief. For poor women, who commonly pursued a variety of employments throughout the year, outdoor relief became a basic element of their incomes, and even the almshouse was a temporary shelter to which they flocked when all else failed. Homework, especially sewing, provided both the leading employment of women, aside from domestic service, and the favorite means of outdoor relief. Consequently, Mathew Carey found that in Philadelphia the rate per shirt paid by private employers was the same as that fixed by charities. When Carey protested that even the U.S. military was paying twelve-and-a-half cents per shirt, the same wage paid by the Provident Society for relief, the secretary of war replied that the subject was "of such delicacy, and so intimately connected with the manufacturing interests, and the general prices of this kind of labour in the city of Philadelphia," that he dared not raise the rate.[47]

The complaint that taxpayers were subsidizing both irregular work habits and employers' profits led legislative committees in Massachusetts in 1821 and New York in 1824 to denounce the whole practice of outdoor relief and to recommend that every recipient of charity be obliged to enter an almshouse and live under its discipline.

45 Smith and Shelton, "Philadelphia Almshouse, 1800," 87, 98.
46 Stansell, 32.
47 Ibid., 11–37; Mathew Carey, *Essays on the Public Charities of Philadelphia* (Philadelphia, 1829), 18–19; Exchange of correspondence with the Secretary of War, printed in Mathew Carey, *Appeal to Common Sense and Common Justice* (Philadelphia, 1822), xii–xiii.

In 1828 the Pennsylvania legislature appropriated funds for the large new Blockley poorhouse in Philadelphia and decreed that after it had been completed, the only relief "granted to the outdoor poor" should be "temporary, and consist entirely of fuel, provisions, clothing, medicines and medical attendance." When Blockley opened in 1835, however, not a single person among the 3,208 on the outdoor rolls reported to the almshouse. A flood of petitions persuaded the legislature to extend the deadline again and again, while Carey angrily denounced the cruel law and summoned his fellow citizens instead to revitalize traditional charities, to reserve certain spheres of employment for poor women and men, and to ostracize employers who "grind the faces of the poor." Twenty years later Philadelphia officials were still dispensing outdoor relief, though with tighter scrutiny of applicants.[48]

"It is not the suppression of poverty that is wanted, so much as the suppression of idleness, extravagance, dissipation, drunkenness, and vice, which are uniformly the parents of poverty," wrote the eminent economist Thomas Cooper. That sentiment was shared by the mercantile and religious leaders who founded New York's Society for the Prevention of Pauperism in 1817. Its goal was to speed the reduction of outdoor relief by taking action against the dissolute habits of the poor. The city's Common Council followed suit, slashing its grants to private charities, which it accused of promiscuous almsgiving. Four years later it reported that "a great portion of the pauperism of this country arises from a reluctance to labor and dependence on the public bounty."[49]

As Stansell has pointed out, the same council session that made that declaration and summoned the state to end outdoor relief also abolished the most familiar historic protection of the living standards of the poor: the assize of bread. The practice by which magistrates had calibrated the price and the size of a loaf of bread according to the current price of wheat was soon to disappear in Philadelphia as well. It had actually been discontinued and subsequently resumed, and, John Binns noted, only fitfully enforced since the beginning of the century. As a symbol of the authorities' historic duty to restrain profiteering in the necessities of life and protect the welfare of working people, however, it had not lost its grip. In New York its abolition also came hard on the heels of a campaign by the mayor and council to stamp

48 Abbott, 2, 5–6; Benjamin J. Klebaner, "The Home Relief Controversy in Philadelphia, 1782–1861," *Pennsylvania Magazine of History and Biography*, 78 (Oct. 1954), 413–23; Mathew Carey, *Appeal to the Wealthy of the Land* (Philadelphia, 1833), 33–4. The act of 1828 is quoted in Carey, *Public Charities*, 30n.
49 Cooper, *Lectures on the Elements of Political Economy* (Columbia, S.C., 1826), 260, quoted in Harris, *Socialist Origins*, 26n; Stansell, 33–5. The quotation is on p. 35.

out the people's custom of letting their hogs feed in the streets. While lawyers appealed in vain to the common law in defense of poor people's pigs, angry crowds of white and black women continued to assault police who were "stealing their hogs" into the 1830s.[50]

The battle over the cost of living faced by the poor resurfaced angrily in the flour riots of 1837. Crowds, contemptuously described by the *Journal of Commerce* as "the very *canaille* of the city . . . several of them . . . colored people, not a few of them noted thieves, and some of them foreigners of the lowest description," hurled barrels of flour out of Eli Hart's store in protest against exorbitant bread prices, echoing an earlier petition to the council for a restoration of the assize. The *Journal of Commerce* replied, "We say, let every man look out for himself. If you weigh the loaf, you know what it weighs, but if it is stamped with the weight, you do not know." Two weeks later it added: "Price is the regulator of consumption. If there is a scarcity it draws supplies from a distance and deals out for consumption with a sparing hand." The *Evening Star* reassured the poor, "If they are in want, the public authorities, on application, will relieve their wants."[51]

Free markets, a safety net of abstemious relief to the worthy poor, and the suppression of "idleness" and "dissipation" thus framed the historic alternative to working people's claims to benevolence from the rich and the magistrates. In the campaign to discipline the lives and aspirations of the poor, however, a special and paradoxical role was played by the efforts of bourgeois women to aid and reform their less fortunate sisters. Not only were the men from the wealthier classes – who embarked on missions to instruct the poor on an unprecedented scale – joined by their wives and daughters, but also benevolent activity was reinforced, and even driven, by a belief that women's special nature equipped and obliged them to elevate the moral tone, not only of their families, but of the whole society. The thousands of women who lived in crowded quarters into which they had to bring the work they performed for pitiful wages, who hawked and peddled oysters, vegetables, and used goods of dubious origins through the congested streets, who served men in grog shops and other "disorderly" houses, or who faced abuse from violent and drunken husbands, seemed obviously and urgently in need of benevolent assistance. As the 1820s came to an end, evangelical women were systematically distributing religious tracts to women in poor neighborhoods while male counter-

50 Stansell, 35; Gary B. Nash, *The Urban Crucible: Social Change, Political Consciousness and the Origins of the American Revolution* (Cambridge, Mass., 1979), 130; Hartog, 140–2, 151–2; Gilje, 228–30.
51 *Journal of Commerce*, Feb. 1, 14, 18, 1837; *Evening Star*, Feb. 15, 1837. Cf. the dignified depiction of the protests in Fitzwilliam Byrdsall, *The History of the Loco-Foco or Equal Rights Party* (New York, 1842), 99–113.

parts sought out workingmen. The newly established Female Moral Reform Society campaigned openly and vigorously against male lust and the injury it inflicted on women.[52]

In a word, at the very time that city governments were attempting to suppress some market activities in which working-class women engaged, and withdrawing their protective arms from others, bourgeois women were actively redefining the character and role of nongovernmental benevolent activities. Both aspects of this development informed the role of gender in the new discourse of class.

During the 1840s and 1850s the new network of benevolent agencies moved to displace city government altogether from its control of outdoor relief. In New York the first session of the legislature to meet under the new constitution of 1846 adopted several measures, which in retrospect defined a new era. One was a general incorporation law for manufacturing, which provided a reliable and accessible legal framework for the direction of the economy through the use of accumulated private capital, subject only to the discipline of the market. The second was the married women's property act, then the most urgent legislative priority for middle-class women, and, as it turned out, a measure of great benefit also to husbands seeking to shelter assets. Third, in response to a massive petition campaign led by the Female Moral Reform Society, seduction and abduction were made criminal offenses. Finally, another general incorporation law simplified the organization and capitalization of benevolent societies.[53]

The Moral Reform Society was among the first to incorporate, under the name American Female Guardian Society, with an advisory board of prominent men; this heralded a resurgence of male direction in organized charity. The society erected a new building, which sheltered as many as two thousand people in the ensuing fifteen years, and devoted special attention to young women who were in danger of falling into a dissolute life. Praised by a male officer, R. W. West, for doing "what no machinery of municipal government could effect," the society received $10,000 from the New York legislature in 1856 in tribute to its success in keeping women off the poor rolls. Philadelphia's city council followed suit the next year by gutting relief appropriations once again and urging the poor to turn to their relatives or to private charities for aid. "Every thing is now in motion," wrote Female Moral Reform activist Sarah Smith Martyn, "and he who would stamp his impress . . . on society, must be at least a practical utilitarian."[54]

52 Ginzberg, 20–44; Stansell, 11–18; Mary P. Ryan, *Cradle of the Middle Class: The Family in Oneida County, New York, 1790–1865* (Cambridge, 1981).
53 Gunn, 235; Ginzberg, 78.
54 Ginzberg, 75, 78, quotations on pp. 123, 100; Rev. John Francis Richmond, *New York and Its Institutions* (New York, 1871), 430–4; Klebaner, 422.

The great age of institution-building under private direction was at hand, and the guiding force of the "practical utilitarianism" that directed it was the New York Association for Improving the Condition of the Poor. During the 1850s the AICP, in conjunction with various other agencies with overlapping membership, extracted funds from the powerful county board of supervisors, created by the constitution of 1846, to build new asylums and orphanages; it also appeared before courts to urge appropriate incarceration for destitute individuals. Its agents and those of affiliated charities hired out orphans and other pauper children from those institutions to private employers, sent them to the West, prevented parents from reclaiming institutionalized children, and during the Civil War enrolled boys in their care into the army and kept half the enlistment bounty.[55]

The desire of Charles Loring Brace, Frederick Law Olmsted, Josephine Shaw Lowell, and other leaders of the AICP to "abolish beggary" and compel "lazy vagabonds to work" inspired the association not simply to share authority with elected officers of the city, but also to usurp public control of relief disbursement. They persuasively portrayed politics as the seedbed of corruption, and privately directed benevolence as the nation's salvation. City officials disbursed relief to win voters' favor. Their powers posed the greatest menace to poor-relief reformers of all, because tax-based benevolence threatened, as the *Chicago Tribune* editorialized in 1874, to make the city "an organized robber," which would use the votes of the many to transfer "the sweat and toil of the thrifty and self-denying" to "the idle, the improvident, the spendthrifts, and the drones of society."[56]

The AICP's leaders also insisted, not only that their donors be shielded against "imposition" by careful screening of applicants for aid, but also that even those who were deemed worthy be obliged to give some equivalent for the charity received, preferably in work, but at the very least in the degradation attendant upon the process of applying. It was, Josephine Shaw Lowell advised her fellow charity administrators, always "a good thing to drive a hard bargain," rather than give "a dollar without . . . equivalent." Easy payment would leave the applicant's "days in idleness and her nights in debauchery."[57]

---

55 Tara Fitzpatrick, "Reared by Industry: Labor Discipline and Prison Discipline in the New York House of Refuge" (unpublished seminar paper, Yale University, 1981). As Michael Katz has written: "Everywhere relief had a mixed economy." *In the Shadow of the Poorhouse: A Social History of Welfare in America* (New York, 1986), 46.

56 Ringenbach, *Tramps*, 15; *Chicago Tribune*, January 2, 1874, quoted in Karen Lynn Sawislak, "Smoldering City: Class, Ethnicity, and Politics in Chicago at the Time of the Great Fire, 1867–1871" (Ph.D. diss., Yale University, 1990), 313.

57 Amy Dru Stanley, "Beggars Can't Be Choosers: Compulsion and Contract in Postbellum America," *Journal of American History*, 78 (March 1992), 1292.

The confrontation between private and state control assumed its most acute form in Chicago after the great fire of 1871. When contributions exceeding $4.4 million poured into the city from around the world, a Relief and Aid Society formed by business leaders successfully demanded that the city council turn all the funds over to it, without the elected government being allowed even to audit the expenditures. In its first report the society specified as its primary objectives "to secure to the real sufferers needed aid; to detect and defeat imposition; [and] to aid in establishing order by withholding encouragement to idleness." So miserly was the society in dispensing the funds that when the great depression struck in 1873 it still had $600,000 left, and it adamantly refused to let the city touch that sum for the newly unemployed.[58]

In New York the reformers engaged in a running battle with the dominant Democratic Party for control of poor relief. The public works projects launched by Mayor Fernando Wood in 1857 to feed the unemployed had been denounced by an enraged AICP as "pseudo-philanthropy" and as an incitement to revolution akin to Paris's national workshops of 1848. During the ensuing decade William Marcy Tweed and his political allies secured control over the county board of supervisors, which had been created by the state to remove such expenditures as relief from the city's control. Tweed's lavish grants to Catholic charities provided a major complaint in what the *New York Times* called the "revolt of the capitalists" against the extravagance of the Tweed Ring. By the time the depression of the 1870s enveloped New York, however, Tweed and his colleagues had been ousted, and the reformed city government spent not one cent on relief to the unemployed. Instead, it dispatched the police to scatter the demonstrators who had gathered in Tompkins Square in January 1874 to demand work relief.[59]

The depression of 1873–8 was a period upon which the AICP could look back with satisfaction. The privatization movement had spread to urban areas throughout the North. In New York City itself pressure from the AICP helped terminate all municipal outdoor relief except coal distribution in 1874, and, to the great satisfaction of Josephine

58 Sawislak, 105–17, 312–25. The quotation is on p. 117. City authorities had not distributed outdoor relief since 1857. Robin L. Einhorn, "The Civil War and Municipal Government in Chicago," in Maris A. Vinovskis, ed., *Toward a Social History of the American Civil War: Exploratory Essays* (Cambridge, 1990), 131–2.
59 Bernstein, 138–40; David Montgomery, *Beyond Equality: Labor and the Radical Republicans, 1862–1872* (New York, 1967), 377–9; Herbert G. Gutman, "The Tompkins Square 'Riot' in New York City on January 13, 1874," *Labor History*, 6 (Winter 1965), 44–70. These issues were replayed, often on a larger scale, in the 1890s. See Carlos C. Closson, Jr., "The Unemployed in American Cities," *Quarterly Journal of Economics*, 8 (Jan. 1894), 168–217, 257–8.

Shaw Lowell, even the distribution of coal to the needy was halted in 1879. Although thirty-four soup kitchens, dispensing free meals from churches and missions to some five to seven thousand people daily despite the objections of the AICP, revealed that not all private charities conformed to the rigid standards espoused by Lowell and her colleagues, the dispensation of poor relief outside of the almshouse in New York had been effectively brought under the control of private agencies. Not until the great depression of the 1890s (and later the crises of 1908 and 1913–14) overwhelmed the capacities of private charities did their leaders cautiously turn back to city and state governments for resources to help them care for the needy and dampen social unrest.[60]

Moreover, the State Charities Aid Association (SCAA), another private agency, which had been created by veterans of the Civil War's Sanitary Commission, secured the power to supervise the relief work of the government. Learning that more than 435,000 people had found lodgings in police stations of New York during 1874 and 1875, the SCAA established its own Night Refuge, in which men could sleep in exchange for an hour or two of work. Police at the stations agreed to select the men who were worthy of such lodging and to send all others to a magistrate to be sentenced to jail for vagrancy. Within one year the number of vagrancy arrests in the city almost doubled, rising to more than one million. In 1881 the SCAA was granted authority by the state legislature to inspect state, county, city, and town charitable institutions on a regular basis. The association's efforts, its leader Joseph Choate assured the legislators, was not guided by "weak or sickly sentimentality."[61]

It is crucial to understand, however, that despite the persistent efforts of such organizations as the AICP and the Charity Organization Society (COS), which sprang up in many cities, they never secured the monopoly on the dispensation of relief that their plan to "abolish beggary" and "compel lazy vagabonds to work" required for success. The state of New York levied a tax on shipmasters for every immigrant they brought into the state, and after 1847 used the proceeds to fund a hospital and a refuge for immigrants in need of such facilities. Nativists' fears of diseased foreigners encouraged the development of those institutions. Child-care centers sponsored by bourgeois women as well as beneficial societies created by immigrants dispensed aid primarily for the purpose of promoting group solidarity.

60 Ringenbach, 83, 93–7.
61 Ringenbach, 10–11; Ginzberg, 190–7. The quotation is on p. 195. The AICP of Pittsburgh won similar authority, and the Western Pennsylvania Humane Society obtained legal authority to intervene in the child-rearing practices of families, despite many conflicts with aldermen. Ingham, 167.

"The mission of our Catholic charities," explained a spokesman, "is . . . preservative." They scrutinized cases more with the objective of conserving their treasuries than of improving the work ethic of recipients. Even when Catholic charities began collaborating with the COS in 1893–4 and received some money from that agency, they refused to send the names of recipients of their funds to the clearinghouse that the COS had established.[62]

Local assemblies of the Knights of Labor often voted contributions to needy members or to members' wives and widows, and many trade unions established regular funds to provide some income for sick, disabled, or unemployed members. During the spring of 1864, while the leaders of the United States Sanitary Commission were soliciting funds from businesses and their employees for a Great Central Fair in Philadelphia, the city's 790-member Typographical Union No. 2 reversed the social dynamics of that famous project by raising $1,274 for the relief of the families of their own eighty-eight members who were in the army; most of the money came from publishing houses and newspapers for whom the union typographers worked. Labor organizations shared the desire, so clearly expressed by the Odd Fellows, to guard members and their families "against what is most to be dread in these unavoidable ills of life" while preserving "the feeling of equality, and the dignity of a *man*." As one lodge member expressed it, "When a poor man receives a benefit, the heart is not made sick and the feelings crushed and degraded by the thought that it is bestowed because he is poor."[63]

Even the federal government became heavily, though deviously, involved in dispensing pensions for the disabled, for widows, and eventually for the elderly, through ever-growing payments to veterans of the Union army and their dependents. Under a law of July 1862 that had provided for monthly payments to all men totally disabled

---

62 On New York's immigrant head tax, see Maldwyn A. Jones, *American Immigration* (Chicago, 1960), 128. On child-care centers see Lynn Weiner, *From Working Girl to Working Mother: The Female Labor Force in the United States, 1820–1980* (Chapel Hill, N.C., 1985), 124; Jane Levey, "The New Haven Mothers' Aid Society and the Day Nursery Idea, 1885–1904" (unpublished seminar paper, Yale University, 1990). On Catholic charities, see Thomas F. Ring, "Catholic Child-Helping Agencies in the United States," in National Conference of Charities and Corrections, *Proceedings of 1896*, 346, quoted in Levey, 46–7; Ringenbach, 101. For evidence of the solidaristic goals of immigrant fraternal lodges in the twentieth century, see Lizabeth Cohen, *Making a New Deal: Industrial Workers in Chicago, 1919–1939* (Cambridge, 1990), 58–71.
63 Minute books of LA 222, Scranton, in Terence V. Powderly Papers, reel 65; Alexander Keyssar, *Out of Work: The First Century of Unemployment in Massachusetts* (Cambridge, 1986), 186–90; Minutes of Typographical Union No. 2, Feb. 13, March 13, May 14, 1864, in author's possession; J. Matthew Gallman, "Voluntarism in Wartime: Philadelphia's Great Central Fair," in Vinovskis, 93–116; *Western Odd Fellows Magazine*, 3 (July, 1854), 6.

and to the widows of men killed in service, and under later legislation that authorized compensation for specific disabilities, pensions based on a scale starting at eight dollars a month for privates, plus two dollars for each child under sixteen, had been awarded to 300,204 men and to 200,825 women by 1885. The social turmoil of 1886 prompted Congress to raise the minimum monthly payment to twelve dollars, and the famous Dependent Pension Act of 1890 awarded pensions to anyone who had been honorably discharged after at least ninety days of service, and who had subsequently been disabled or widowed for any cause. That act increased the number of people on federal pension rolls to 999,446 by 1902 and consumed 40 percent of the federal budget on the eve of the war with Spain ($165.3 million in 1893).[64]

By the end of the century, therefore, some 30 percent of all white males between the ages of fifty-five and fifty-nine, and 18 percent of those between sixty and sixty-four, were drawing more than one-third of the average employee's annual income from federal transfer payments. Moreover, one out of every six widows in the largest age cohort (forty-five to fifty-four) was eligible for the same amount, unless she had remarried. Isaac Rubinow calculated that in 1909 between one-half and two-thirds of all native-born persons over the age of sixty-five outside of the South were receiving military pensions. Although his estimates may be skewed by underestimating the number of soldiers who were foreign born, his conclusion that pensioners were numerous but a select group of largely native-born whites in communities whose foreign-born population was constantly expanding, has been seconded by Amy E. Holmes's scrutiny of the widows who benefited from the 1890 act.[65] Consequently, at the very time charity reformers were tightening their scrutiny of applications for relief from impoverished working people of largely foreign origins, Civil War pensions provided a significant contribution to the incomes of the aging members of the population that had reached maturity in this country in the bloody 1860s.

Even at the municipal level, incessant protests from the working class prevented the permanent removal of poor relief from control by elected officials. That protest most often took the form of action: individuals and families refusing to enter almshouses, asking for overnight accommodations in police stations, cajoling and threatening visitors from benevolent agencies who determined eligibility, and at

---

64 Vinovskis, 22–3, 27, 172; Theda Skocpol, *Protecting Soldiers and Mothers: The Political Origins of Social Policy in the United States* (Cambridge, Mass., 1992), 102–51.
65 I. M. Rubinow, *Social Insurance, With Special Reference to American Conditions* (New York, 1913), 404–9; Amy E. Holmes, "'Such Is the Price We Pay': American Widows and the Civil War Pension System," in Vinovskis, 171–95.

times joining in large public demonstrations demanding relief. Workers articulated their opposition to the beliefs of charity reformers in
two distinct and quite contradictory ways. One had been expressed as
early as 1828, when a writer in Philadelphia's *Mechanics' Free Press*
voiced a position that socialists would later repeat again and again. He
said, "I think that no such things as *charities* should exist; for though it
is very proper that schools should be instituted for the instruction of
youth, and asylums provided for the aged, the sick and the infirm, yet
these things ought not to be left to the uncertainty of private charities,
but to be institutions founded and supported by the government
itself."[66]

Socialists of the 1880s carried the argument one step further. They
sought to abolish the system of employment for wages, which left
people without work or income. All the wealth of the rich, they
argued, had been created by the labor of the poor. Workers were fully
entitled to get some of it back in their hour of need. In Chicago, Social
Revolutionaries seized the occasion of the most reverent holidays to
display the miseries of working-class men, women, and children and
their contempt for the social order before the homes and meeting
places of the city's most prominent bourgeoisie. A circular that summoned more than two thousand people to march on a cold and rainy
Thanksgiving Day in 1884 proclaimed:

> Next Thursday . . . when our Lords and Masters are feasting on
> Turkey and Champagne, and offering prayers of gratitude for
> the bounties they enjoy, the wage-slaves of Chicago, the un-
> employed, the enforced idle, the tramps – and the homeless and
> destitute – will assemble on Market Street, between Randolph
> and Madison Streets, to mutter their curses loud and deep
> against the "Lords" who have deprived them of every blessing
> during the past year.[67]

The Thanksgiving Day assembly was no mob, but a procession
whose thorough organization made it all the more awesome as it
wound through the city's finest neighborhoods, lampooning the rich,
shouting "Vive la Commune," and foretelling the workers' pending
seizure of all means of production. Ten years after that, the irrepressible Morrison Swift and his socialist comrades led equally large
crowds through the streets of Boston demanding "the right to work."
It was not charity they sought, but municipal and national enterprises

---

66 *Mechanics' Free Press,* June 28, 1828.
67 Quoted in Avrich, 144. See also Bruce C. Nelson, *Beyond the Martyrs: A Social History
   of Chicago's Anarchists, 1870–1900* (New Brunswick, N.J., 1988), 141; Hartmut Keil
   and Heinz Ickstadt, "Elemente einer deutschen Arbeiterkultür in Chicago zwischen
   1880 und 1890," *Geschichte und Gesellschaft,* 5 (1979), 103–24.

that would provide remunerative employment to everyone who needed it.[68]

Most leaders of immigrant communities, and especially Catholics, did believe in charity – to benefit the giver and the community, as well as the recipient. But ethnic aid societies used the voting power of their constituents to solicit government funds, and their solidaristic intentions allowed some evasion of the AICP's screens against "lazy vagabonds." The belief that poverty would be suppressed not by crusading against "idleness, extravagance, dissipation, drunkenness, and vice," as Thomas Cooper had advocated, but rather by guaranteeing a job for every honest man, was widely favored in Irish-American circles. In Butte, Montana, the Ancient Order of Hibernians defied both the cult of the free market and evangelical supervision of the poor by tightly regulating access to and dismissal from jobs in and about the copper mines, and by providing financial aid to disabled or widowed residents. Many members would have agreed with the writer in the *American Catholic Quarterly Review* who had attributed the severe unemployment of the 1870s to the recent influx of women and Chinese into the labor force, but who also considered it the duty of the government to undertake public works, and of the church to colonize the poor in the West, so that all men could find remunerative employment. The *Irish World* summed up their contempt for evangelical reformers in an editorial describing a jobless man returning to his hungry family:

> Now, ye "Revivalists" – ye MOODYS and ye SANKEYS – where is your "revival"? . . . Is it your screaming and spasmodicking . . . that will save . . . ye "from the wrath to come?" . . . Is not the voice of the Divine Redeemer ringing in your ears? "I was hungry, and ye gave me not to eat; naked and ye clothed me not; sick and in prison, and ye visited me not; houseless and ye took me not in."[69]

The Crime of Idleness

Despite the protests of the *Irish World*, the Association for Improving the Condition of the Poor believed that, even when it had wrested control of poor relief away from corrupt elected officials, there was still a need for police regulation of the "debased poor." Such people,

68 Keyssar, 225–31.
69 David M. Emmons, *The Butte Irish: Class and Ethnicity in an American Mining Town, 1875–1925* (Urbana, Ill., 1989), 139–41, 159–67; David M. Emmons, "'Refuge of the Exile': The Social Welfare Policies of Butte's Ancient Order of Hibernians, 1880–1925" (unpublished paper); [anon.] "The Labor Question," *American Catholic Quarterly Review*, 3 (Oct. 1878), 721–46; *Irish World and American Industrial Liberator*, Dec. 2, 1876.

the association argued in 1850, "love to clan together in some out of the way place, are content to live in filth and disorder with a bare subsistence, provided they can drink, and smoke, and gossip, and enjoy their balls, and wakes, and frolics without molestation."[70]

Massachusetts led the way to new legislation with an act of 1866 increasing the punishment meted out to "idle persons who, not having visible means of support, live abroad without lawful employment . . . or place themselves in the streets, highways, passages, or other public places to beg or receive alms" to six months forced labor. "The low nature of the vagrant lacks any principle or purpose impelling him to labor," explained Edward Pierce of the Massachusetts Board of Charities.[71]

Although there was abundant precedent for legal prosecution of vagrants, Pierce's stress on "impelling" people "to labor" placed discussion of government policy toward men and women without work squarely in the context of the national consolidation of a system of employment at will. In the early years of the century, individuals who were charged before magistrates with being an "idle and disorderly person" had usually been brought by night watchmen or by residents of the area where they were found, on suspicion that they represented a peril to the neighborhood or were runaway servants, "poor Creatures . . . very ragged and swarming with bodily Vermin," or both. Summary incarceration of drinkers, beggars, people without evident means of support or homes, and those who harassed pedestrians in the finer residential and shopping areas had increased steadily since the 1810s, and especially after the organization of uniformed police forces. By the 1850s, as we have seen, officials in New York and Philadelphia on occasion ordered police dragnets to sweep such people (momentarily) from the streets. The unseen hand of the market called forth police coercion that was quite visible.[72]

Individuals had also been legally forced to work for and remain with particular masters. Specific enforcement of labor contracts had virtually disappeared from the experience of white men and women by the 1850s, but almost four million black people remained in absolute bondage, and African Americans who were not slaves still encountered various forms of indentured servitude from Maryland to Illinois. It was, therefore, the destruction of slavery by the Civil War and the Thirteenth Amendment that cast the relationship between vagrancy prosecution and freedom of contract into sharp focus.

70 Report of AICP in 1850, quoted in Bernstein, 181.
71 Stanley, "Contract Rights," 131, 141. Stanley attributes the new severity of Massachusetts' laws to the experience of Pierce and others with proletarianizing former slaves in the South during the Civil War.
72 Philadelphia Prisoners for Trial Docket, 1796–1802; Smith and Shelton, "Philadelphia Almshouse, 1800–1804," 194.

The Freedmen's Bureau and the U.S. Army had frequently coerced former slaves into signing and fulfilling annual contracts with planters throughout the occupied areas of the Confederacy, especially in Louisiana. The Black Codes enacted by the legislatures of the restored southern states in 1865–6, however, had openly applied the doctrine of specific performance to all black residents. South Carolina, for example, recognized the capacity of African Americans to make contracts, own property, sue, and be sued, but it also established separate courts and penalties for offenses with which "persons of color" were charged, barred them from the practice of "artisan, mechanic, or shopkeeper, or any other . . . employment, or business (besides that of husbandry, or that of servant under a contract for service or labor)" without an annual license from a district judge, and declared that "all persons of color who make contracts for service or labor shall be known as servants, and those with whom they contract as masters."[73]

The contrasting doctrine of "freedom of contract" was quickly and forcefully spelled out by General Daniel Sickles, commander of the South Carolina district, who issued an order in January 1866 nullifying the Black Code and setting forth his own decree (of twenty-three articles) defining "the rights and duties of the employer and the free laborer respectively." Sickles's regulations began with the principle that "all laws shall be applicable alike to all the inhabitants." Subsequent provisions asserted that "all lawful trades or callings, may be followed by all persons, irrespective of color or caste," that no special licenses could be required of one race, and that "no person will be restrained from seeking employment when not bound by voluntary agreement, nor hindered from traveling from place to place, on lawful business." Extending workers' rights beyond those enjoyed by northern workers, Sickles prohibited the eviction of freed people from plantations "where they have been heretofore held as slaves," even if they refused to take jobs there, provided they were seeking work elsewhere (though those who had arrived since emancipation had to leave the premises within ten days of their refusing terms of employment approved by the Freedmen's Bureau).

Sickles's order also asserted that the vagrant laws of South Carolina "applicable to free white persons, will be recognized as the only vagrant laws applicable to the freedmen," but he went on to add that nobody should be charged with vagrancy "if they shall prove that they have been unable to obtain employment, after diligent efforts to do

73 Leon Litwack, *Been So Long in the Storm: The Aftermath of Slavery* (New York, 1979), 366–75; Eric Foner, *Reconstruction: America's Unfinished Revolution, 1863–1877* (New York, 1988), 199–215. The quotations from the South Carolina code are in Edward McPherson, *The Political History of the United States of America during the Period of Reconstruction* (Washington, D.C., 1875), 34–6.

so," a provision on the face of it more lenient than the tramp acts soon
to appear in the North. Other provisions, however, coupled contemporary Yankee poor relief practice with the contract enforcement
earlier instituted by the Freedmen's Bureau. They instructed local
commanders to issue rations only to "destitute persons who are unable
to work," being careful "not to encourage idleness or vagrancy," but
also to make regulations hiring out convicted vagrants to planters for
a period not to exceed one year if employment could not be found for
them on government work.[74]

Three months later Congress passed the Civil Rights Act over
President Johnson's veto, both establishing the principle of a single
code of law for all races and eliminating the last remnants of
masters' rights to bring criminal charges against absconding servants. Only one month after the new federal law went into effect
Massachusetts adopted its stringent new vagrancy law. Although
antebellum developments in the North are slighted by Amy Stanley's conclusion that "the lessons of emancipation [had] quickly
travelled north, where they guided the cures devised for depend-
ency," she is absolutely right to point out that the triumph of wage
labor as a national system, codified in the doctrine of freedom of
contract, had precipitated a new debate over how to deal with
workers who did not work. The thousands of wandering unemployed turned loose by the depression of the 1870s, and the tumult
of the strikes that traversed the land in July of 1877, focused that
debate on the problem of the "tramp."[75]

A conference of boards of public charities agreed in 1877 that
new state legislation was needed to prevent people from begging
and wandering about without employment. Charles Loring Brace
proposed that a pass system should be adopted, along the lines of
the French or Belgian *livret*, to reveal a man's employment record
and certify his *bona fides*, if he claimed to belong to a craft in which
traveling was commonplace. Most delegates opposed any restrictions on freedom of movement as injurious to the economy, and
instead favored incarceration of those who could not prove they
had a job or were on the way to one. In what may have been the
country's first campaign for uniform state legislation, they urged
that similar statutes should be adopted in all states to leave no
advantage to moving about. The influential dean of Yale Law School,
Francis Wayland, added, "Harsh as it may seem," the law should
treat "those who honestly desire employment, but can find nothing
to do, [and] are reduced to the necessity of begging from door to

74 McPherson, 36–8.
75 Stanley, "Beggars," 1,286.

door," in the same manner that it deals with "those who are unwilling to labor."[76]

Tramp acts were soon adopted by all industrial states, and also by some agricultural states like Iowa. By 1896 forty of the forty-four states had enacted some such measure. The acts shifted the emphasis in the definition of the crime from begging to wandering without work. In addition they converted into felonies certain deeds, when perpetrated by tramps, that were misdemeanors when committed by others. They also provided that state governments would reimburse localities the expenses of incarcerating tramps. Sidney Harring's study of Buffalo revealed that police there arrested more than two thousand people each year under such a law between 1891 and 1897, including Jack London, who had ridden the rails to see Niagara Falls. They seized 4,716 people as tramps in 1894 alone, in addition to even greater numbers charged under the older vagrancy and drunk-and-disorderly rubrics.[77]

Workers' reaction to tramps was ambivalent, but the labor press was quick to condemn the new laws as "worthy of the days of fugitive slave laws." In the popular dime novels of the 1880s the tramp appeared as a treacherous figure, as dangerous to the republic as was the capitalist. During the strikes of 1877, strikers' committees in many midwestern railroad towns barred all strangers from their communities. An editorial in the *National Labor Tribune* condemning the "Filthy Huns" who had emigrated to Pennsylvania, warned, "Already bands of these Hungarians roam the country unemployed and cast off by persons [capitalists] worse morally than themselves, [who are] responsible for this influx of pariahs." Yet the most respectable workman knew that he could be the next accused tramp. As if in direct response to Dean Wayland's call for harsh treatment of unsuccessful job seeker and casual drifter alike, a cartoon in the *Irish World* had depicted "American Labor" as a man clad in rags, standing on an auction block. A notice on the block was inscribed: "Knocked Down to the Highest Bidder." In the background loomed a huge prison. The jailer holding shackles was the *only* bidder.[78]

Samuel Gompers corrected Senate investigators who referred to "tramps" in 1883, saying, "I should call them, workingmen who for a

76 Ringenbach, 20–3; Stanley, "Beggars," 1,277.
77 Sidney L. Harring, "Class Conflict and the Suppression of Tramps in Buffalo, 1892–1894," *Law and Society Review*, 11 (Summer 1977), 873–911. The New York statute is quoted on p. 881; Ringenbach, 22–3.
78 *Workingman's Advocate*, Jan. 15, 1876, quoted in Stanley, "Beggars," 1,281; Mary C. Grimes, *The Knights in Fiction: Two Labor Novels of the 1880s*, with afterword by David Montgomery (Urbana, Ill., 1986); Michael Denning, *Mechanic Accents: Dime Novels and Working-Class Culture in America* (London, 1987), 149–57; J. A. Dacus, *Annals of the Great Strikes in the United States* (Chicago, 1877); *National Labor Tribune*, Aug. 26, 1882, quoted in Krause, 216–7; *Irish World*, Dec. 30, 1876. Front page.

time have become superfluous in society, men rather, whom the employing class have made superfluous." The previous year he had defended state assemblyman Edward Grosse (author of the famous tenement house cigar prohibition) from the criticism of socialists by reminding them that Grosse "was the only assemblyman who dared oppose the infamous tramp law now upon the statutes of the State." The Washington *Craftsman* responded to Connecticut law by observing that "had Christ lived in Connecticut, he would have been imprisoned for asking for a drink of water."[79]

During the depression of the 1890s trade unions worked directly with city governments in such cities as Chicago and Denver to feed and house the unemployed, and demonstrators in Boston demanded "municipal factories where the unemployed can work for themselves." Populist Governor Lorenzo Lewelling of Kansas declared his state's tramp act unconstitutional and ordered the police not to molest people without homes or jobs. "The right to go freely from place to place in search of employment, or even in obedience of a mere whim," his circular proclaimed, "is part of that personal liberty guaranteed by the Constitution of the United States to every human being on American soil."[80]

A "tramp census" conducted by Trinity College professor John J. McCook in 1892–3 revealed the significance of these laws: The demographic characteristics of tramps (sex, nativity, trade, and literacy) were virtually indistinguishable from those of industrial workers generally. Similarly, the German Society of Chicago discovered in the same years that most of the growing number of tramps it encountered were not recent arrivals in the United States, but rather residents of many years' standing, and very often skilled workers.[81]

In place of the master-and-servant law, which had required a worker to complete a contract with a particular employer, the principle of employment at will was now supplemented by laws requiring the free worker to have *some* employer. A commentary on criminal law from the 1890s made the point clear: "There is, in just principle, nothing which a government has more clearly the right to do than to compel

79 Stuart B. Kaufman, ed., *The Samuel Gompers Papers* (4 vols., Urbana, Ill., 1986–91), vol. 1, 342, 258–9; *Craftsman*, Dec., 19, 1885, quoted in Gutman, *Work, Culture, and Society*, 96.
80 Closson; Keyssar, 349; "The Tramp Circular," in Lawrence Goodwyn, *Democratic Promise: The Populist Moment in America* (New York, 1976), 597–9. The quotation is on p. 598.
81 Harring, "Class Conflict," 881, 886–7; John B. Jentz and Hartmut Keil, "From Immigrants to Urban Workers: Chicago's German Poor in the Gilded Age and Progressive Era, 1883–1908," *Vierteljahrschrift für Sozial- und Wirtschaftsgeschichte*, 68 (1981), 95. On McCook's research, see Adela Haberski French, ed., *The Social Reform Papers of John James McCook: A Guide to the Microfilm Edition* (Hartford, Conn., 1977).

the lazy to work; and there is nothing more absolutely beyond its jurisdiction than to fix the price of labor."[82]

Arms and the Man

The armed forces at the government's disposal in the nineteenth century provided both the most formidable instrument for compelling people to conform to its wishes and an effective agency for reducing the possibility that government would need to resort to compulsion. Time and again working people were confronted by rifles and bayonets wielded by men wearing uniforms of a state militia or the regular army. Louisiana's slave rebellion of 1811, Maryland's canal strikes of the 1830s, the urban riots of the 1840s, the draft riots of the 1860s, and the great strikes of 1877 provided precedents for the incessant mobilization of troops against strikers in the 1890s. All these events informed debates over the organization and role of the country's military power, and all of them contributed to a protracted debate among working people about what role they should play in military life.

Military service also incorporated workers into the polity, but not in the comprehensive manner of European states. No peacetime conscription existed in the United States, and the obligation of all free males to serve in the state militia fell into disuse long before the Civil War. In continental Europe military service, years of obligatory reserve duty, and veterans' clubs provided a crucial arena in the struggle between governments and socialists for the hearts and minds of workingmen. Despite widespread popular hatred of conscription, important aspects of social life were shaped around it. For example, a government survey of 1872 in France found that working-class children commonly went to work immediately after their first communion (age twelve or thirteen), but that boys lived with their families, to whom they turned in their earnings, until they left for the army, after which they were considered independent and eligible for marriage. The only such benchmarks provided by the United States to locate rites of passage for males were the age of leaving school (which did not become clearly demarcated and enforced until the later part of the century) and voting age.[83]

---

82 Joel Bishop, *New Commentaries on the Criminal Law* (2 vols., Chicago, 1892), vol. 1, 273–4.

83 Dieter Groh, *Negative Integration und Revolutionärer Attentismus: Die deutsche Sozialdemokratie am Vorabend des Ersten Weltkrieges* (Frankfurt/M, 1973), 55–6; Alfred Kelly, *The German Worker: Working-Class Autobiographies from the Age of Industrialization* (Berkeley, Cal., 1987), 37, 90–6, 270–1; Michelle Perrot, *Les ouvriers en grève. France, 1871–1890* (2 vols., Paris, 1974), vol. 1, 314; Eugene Weber, *Peasants into Frenchmen: The Modernization of Rural France, 1870–1914* (Stanford, Calif., 1976), 292–302.

Citizenship and combat had been coupled in American thinking since the founding of the republic. As J. G. A. Pocock has argued, the republican doctrines of Italian city-states, which strongly influenced the thinking of the revolutionary generation, had identified civic virtue inseparably with the bearing of arms. Both the gender and the racial dimensions of nineteenth-century republicanism were deeply entangled with the recognized obligations and privileges of military service. "Americans learned at home how to be mothers and fathers, and at school how to behave as jurors, magistrates, and voters," Jean H. Baker has astutely observed, and the centerpiece of their studies was the history of the Revolution, which was framed by its battles and its field commanders. Not only was the pageantry used by political parties to stir mass enthusiasm routinely spiced with flags, uniforms, and martial airs, but from the 1850s through the 1870s, paramilitary units, like the Know-Nothings' Wide Awakes and the Democrats' Red Shirts, infused a bellicose tone into mobilizations of the electorate.[84]

Nevertheless, the imposition of conscription by the Confederacy and by northern state governments in 1862, and by the federal authorities in 1863, provoked such intense opposition that units of the invalid corps had to impose the provost marshall's authority in Pennsylvania's anthracite fields. Confederate cavalry was needed to bring in conscripts from the uplands of Alabama and North Carolina, while in New York City the bloody riots of July 1863 effectively nullified conscription in the city for the remainder of the war. Elsewhere in the North, virtually all local governments increased their taxes to fund the payment of bounties to volunteers (who were increasingly often outsiders to the community), whose enrollment would reduce their draft quotas. Even though slaves volunteered for the U.S. Army in large numbers during the Civil War and subsequently linked their claims to citizenship to military performance, they, too, vigorously resisted being forcibly impressed into the forces. Most working people wished their involvement with military service, like their involvement with electoral politics, to be celebrated, but voluntary. They also resented all attempts to impose a military discipline on civilian life. As the *Irish World* editorialized in the spring of 1877:

> General SHERMAN in his speech at the banquet of the New York
> Friendly Sons [of St. Patrick] gave us all to understand that the
> laws which govern the ordinary affairs of civil life ought to be
> copied from the regulations enforced in the camp. The General,
> it is supposed, understands drill. Let him stick to his profession.
> When THOMAS JEFFERSON is put aside as obsolete, but not until

84 Pocock, 90–167; Baker, 71, 282–6. On paramilitary organization of midcentury
   political parties, see this volume, Chapter 3

then, will people go to WILLIAM TECUMSEH for instruction in civil or political affairs.[85]

The Militia Act of 1792 had provided for enrollment of every able-bodied free white male between the ages of eighteen and forty-five into the militia of his state, and required him to provide his own weapons and equipment. It empowered the president to call out the militia for action against foreign or domestic enemies, but in practice, Marcus Cunliffe has argued, "the state militias were local armies, or at least local agglomerations," which functioned under the directions of state legislatures and governors. The "well regulated militia," envisioned by the Constitution as the bulwark of the republic's security proved ineffective from the start. Campaigns against Native Americans from the 1790s onward were conducted primarily by the small regular army. The regulars also overcame the suspicion of the Jeffersonians by providing the effective enforcement of the embargo against imports from Britain in 1808 as well as the main fighting force of the War of 1812, when the governors of Massachusetts and Connecticut refused even to call out their militias.[86]

During the next twenty years working people literally ridiculed the militia into oblivion. Michael Floy, an ardent Methodist and Democrat who despised militia musters, was delighted to observe late in 1835 "a company of men dressed up in a fantastical manner," parading through New York's streets to "ridicule the militia system." One man among them "rode a jackass which I suppose was not much larger than a good-sized hog; one had a cap on which was full as large as a hearth rug; their faces were painted of various colors, as black, yellow, red, with trousers of different colored patches, giving them such a woebegone appearance as to make a person smile." Nine years earlier the Eighty-fourth Regiment of Philadelphia's Northern Liberties had elected as its colonel a short, hunchbacked stable cleaner called John Pluck, who exchanged jokes with his officers and men in public comedy to the delight of great crowds. The "Bloody 84th" toured New York, Richmond, Providence, and Boston, drawing large and appreciative audiences, until Pluck was court-martialed by his superiors, later to die a pauper in the Blockley almshouse. Its escapades were

---

85 *Irish World*, March 31, 1877; Vinovskis, 48–58, 128–9; Grace Palladino, *Another Civil War: Labor, Capital, and the State in the Anthracite Regions of Pennsylvania, 1840–68* (Urbana, Ill., 1990); Albert B. Moore, *Conscription and Conflict in the Confederacy* (New York, 1924); Bernstein; Ira Berlin, *Freedom: A Documentary History of Emancipation, 1861–1867* (5 vols., Cambridge, 1982–   ), series 2, 8–10, 167, 175.

86 Marcus Cunliffe, *Soldiers and Civilians: The Martial Spirit in America, 1775–1865* (Boston, 1968), 184–5; W. E. Birkhimer, "The Army: Its Employment during Time of Peace, and the Necessity for Its Increase," *Journal of the Military Service Institution of the United States*, 19 (July 1896), 188–9.

repeated early in the 1830s in the Northern Liberties, when a Democratic politician led marches by the "Hollow Guards," in New Haven,
where commander Timothy Tremendous marched as "The Bull-Work
of Our Country," and in New York, where, as we have noted, Michael
Floy recorded the parodies in his diary.[87]

During the 1840s one northern state after another abolished the
fines and threats of imprisonment that had once supposedly enforced
militia duty upon all adult white males. Indiana reported in 1841 that
it had not assembled its militia once in the previous ten years. By that
time, however, another type of military force had made its appearance – one better suited to bourgeois society. It was the volunteer
company. Electing (or being raised by) their own officers, providing
their own uniforms, equipment, and drill instructors, screening
applicants for membership, and organizing parades, dinners, and
club rooms for the benefit of members and their families, volunteer
companies were typically led by prominent professional, political, or
business leaders, but were open to workingmen whose conduct was
acceptable to the officers. Many of them organized along ethnic lines,
and even after the urban riots of the 1840s inspired authorities to
suppress the use of names like Montgomery Hibernia Greens in
northeastern cities, Irish, German, Norwegian, and other such legions
proliferated in the Middle West right through the Civil War.[88]

A Massachusetts law of 1840 incorporated volunteer companies as
the state's "active militia" while putting an end to the requirement that
every male report for periodic musters. Private military academies
sprang up in many parts of the North between the 1820s and the
1850s, training many future officers of such companies. Former President John Adams expressed the fear that "a select militia might soon
become a standing army, or a corps of Manchester yeomanry" (refer-
ring to the volunteer corps that had shot down demonstrating workers
in England's Peterloo massacre of 1819). Membership in many of the
most durable volunteer units, like Pennsylvania's First State Fencibles
and all cavalry contingents, was simply too expensive for workers to
afford, and they represented just what Adams had feared. There were,
however, other units with many workers in their ranks, among them
the companies raised during wartime, the ethnic companies, and even
the splendidly attired Zouave Guards, which became fashionable in
1859. In 1861 and 1862 large foundries and iron mills in Philadelphia, Johnstown, and probably elsewhere in Pennsylvania, raised units

87 Michael Floy, Jr., *The Diary of Michael Floy, Jr. Bowery Village, 1833–1837*, R. A. E.
Brooks, ed. (New Haven, CONN., 1941), 26; Davis, *Parades*, 78–82; Faler, 129.
88 Cunliffe, 205–33; Robert Reinders, "Militia and Public Order in Nineteenth-Century
America," *Journal of American Studies*, 11 (April 1977), 85–7; Montgomery, "Shuttle";
Ella Lonn, *Foreigners in the Union Army and Navy* (Baton Rouge, La., 1951).

of their own, with workers serving as the enlisted men and company officials as officers. Not until the end of the 1850s, however, had New York and Massachusetts developed effective machinery for mobilizing their volunteer units for large-scale action. The fact that they were the first states to do so accounts for the large number of their citizens who fell at Bull Run. By the war's end more than 2,653,000 men had been mustered into the forces under federal command. Of them, 42 percent were identified as mechanics and laborers.[89]

It was the volunteer companies and the military academies that nurtured the cult of personal honor and physical courage, which Gerald F. Linderman has shown molded the behavior of soldiers in the first years of the Civil War. Theirs was a vision of "manliness" in the service of the republic, which was an unfriendly relative of the "masculine bravado" and "group loyalty" which Elliott Gorn discerned in the brawls of New York's streets, saloons, and polling places. Men who stood erect in their ranks while under fire and who were paroled by their battlefield captors on no more security than a personal pledge to go home, came from the same society as those who had marched in honor of "Butcher Bill" Poole after he was shot in a New York barroom. Bourgeois moral reformers, however, saluted the former and did all in their power to curb the latter. The United States Sanitary Commission considered it part of its mission to reinforce the bravery and stoicism essential to its conception of manliness, not only under enemy fire, but also under the surgeon's knife. When a mortally wounded soldier told the commission's leader, Mary Livermore, of his fear of death and hell, she responded, "Stop screaming. . . . If you *must* die, die like a man, and not like a coward."[90]

As Linderman argues, the cult of courage was underwritten by the soldiers' many ties to home. The letters, newspapers, visits of chaplains and Sanitary Commission workers, and the salutations even of strangers made one soldier remark, "We fought with the feeling that we were under the straining eyes of those who loved us and had sent us forth." Long before the end of the war, however, the devastating fire of rifles that could lay waste to a charging column at half a mile's

89 Cunliffe, 200 (quotation from Adams), 203–53; Thomas S. Lanard, *One Hundred Years with the State Fencibles . . . 1813–1913* (Philadelphia, 1913); David Montgomery, "William H. Sylvis and the Search for Working-Class Citizenship," in Melvyn Dubofsky and Warren Van Tine, eds., *Labor Leaders in America* (Urbana, Ill., 1987), 20–1; John Bennett, "The Iron Workers of Woods Run and Johnstown: The Union Era," (Ph.D. diss., University of Pittsburgh, 1977), 147–50; Montgomery, *Beyond Equality,* 93–5; Benjamin A. Gould, *Investigations in the Military and Anthropological Statistics of American Soldiers* (New York, 1869), 5, 10–14, 209–10, 215, 217. On Peterloo, see Thompson, *Making,* 681–91.
90 Gerald F. Linderman, *Embattled Courage: The Experience of Combat in the American Civil War* (New York, 1987), 1–112. The quotation from Livermore is on page 30.

distance, the end of battle-field paroles, the abundance of conscript and bounty-hunting reinforcements, the emergence of a seasoned cadre of commissioned and noncommissioned officers from the ranks of those early volunteers who had survived, and open warfare against enemy civilians, had not only eroded soldiers' faith in the protective shield of personal virtue, but also widened the social distance between officers and men. The societal distempers that the AICP had fought in the streets of New York were now rampant among the soldiers themselves.[91]

By the time the Confederate armies surrendered, 37 percent of the men of military age in the loyal states had served at least some time in the army. After a few mammoth victory parades by what was then surely the most formidable military force in the world, the U.S. Army was quickly demobilized, shrinking within a year from more than one million men to 54,000. By 1874 its numbers had dropped to 25,000 enlisted men and 2,161 officers. Equally abrupt was the decline of interest in volunteer companies. Outside of the South, where military and paramilitary organizations fought for and against the Reconstruction governments until the late 1870s, only a handful of volunteers could be mobilized for such actions as the suppression of Chicago's strikes for the eight-hour day in 1867, or escorting a parade of Orangemen through New York's Catholic neighborhoods in 1871. Not only were there no reserve units such as those that kept workers involved and under surveillance in Europe, there was precious little organization of veterans or even publication of writings about the war and military life. In 1878 fewer than 2 percent of the veterans of the Union Army even belonged to the Grand Army of the Republic. The nation's effective gendarmerie, whether in continuing wars against Native Americans, occupying Chicago after the 1871 fire, or ousting Democrats from the statehouse in New Orleans, was the regular army.[92]

The enlisted ranks of the regular army had long been constituted primarily of men from poor circumstances. Serving five year terms for a pay of ten dollars a month on the eve of the war, and commanded by officers with West Point training, they developed, in Marcus Cunliffe's words, "professional styles which had little in common with the folklore of amateur soldiering." Almost half of them were foreign born by 1840. In 1859 some nine thousand of the sixteen thousand enlisted men (56 percent) had been born abroad. After the war important

91 Linderman, 113–240; Ira S. Dodd, quoted in ibid., 93. See also Reid Mitchell, "The Northern Soldier and His Community," in Vinovskis, 78–92.
92 Gould, 10–4, 209–17; Stephen Skowronek, *Building a New American State: The Expansion of National Administrative Capacities, 1877–1920* (Cambridge, 1982), 86–7; Reinders, 91; Linderman, 270–1. On black paramilitary mobilization, see Julie Saville, "A Measure of Freedom: From Slave to Wage Labor in South Carolina, 1860–1868" (Ph.D. diss., Yale University, 1986), 232–40. On General Sheridan's occupation of Chicago, see Sawislak, 63–80, and of New Orleans, see Foner, *Reconstruction*, 553–5.

units of black soldiers were added to the army, but its growing involvement in the suppression of strikes after 1877 also inspired the army to
focus its recruiting efforts on rural youth rather than those from the
large cities, while also reducing the term of service to three years. That
policy, wrote Lieutenant W. E. Birkhimer, might not have produced
"better soldiers," but it did help "the people generally . . . know more
about the army than ever before . . . [and] appreciate it more than
formerly."[93]

The strikes of 1877 revitalized interest in both the regular army and
volunteer companies, or National Guard, as they had come to be
called. Secretary of War George McCrary warned Congress that "as
our great cities become more numerous . . . there may be great danger
of uprisings of large masses of people for the redress of grievances,
real or fancied . . . [in which] the sympathies of the communities in
which they occur . . . renders the militia unreliable . . . [and calls for
the qualities of] the trained and experienced soldiery." Career officers, who were largely longtime Democrats like Sherman and Mc-
Clellan (since eminent Republican officers ran for public office),
advocated reform of the army along Prussian lines. They were challenged by officers of state national guards, who initially obtained
funds directly from local businessmen to rebuild their units and armories, but in 1887 managed to double the level of federal appropriations for state units. The Pennsylvania legislature (like several others)
had responded to the strikes of 1877 by signaling the need for a
military defense against the "large numbers of illiterate and unprin-
cipled men concentrated in certain localities, many of whom are
foreigners, and imbued with the spirit of foreign communism, which
is spreading in this country . . . " Pennsylvania reorganized its militia
laws, incorporating volunteer companies as a National Guard and
assigning all other able-bodied men to an "inactive militia." Other
northeastern states quickly followed suit, and so expanded their expenditures that the "active" strength of the National Guard had grown
to a hundred thousand men by 1892, seventy thousand of whom were
in the industrial states.[94]

In the decade between 1886 and 1895, state governors called out
their units of the national guard 328 times. In one-third of the mobilizations the cause was explicitly listed as "labor troubles," but numerous other disturbances also arose out of workplace disputes, for
example the dispatch of soldiers to return convicts whom miners had
set free in Tennessee. No fewer than ninety-one guard actions had

93 Cunliffe, 119–20; Skowronek, 86–7; Birkhimer, 190.
94 Skowronek, 89–93, 101–11; Reinders, 96; Pennsylvania, *Journal of the Senate of Pennsylvania,* 1878 (Harrisburg, Pa., 1879), 1,065.

been caused by attempted lynchings or by outbreaks classified as "race troubles (negroes and whites)." That description usually referred to the suppression of some collective action by African Americans, but it could include anything from evicting black squatters to enforcing laws against gathering oysters. General Coxey's Industrial Army of the Unemployed, on its march from the West Coast to Washington in 1894, was dogged constantly by the national guard, which was called out nine different times against it.[95]

During the same years a rash of murals of Civil War battles, monuments to the war dead, and writings in praise of the soldiers' deeds in those glorious days spread over the land. War veterans were hailed by a former colonel from Vermont as "the aristocracy of the land," and the membership of the Grand Army of the Republic swelled to 428,000 in 1890, the year of the generous veterans' pension act (available to 41 percent of all surviving Union veterans). Although skilled workers, clerks, and shopkeepers constituted the bulk of the organization's membership, they were overwhelmingly native-born whites. Former commissioned officers were clearly the most likely to be elected to leadership in both rural and urban posts, though the popular "campfires" celebrated the days when brothers-in-arms used to drink "from the same canteen." The ceremonies of the GAR symbolically froze American life in the 1860s. The war they commemorated was the redemption of the nation-state, with even the mention of slavery marginalized by the 1880s. Southern veterans of the Union army, white as well as black, were effectively discouraged by their neighbors from joining such observances, but there were comradely joint reunions of Union and Confederate veterans as the century approached its end. Civil War service came to be depicted as a badge of the true American, as distinct from the recently arrived immigrant (in blithe disregard of the foreign birth of many soldiers).[96]

By the early 1890s, therefore, both regular army units and state volunteer companies were employed separately or together to enforce orders of governors or judges directed at the behavior of local residents, and a powerful veterans' organization had mythologized the armed citizen, defender of the republic. Military journals devoted many articles to the logistics of mobilization, proper uses of cavalry

95 Winthrop Alexander, "Ten Years of Riot Duty," *Journal of the Military Service Institution of the United States,* 19 (July 1896), 1–62. A summary of actions is on p. 26.
96 Linderman, 275–97. The quotation from William Ripley is on p. 286. Stuart McConnell, "Who Joined the Grand Army? Three Case Studies in the Construction of Union Veteranhood, 1866–1900," in Vinovskis, 139–170. The description of campfires is on p. 169. The interpretation of the Civil War that dominated the 1880s and 1890s can be found in James Ford Rhodes, *History of the United States from the Compromise of 1850 to the Final Restoration of Home Rule at the South in 1877* (5 vols., New York, 1893–1904).

against crowds, the accomplishments of Gatling guns and other rapid
fire weapons, the problems caused by governors who might sym-
pathize with the offenders (like Illinois's John Peter Altgeld), and the
need to keep amateurish sheriffs, marshalls, and citizen posses away
from the scene. The ruling of the U.S. Supreme Court in the case of
the 1894 Pullman Boycott inscribed the military's role into legal
doctrine, and in so doing made explicit the police role of armies in a
market-driven economy:

> The entire strength of the nation may be used to enforce in any
> part of the land the full and free exercise of all national powers
> and the security of all rights entrusted by the Constitution to its
> care. The strong arm of the national government may be put
> forth to brush away all obstructions to interstate commerce or to
> the transportation of the mails. If the emergency arises, the army
> of the nation, and all its militia, are at the service of the nation
> to compel obedience to its laws.[97]

The prominence of military activity against workers during the last
quarter of the century and the revised cult of manly service to the
republic provoked an ardent debate within the labor movement, and also
between the movement and its foes, about the relationship of citizenship
to the bearing of arms. One aspect of the controversy involved the
expediency of attempting to pursue workers' goals through military
organizations. Another was the menace of military power used to thwart
those goals.

The large concentration of workers in the ranks of the Union Army
had provided an attractive arena for proselytizing by a variety of
political movements. The Fenian Brotherhood had recruited openly
and effectively among Irish-American soldiers, holding out before
them the prospect of two hundred thousand armed veterans landing
in Ireland under the command of General Philip Sheridan to win
their homeland's freedom. Despite suspicious surveillance by white
officers, Major Martin Delany had admonished black soldiers to rely
on no one but themselves in their future quest for rights and property.
General August Willich of the Thirty-second Indiana Regiment was
but the most prominent of the officers who regularly educated their
troops with a Marxist interpretation of the war in which they were
engaged. A lieutenant in another Indiana regiment, who had been a

---

97 *In Re Debs*, in Henry Steele Commager, *Documents of American History* (2 vols. in one,
3rd edition, New York, 1947), vol. 2, 164. In 1903 the Dick Law passed by Congress
incorporated the National Guard into the national military system and ended the
anomaly of compulsory service that was never enforced, as it had existed since the
Militia Act of 1792.

leader of the ship carpenters' union in his home town, wrote the editor of *Fincher's Trades Review* asking for copies to distribute. He explained:

> There are many mechanics in this army, and the time will come when they will be going home to pursue their different kinds of labor. A great many of them do not know anything about what their fellow men are doing at home for their benefit, so I am trying to instill into their minds what is going on.[98]

Moreover, labor activists wasted little time cultivating their own mythology of the war and emancipation. William Sylvis reminded his fellow iron molders, "While armed treason and rebellion threatened our institutions with destruction, while the proud and opulent of the land were plotting the downfall of our government, the toiling millions stood like a wall of adamant between it and the destructive elements of revolution, between the country and all its foes." Similarly, Ira Steward spoke for the trade unionists of Boston when he resolved that "the workingmen of America will in future claim a more equal share in the wealth their industry creates in peace and a more equal participation in the privileges and blessings of those free institutions, defended by their manhood on many a bloody field of battle." By 1885 even William Mullen of Virginia could stand before a general assembly of the Knights of Labor and praise the "true and patriotic sons of our common country" who had been incarcerated by the Confederates in Libby prison "as prisoners of war for being engaged in a struggle to liberate a race of people from the galling yoke of slavery." Mullen's purpose was to remind his audience that there "still remains a battle to be fought for the establishment of universal freedom."[99]

Some workers concluded that their class needed its own armed forces to fight that coming battle. The Geneva congress of the International Workingmen's Association had denounced standing armies and advocated a militia system of national defense, but it had also accepted unanimously an amendment proposed by German delegates recommending that all sections form their own military drill societies as the first step toward arming all the people. That call was taken up in Chicago by the Workingmen's Party of Illinois in 1875, when it formed its armed educational and defense league (*Lehr-und-Wehr Verein*). During the next ten years German workers copied Chicago's example in Cincinnati, San Francisco, Philadelphia, Denver, St. Louis, and other cities. Their contin-

98 Montgomery, *Beyond Equality*, 94–5, 129–31; Berlin, *Freedom*, Series 2, 739–41; *Fincher's Trades Review*, May 27, 1865.
99 James C. Sylvis, *Life, Speeches, Labors and Essays of William H. Sylvis* (Philadelphia, 1872), 139–40; *Daily Evening Voice*, Nov. 3, 1865; Peter J. Rachleff, *Black Labor in the South: Richmond, Virginia, 1865–1890* (Philadelphia, 1984), 138–9.

gents contributed a martial spirit to parades, picnics, and dances and dissuaded "Irish hooligans" from disturbing socialist festivities, while they also promised an effective rebuff to police, soldiers, and Pinkertons who attacked strikers. They reminded citizens that Europe's revolutionary heritage had at least as much to offer the workers as did America's. [100]

By no means were all recruits to workers' armed contingents Germans. French, Irish, and English-speaking riflemen also marched in Chicago's demonstrations of the 1870s, and the stalwart Bohemian Sharpshooters encouraged workers and frightened their foes until 1886. The Detroit Rifles enjoyed the support of the Knights of Labor in their city during the early 1880s, and they promised to "keep Pinkerton's men at a distance." Nor were all armed units socialist. In the wake of the July strikes and the hangings of alleged Molly Maguires in 1877, the *National Labor Tribune* reported military companies drilling nightly in "Shanty Hill, Callaghan's Corner, Sandy Banks, and kindred 'classical' suburbs" of Scranton, Pennsylvania. On the fourth of July, 1886, residents of western Pennsylvania's coal fields saw hundreds of Slovaks and other immigrants from the Kingdom of Hungary march in military attire behind their director general, Josef Stefanki, who wore the "uniform of the Revolution of 1848." A banner at the head of the procession proclaimed: "Live Forever the United States."[101]

When Chicago's Social Revolutionaries organized a grand parade and picnic in the spring of 1878, the city called its entire police force to duty for the day, while two regiments of the Illinois National Guard assembled in the armories. Less than a year later the state assembly amended its military code so as to forbid "all bodies of armed men except the regular State militia and United States troops from associating, drilling or parading with arms in any city" without the license of the governor. The ban provoked the *Lehr-und-Wehr Verein* to march in open defiance year after year through Chicago's streets, and in response the size and armaments of the national guard were increased steadily. When the Social Revolutionaries staged their confrontational Thanksgiving Day demonstration on behalf of the unemployed in 1884, the militia practiced its street drill nearby. The conviction in

100 International Workingmen's Association, *La Première Internationale. Recueil de documents publié sous la direction de Jacques Fréymond* (2 vols., Geneva, 1962), vol. 1, 52; *Chicago Tribune,* June 4, 1875; Henry David, *History of the Haymarket Affair: A Study in the American Social Revolutionary and Labor Movements* (New York, 1936), 60–1; Avrich, 160; Nelson, *Beyond the Martyrs,* 138, 158.

101 Nelson, *Beyond the Martyrs,* 151; Richard J. Oestreicher, *Solidarity and Fragmentation: Working People and Class Consciousness in Detroit, 1875–1900* (Urbana, Ill., 1986), 134–5; *National Labor Tribune,* Aug. 18, 1877, quoted in Mary Ellen Freifeld, "The Emergence of the American Working Classes: The Roots of Division, 1865–1885" (Ph.D. diss., New York University, 1980), 418; Krause, 224.

Court of the *Verein*'s Major Herman Presser for leading an armed parade in defiance of the law led to seven years of appeals, until the United States Supreme Court early in 1886 upheld the prohibition as constitutional. In the wake of the Haymarket bombing the following May, police raids singled out the armed units with special venom, and by April 1887 all public trace of them had disappeared.[102]

Armed men marching behind red and black flags to the accompaniment of revolutionary anthems and slogans also alienated many English-speaking workers. During the Chicago preparations for the eight-hour–day struggle of May 1, 1886, the Knights of Labor and trade unionists of British and Irish backgrounds organized separately from the dense network of social revolutionary clubs, newspapers, armed units, trade unions, and neighborhood groups, which drew strength primarily from German, Bohemian, and Scandinavian immigrants. Editor Andrew Cameron of the *Workingmen's Advocate* proclaimed (as he often had before), "I am opposed to any movement toward joining with those who carry the red flag of Socialism [from] Europe to the democratic-republicanism of America." In Cincinnati the machinists' strike committee refused to join a parade which featured red flags and a rifle corps, despite supporting the eight-hour day.[103]

More vexing to workers who derived their political views from the republican, rather than the socialist legacy, was the question of whether or not they should participate in the national guard itself. Patrick Ford of the *Irish World* took note of the many instances during the July strikes of 1877 in which members of the militia had demonstrated their sympathy for the strikers. He concluded (as did many of his socialist contemporaries in Europe) that it was far safer to entrust the security of the republic to a volunteer military force whose members retained their everyday ties to civil society than to professional soldiers or police. His reasoning is worth reproducing at length, because it inverted the categories of discourse used by the reformers of the AICP:

> The police, many of whom have found their way into their places got through partisan influence or other unworthy agency, and who, from their contact with brothel keepers, ward politicians, and rum sellers, have become demoralized in the service, may be relied upon for any sort of beastly work. The men who

102 Nelson, *Beyond the Martyrs*, 139–41, 216–18; David, 136–7.
103 Bruce C. Nelson, "'We Can't Get Them to Do Aggressive Work': Chicago's Anarchists and the Eight-Hour Movement," *International Labor and Working-Class History*, 29 (Spring 1986), 1–13. The quotation from Cameron is on p. 10. Steven J. Ross, "Workers on the Edge: Work, Leisure, and Politics in Industrializing Cincinnati, 1830–1890" (Ph.D. diss., Princeton University, 1980), 426, 483.

compose the regular army – a necessary evil at all times – may be put down on the same page. Poor fellows! Misfortune and Hard Times have forced you to take up the trade of killing men for a living. But the Militia, fresh from the people, are in sympathy with the people, *and their fraternization may be counted on in every just uprising.*[104]

Subsequent events inspired working people, including many readers of the *Irish World*, to question whether the state militias were securing the republic or safeguarding its wealthy enemies. Patrick Ford himself accused national guardsmen in Scranton of preventing an alderman from arresting W. W. Scranton, the city's most eminent businessman, on murder charges, after he had led vigilantes through the streets during the strike to shoot at assembled groups of people. They should, "blue blood or no blue blood, be brought before the bar of justice to answer," a local paper thundered. Late in March 1884, when two Cincinnati murderers with good political connections were given ridiculously light sentences, an angry crowd burned down the county jail and courthouse. It took seven thousand militiamen two days of fighting to bring the city under control, leaving thirty-five dead and nearly two hundred wounded, most of them workers from the city's factories and workshops. One national guard unit refused to take up arms against the citizens, and less than a quarter of the soldiers from another local regiment reported for duty. In response to the conflict, Cincinnati's typographical union resolved that membership in the militia was "inconsistent with the duties and obligations of trade unionists," and it requested all workers to withdraw "at the earliest day practicable." Two years later the city's employers refused to reduce the hours of labor to conform to a new state law, which made eight hours a legal day's work. When thousands of workers paraded through the streets to demand obedience to the law, they found their city infested by almost two thousand guardsmen, eight Gatling guns, and a battery of heavy artillery – defending the manufacturers who defied the law![105]

Some offhand remarks by Terence Powderly, the leader of the Knights of Labor, focused press attention on the questions of who national guardsmen were and whom they served in the summer of 1886. Addressing a convention of the Eastern Green Glass Bottle Blowers Association in Atlantic City, New Jersey, he found a regiment

104 *Irish World*, Aug. 4, 1877. For varieties of militia behavior, see Philip S. Foner, *The Great Labor Uprising of 1877* (New York, 1977).
105 *Irish World*, Aug. 25, 1877; Steven J. Ross, *Workers on the Edge: Work, Leisure, and Politics in Industrializing Cincinnati, 1788–1890* (New York, 1985), 264–9, 274–87. The typographical union is quoted on p. 269.

of national guardsmen marching past the hotel with fixed bayonets.
"We looked into their faces," said Powderly to the delegates, "and saw
that some of them were men of means, and some of them mean men."
Warming to his audience's laughter, Powderly asked, "Who are they?
They are clerks, they are tradesmen." He then waxed eloquent, though
with dubious consistency:

> It has been demonstrated that two-thirds of the regiments of
> each State are members of the Knights of Labor and that when
> their time expires they will not re-enlist. Let the men who are in
> the banks and in the railroads – let the men who oppress labor
> fill up these ranks. Then, when the two sides are arrayed against
> each other, we will see who will win. They will be too cowardly to
> do it.[106]

A flurry of press commentary followed these remarks, many editors
agreeing with those of the New York *Tribune* that Powderly was guilty
of "unpardonable demagogism." But the Philadelphia *Times* made the
astute observation that politicians were wary of the subject. For them,
to denounce Powderly would alienate workers; to remain silent would
enrage conservatives.[107]

There have been been few studies of the actual social composition
of the late nineteenth-century national guard. Wisconsin's has been
examined; there, somewhat more than half of the enlisted men were
workers, while the officers came from professional and business ranks.
More revealing is the evidence from Ohio, where young urban crafts-
men and apprentices provided many guardsmen, but coal miners
were conspicuously absent. Whatever their origins, militiamen's encounters with strikers took on an increasingly harsh quality during the
many mobilizations of the 1890s. In Briceville, Tennessee, soldiers
patrolling the town were turned away from a miners' dance, and in
revenge precipitated a fight, hanged a miner, and refused to allow the
body to be cut down. Two years later, troops who were occupying
Homestead, Pennsylvania, crossed the Monongahela River to pursue
sympathetic strikers from Duquesne through the hills and march
them off in manacles to Pittsburgh. The regimental chaplain later
preached a Sunday sermon for strikebreakers in the Homestead mill,
while a thousand soldiers stood guard.[108]

---

106 New York *Daily Tribune,* July 16, 1886.
107 Knights of Labor Scrapbooks, Powderly Papers, reel 69.
108 Reinders, 96–8; Karin A. Shapiro, "The Tennessee Coal Miners' Revolts of 1891–
    92: Industrialization, Politics, and Convict Labor in the Late Nineteenth-Century
    South" (Ph.D. diss., Yale University, 1991), 229–33, 291–304; James Howard
    Bridge, *The Inside History of the Carnegie Steel Company: A Romance of Millions* (New
    York, 1903), 238–9.

Strikers and their sympathizers often shouted defiance and hurled rocks and other missiles at troops who had been amassed against them. Around Baltimore's Camden Depot and Chicago's Halsted Street viaduct, crowds kept soldiers engaged in battle for hours, and in Pittsburgh workers drove the militia from the city. Military commanders wrote many articles during the 1880s and 1890s on the most effective tactics to use against men and women hurling objects from rooftops and about the employment of cavalry to sweep crowds from streets and sidewalks. Nevertheless, although working people engaged in gun battles with Pinkertons and with deputy sheriffs, they rarely shot at soldiers after the 1870s. Most famously, the Advisory Committee, which had directed the successful combat against the Pinkertons in Homestead, organized a welcoming ceremony for the arriving troops (only to find that the army moved into their town in battle formation before dawn). A Knights of Labor lecturer in Tennessee captured the blend of physical and symbolic power that constituted the army's role in securing the state's hegemony. "While I am a labor man I do not propose to become a criminal nor will I fight against any State," wrote J. C. Roberts to Powderly. "I tried fighting for four years in the confederate service and know from experience that it is both expensive and dangerous."[109]

"To every thoughtful and intelligent workingman," wrote "Civis" to the *Journal of the Knights of Labor,* "it should be quite plain that he has no business in the National Guard." Samuel Gompers agreed. He advised the 1892 convention of the American Federation of Labor that "membership in a labor organization and the militia at one and the same time is inconsistent and incompatible." By 1894 national unions of painters, brewery workers, and stonecutters, as well as the American Railway Union, had all prohibited their members from joining the military. That year Gompers also called for the defeat of a proposed amendment to New York's constitution that would have made every young man eligible for guard duty. "Then the men who will refuse to perform military duty and shoot down their fellow workers, will be denounced and charged with treason to the State," he warned.[110]

As the century closed, then, the regular army and state national guard units had been routinely arrayed, in the Supreme Court's words, as the "strong arm of the national government . . . to brush away all obstructions to interstate commerce . . . [and] to compel

---

109 Foner, *1877*, 46–54, 151–6; Krause, 334–8; *Journal of the Military Service Institution of the United States;* J. C. Roberts to T. V. Powderly, Dec. 22, 1891, Powderly Papers, reel 37.
110 *Journal of the Knights of Labor,* Aug. 16, 1894, quoted in Reinders, 99; Montgomery, *Fall,* 363; Gompers at 1892 convention, quoted by Skowronek, 105; Gompers to James Lynch, October 26, 1894, in Kaufman, *Gompers Papers,* vol. 3, 594.

obedience to its laws."[111] The use of military power as the ultimate bulwark of a free-market economy had left many workers perceiving the nation's armed forces as their enemy, not as the defender of their liberties. Although it was impossible to resist such a force, labor organizations could and did urge their members to withdraw from the military service of the republic, which their arms had helped preserve in the 1860s. As the twentieth century dawned, the challenge posed by military might and military service rapidly became more urgent and more difficult. Troops paraded through strike-bound cities and mining camps more often than ever between 1900 and 1922, while America's growing role in a world of ominous international conflict justified the steady increase of military and especially naval forces. With the country's entry into World War I, conscription returned to working-class homes. The arguments and remedies of the nineteenth century appeared to have little meaning in Flanders' fields. They had, however, already set firm limits to the actions and the thinking of workers in the capitalist republic.

Police Powers and Workers' Homes

Although the law had found ways to "compel the lazy to work" and to uphold the authority of the employer to fix the terms of employment without interference from the state, from unions, or from crowds, the homes and neighborhoods in which working men and women resided nevertheless continued to breed defiance to bourgeois dreams of order based on market relations throughout the nineteenth century. Not the smallest part of the problem faced by the AICP and other reformers when they attacked the disorder in working-class districts was that the taproot of that disorder was the market system itself – most obviously the free market in real estate.

In contrast to the enclaves of respectable urban life that the middle and upper classes had created for themselves by mid-century, the bustle and squalor of working-class neighborhoods mocked bourgeois dreams of "new labour habits and a new time-discipline." The intermingled habitats, industry, street life, taverns, and popular theaters that urban growth folded in upon each other spawned plebeian cultures that contested the efforts of business and evangelical reformers in daily social intercourse, at the ballot box, and through violent crowd action. Philadelphia's Moyamensing firehouse riots and New York's Astor Place theater bloodshed in 1849 foretold eruption of "the volcano under the city," which came

111 *In Re Debs,* in Commager, vol. 2, 164.

to pass in the draft riots of 1863 and the nationwide strikes of July 1877. These events persuaded prominent public figures that the free market in urban real estate produced social chaos. The police powers of the state had to be invoked to reshape the physical infrastructure of daily life.[112]

For most workers urban homes were rented homes. As urban populations swelled during the early nineteenth century and the practice of employment at will spread from craft to craft (and became enshrined in law), the dependence of the men and women Mike Walsh called "devoid of all other means of support but their labor" was not only that of wage earners, but also that of renters of dwelling places. The evolving relationship of wage labor to alienation from real estate has been most thoroughly studied in the case of New York City.

A closed elite of landed families had ruled eighteenth-century New York through a royal charter that had made the city itself a landowning corporation, governed by those whom it admitted to the "freedom of the city." Through the sale of common lands and especially of water lots, the corporation both obtained its revenues and organized the private actions of individuals, requiring them by the obligations of freemen and by the terms of land sales to build wharfs, abate nuisances, and guard the community against crime, fire, and disease. Holders of large tracts of land, foremost among them the Trinity Church, also leased out many lots for long terms, but under conditions strictly specifying their use. Between 1790 and 1810 the rapidly growing city sold off much of its common land and leased other tracts without deed restrictions on future use while it instituted its first public services, financed by assessments on the property of beneficiaries. As Hendrick Hartog explained the transition, the city depended less and less on its own property as a source of revenue and a means of shaping private activity to public purposes, and turned instead to the state legislature for grants of authority to raise tax revenues and regulate municipal life. The constitution of 1846 concluded the process by eliminating all prerevolutionary royal grants and making all municipalities local agents of the state, executing those functions that the legislature had authorized.[113]

The transformation can be understood as the triumph of Jeffersonian Democracy in the city and state government of New York. In fact, the revolt of the tenants against the remaining feudal obligations

112 Bernstein, 57–8, 183–5, 254–5; Griscom; William Osborn Stoddard, *The Volcano under the City, by a Volunteer Special* (New York, 1887).
113 Hartog, 93–132, 203–22; Blackmar, 14–43. Unlike Blackmar, Hartog slights the role of private landholders themselves in controlling development through the terms of leases.

on the Van Rensselaer and other Hudson Valley estates in the 1840s, the power of Mike Walsh's Subterranean Democracy in city politics, and the success of the Democrats' "stop and tax" policy in shifting the initiative in the state's economic development decisively away from the legislature and to private capital, were the immediate causes of the 1846 constitutional convention. What concerns us here, however, are the consequences for workers of the sales of land to private pro-prietors for uses that the owners determined.[114]

Several years of debates and surveys had produced the famous grid of 1811, by which all of Manhattan north of the already-built portions of the city was laid out in rectangles for future public sale. As Elizabeth Black-mar has demonstrated, the consequences of this way of creating a free and open market in real estate were by no means as egalitarian as the Jeffersonian rectangular blocks on the city map would suggest. Blackmar contends that "the neutral market had carried a new class dynamic into the process of residential neighborhood formation, and it persisted through the rest of the century." Vast stretches of vacant land surround-ing the city remained in relatively few hands. As Henry George argued in *Progress and Poverty*, unused land on the city's outskirts created an artificial scarcity of land for use within the growing city. New landowners joined descendants of the colonial rentier class in extending long-term leases to builders, with conditions carefully defining what was to be built, so as to maximize the landowners' returns. In this way, writes Blackmar, large land tracts were transformed "into the uniform block fronts that stabi-lized land values." In the 1830s the lure of rents and profits from commercial building, she concludes, "had attracted capital beyond what the city's businesses or residents could pay back in rents." The panic of 1837 sent land values plummeting and brought ruin to the city's many construction workers.[115]

Second, the competitive housing market itself, argues Blackmar, and especially "the purchasing power that permitted elite New Yorkers to claim blocks for their exclusive use," added to the value of real estate in the more elegant neighborhoods while depressing values in less fortunate areas, so that a high return could be acquired in the latter only by multiplying the number of dwellings and surrounding homes with manufacturing and commercial activities. Despite the rapid increase in population, few new residential buildings went up in the poorer neighborhoods. Instead, rooms were added where court-

---

114 On the tenant revolt, see Henry M. Christman, *Tin Horns and Calico: A Decisive Episode in the Emergence of Democracy* (New York, 1945); David M. Ellis, *Landlords and Farmers in the Hudson-Mohawk Region, 1790–1850* (Ithaca, N.Y., 1946).

115 Hartog, 158–61; Blackmar, 104, 203, 185–205; Henry George, *Progress and Poverty: An Inquiry into the Cause of Industrial Depression and of Increase of Want with Increase of Wealth* (New York, 1935, first edition 1879).

yards had once let in some light and air, and high rents forced larger numbers of people to crowd into existing quarters. By the time tenement construction got under way in the mid-1840s, ostensibly for better-paid workers, massive immigration from Europe simply overwhelmed the already-overburdened supply of housing for working people.[116]

Finally, the rising portion of incomes that working people had to devote to rent diminished their ability to acquire their own property in cheaper areas. "The workingman who lives in a city tenement," wrote the popular Knight of Labor Phillips Thompson late in the century, "pays a larger proportion of his earnings to the landlord for the privilege of existing and employing his faculties in some form of productive industry, having apparently very little direct connection with the soil, than does the small farmer whose subsistence is wholly and directly drawn from the land." The possibility of escape to the outskirts of the city, to build one's own shanty or raise one's own food, was blocked again and again by enclosures of common lands and evictions of squatters. In 1821 and 1826 fences were torn down and residences of landlords attacked by irate men and women who had formerly used lands to the north of the city. Among them were many butchers, who were allowed to ply their trades outside of rented stalls in the city market only north of the city limits. Whole villages of squatters, many with tidy homes they had erected themselves, were evicted to make way for Central Park.[117]

All three of these developments were duplicated in every industrial town, though not always effecting so total a transformation as occurred in New York. Jonathan Prude found native-born artisans in textile towns of the Blackstone Valley in Massachusetts likely as late as 1850 to own their homes (and to enjoy unchanged patterns of work), but the transient mill hands boarded or rented. Alan Dawley concluded that the extinction of master shoemakers in Lynn, Massachusetts, also rendered the town's fabled home-owning workers a myth.[118] The 1840 tax rolls of Manayunk, a spinning mill and hand-loom weaving center adjacent to Philadelphia, revealed very few workers with any real estate. The few who owned buildings were carpenters, masons, and blacksmiths. The most desolate conditions were reported by Philadelphia street preacher Benjamin Sewell, most of whose im-

116 Blackmar, 104, 203–13.
117 Phillips Thompson, "The Land Question," in Terence V. Powderly and A. W. Wright, eds., *Labor Day Annual* (Toronto, 1893), 18; Gilje, 221–2; Roy Rosenzweig and Elizabeth Blackmar, *The Park and the People: A History of Central Park* (Ithaca, N.Y., 1992), 63–81.
118 Prude, 69–78, 183–94; Dawley, 51–3. Cf. Klaus Tenfelde, "Germany," in van der Linden and Rojahn, vol. 1, 252–3, on renting and home ownership among workers in late nineteenth-century Germany; and Hartmut Kaelble, *Industrialisation and Social Inequality in 19th-Century Europe* (Leamington Spa, 1986), 105–27.

poverished neighbors disappeared after dark into habitations for which they paid in advance by the night: six cents if there was no floor, twelve cents if there was flooring.[119]

Although real incomes of working-class families rose significantly between 1850 and 1900, fewer than 25 percent of all homes were owned by the families that inhabited them in the cities of the East and the Ohio River Valley at the time of the 1890 census. Stephan Thernstrom sampled 1,000 wage earners in Boston in 1870 and found only 11 percent of them owning the dwellings in which they resided. In Boston's suburbs, Sam Bass Warner, Jr., adds, only a quarter of the resident families of *all* classes owned their homes. Even in Philadelphia, where four hundred building-and-loan associations helped people finance their own homes by 1874, the first census to inquire into the subject (1890) found a level of ownership like that of Boston's suburbs: less than 25 percent of the entire population of households. In southern cities and in northern textile towns the rate of ownership was considerably lower than that.[120]

A somewhat different pattern emerged in Detroit, Toledo, Grand Rapids, St. Paul, and a few other cities in the interior of the continent, all of which manufactured consumer goods that depended more on rail than water transportation. Although the waterfronts of these cities conformed to the New York pattern, the major factories were located along rail lines in low-rent areas, and housing developers quickly learned to erect modest single-family dwellings in the vicinity of those enterprises and to offer them for sale on easy terms. Residents of such tracts could empathize with the fictional "Larry Locke, Man of Iron," who at the conclusion of his successful strike against the mill owners, remained, in the words of the story,

---

119 Manayunk tax rolls of 1840 (Pennsylvania Historical Society); Sewell, 323–4.
120 Gregory R. Zieren, "The Propertied Worker: Working Class Formation in Toledo, Ohio, 1870–1900" (Ph.D. diss., University of Delaware, 1981), 146–8; Stephan Thernstrom, *The Other Bostonians: Poverty and Progress in the American Metropolis, 1880–1970* (Cambridge, Mass., 1973), 98; Sam B. Warner, Jr., *Streetcar Suburbs: The Process of Growth in Boston, 1870–1900* (Cambridge, Mass., 1962), 26, 119–20; John F. Sutherland, "Housing the Poor in a City of Homes: Philadelphia at the Turn of the Century," in Allen F. Davis and Mark H. Haller, eds., *The Peoples of Philadelphia: A History of Ethnic Groups and Lower-Class Life, 1790–1940* (Philadelphia, 1973), 182; Margaret Marsh, "From Separation to Togetherness: The Social Construction of Domestic Space in American Suburbs, 1840–1915," *Journal of American History,* 76 (Sept. 1989), 511; U.S. Census, *Historical Statistics,* 2,646; Christian Topalov, "Régulation publique du capitalisme et propriété de masse du logement: la 'révolution hypothécaire' des années 1930 aux Etats-Unis," *Economie et Société,* 5 (1988), 51–99. Only after the New Deal underwrote long-term, low-interest loans covering most of the price did home ownership become the norm among urban Americans – including 70 percent of AFL-CIO members before 1980.

known to-day as one of the best practical men in the iron trade and has long turned his little shanty on the rocks into a handsome [and mortgage-free] house, for he would not sell the house where he had first seen Molly. . . . I'll live in it all my days just to make me remember that a man's got to stick to his colors if he hopes to win in the fight between labor and capital.[121]

Toledo, where 93 percent of the population lived in single-family dwellings in 1900, was not a high-wage city. The workers most likely to own their dwellings were Polish immigrants, 63 percent of whom were home owners. As Gregory Zieren has pointed out, ethnic culture alone does not explain this pattern. In other major American cities hardly 10 percent of the Poles had bought their houses. Furthermore, in the parts of Toledo where land was cheapest, even native-born white workers, who ranked near the bottom of ethnic groups in home ownership there as elsewhere, tended to buy. Toledo's widely dispersed residences placed the franchises of traction companies at the very center of local political controversy, as was also the case in Cleveland, Detroit, and Milwaukee. Popular insistence that street car companies constantly extend their network of lines and hold fares down to the three or four cent level for the use of the widely dispersed workers and their families provided the issue that propelled to power reform mayors like Golden Rule Jones, Tom Johnson, and Newton D. Baker. Even in those cities, however, most workers rented one of the characteristic single-family dwellings or duplexes. What made the cities remarkable is that 40 percent or more of the inhabitants were home owners.[122]

In New York, as in most other cities, political struggles hinged directly on the cost and character of rental housing. Before the legislature ended landlords' right to claim personal belongings for unpaid rent in 1846, the role of magistrates in evictions and in distress proceedings provided no end of grist for the mills of both labor and evangelical reformers. Lawsuits against landlords for not maintaining rented premises suitably frequently found jurors and judges on opposing sides. By the 1840s, however, the needs of rent-paying wage earners were articulated in programmatic form. Leader George Henry Evans of the National Reform Association called for a legal limit to the amount of urban land one person could own, in addition to his famous demand for free access to plots on the public domain. He also

121 Zieren, 37–78, 146–8; Capt. Fred Whittaker, "Larry Locke, The Man of Iron; Or, A Fight for Fortune. A Story of Labor and Capital," *Beadle's Weekly*, 2 (Jan. 12, 1884), 7. The edition of "Larry Locke" reproduced in Grimes, 135–326, has a somewhat different ending, but retains the mortgage-free home.
122 Zieren, 96–128.

advocated salaries for aldermen, ending the fee system of justice, and poor relief as a right, not as charity.[123]

A Tenant League called on the city government in 1848 to rescue the working people from the ravages of the free market in real estate. Its leader, M. T. O'Connor, advocated a triple tax on unimproved land, the sale of city lots to homesteaders on easy terms, a prohibition on rental of cellars, and a repeal of the fire limit law, which required brick construction north of Fourteenth Street.[124] All of the league's proposals reappeared in one form or another in the political demands of urban workers during the ensuing half-century.

After the Chicago fire the newly elected "Fireproof Administration" attempted to require brick construction throughout the Windy City, only to encounter adamant resistance not only from workers but also from the business and professional leaders of the predominantly German North Side. Brick construction meant tenements and "smoking machine shops, mills, and lumber depots," argued Anton Hesing of the *Illinois Staats-Zeitung*. Workers could build their own cottages out of wood. "Those are not *true* Americans – no matter where born," Hesing thundered, "who would consign our laboring classes to the condition of *proletaires* by depriving them of a chance to live under their own roofs."[125]

Democratic institutions provided an effective defense for Chicago's workers, first because their cause was championed by a powerful ethnic elite, and second because it was the Germans who demanded an unrestrained market. The Fireproof Administration wished to regulate land use in the larger interest of the city's businessmen. The long-term consequences of the German householders' political victory, however, did not reproduce the style of living enjoyed by their fellow Germans in Toledo. By the time of the Haymarket Affair it was evident that the "friendly flower-framed little houses" promised by Hesing had become dark duplexes crowded in by apartment buildings and workshops.[126]

A remarkably different approach had been attempted by New York's workers. An unprecedented wave of strikes in 1850 prompted the Tammany Hall Democrats to donate a wing of the new city hall to the use of an Industrial Congress, made up of delegates from all workers' organizations. A committee of that congress, chaired by carpenter Benjamin Price, sought legislative remedies for what it called the

123 Blackmar, 227–35; Bridges, 115.
124 Blackmar, 247.
125 *Illinois Staats-Zeitung*, Oct. 20, 1871; Anton C. Hesing to *Chicago Republican*, Jan. 18, 1872, quoted in Sawislak, 182, 191.
126 Hartmut Keil, ed., *German Workers' Culture in the United States, 1850 to 1920* (Washington, D.C., 1988), 30–1, 51.

accumulation of "immense wealth regardless of the misery and distress thereby entailed upon hundreds and thousands . . . [of] fellow beings," through the creation of an elected inspector of rents, who was to be empowered to halt the payment of rents on unfit tenements, and of district surveyors, who would inspect all buildings and prohibit occupancy of unfit ones. The second effort – that which sought to impose legal standards on the construction and use of dwellings – placed at least part of the labor movement in alliance with the Association for Improving the Condition of the Poor, and it led eventually to the tenement house law of 1867, based on AICP proposals, but introduced into the legislature by Assemblyman Patrick Keady, former president of the Brooklyn painters' union.[127]

Although lax enforcement by the city government neutralized the effects of the 1867 law (aside from the eviction of thousands of people from cellars), the effort to regulate tenement houses had revealed that workers' homes played as decisive a role as their jobs in the class conflict over the social discipline required by a market-driven capitalist economy. Labor activists like O'Connor, Price, and Keady, who joined with bourgeois reformers (albeit on their own terms) in the quest for governmental regulation of the housing market, often found the support of their own constituents halfhearted at best. In 1835 the Trades' Union had opposed the plan to create a professional city fire department, seeing behind it a scheme of the insurance companies and property owners to saddle "the whole of the expense" on tenants, by "raising the rents of our already overburdened citizens." Frugal government, not more government, had been George Henry Evans's favorite rhetorical theme. The men and women who suffered most from dismal housing were so deeply enmeshed in networks of subleasing and petty credit that they were often frightened by reformers' attacks on their immediate exploiters. As Elizabeth Blackmar observed: "While such reformers as [John] Griscom attacked the rapacious greed of working-class sublandlords, many tenants were sympathetic to these community creditors, who, by 'extending' the wage, sustained working-class families within the bounds of the legal economy. Then, too, tenants knew well that landlords repaired housing in order to increase rents."[128]

Nevertheless, the discernible role of rents connecting the struggle to live on wages with the barrenness of urban living for working-class men and women explains the widespread popularity of the Single-Tax movement. Henry George proclaimed that "private property in land is a bold, bare, enormous wrong, like that of chattel slavery." Seeking a

---

127 Bernstein, 85–92, 187–8. In 1835 the common council of New York had explicitly refused to provide rooms for the use of the National Trades Union. Bridges, 108.
128 Bridges, 108, 115; Blackmar, 262.

remedy that would "approach the ideal of Jeffersonian democracy" by reducing the need for and exercise of government's coercive powers, he concluded that government might "become the administration of a great co-operative society," if the market value of unimproved land was transferred by taxation to the community, whose work he believed had created that value, and all other taxes abolished. Then a new kind of city could arise: "We could establish public baths, museums, libraries, gardens, lecture rooms, music and dancing halls, theaters, universities, technical schools, shooting galleries, play grounds, gymnasiums, etc. . . . and in a thousand ways the public revenues [could be] made to foster efforts for the public benefit."[129]

The huge vote garnered by Henry George's campaign for mayor of New York in 1886 represented for many reformers the high-water mark of that decade's labor struggles. George singled out the rentier class – not the entrepreneurs, developers, or sublettors – as the wealthy parasites living off the toil and suffering of others. "We are wage-workers and tenants," said George's daily campaign organ. "We should vote for a man who proposes to use his best endeavors to bring about legislation by which wage-slavery and land monopoly shall be abolished." His election campaign involved many more women than did most organized activities of the late–nineteenth-century labor movement, not only because it was neighborhood-based, but also because its demands touched the lives of housewives as well as those of men and women who earned wages outside of their homes. Although socialists shunned the Anti-Poverty Society, led by Rev. Edward McGlynn in conformity to George's teachings, Irish-American women were conspicuous at its meetings and especially in the public gatherings convened to defend McGlynn after he had been defrocked by the church.[130]

The connection between alienation from the land and the rigors of the wages system was constantly reiterated by labor reformers of the 1880s. General Master Workman Terence V. Powderly of the Knights of Labor believed "the key note that will reach the American heart," was the workers' experience of

> the alien land lord who first drives his victims from Irish soil and heads them off in this land by buying (stealing) up the land and compels his slave to go up into an eight story tenement in a large city and live on a crust of bread or pay an exorbitant price for land which God made for all honest men instead of for thieves.[131]

129 George, 358, 455, 456.
130 David Scobey, "Boycotting the Politics Factory: Labor Radicalism and the New York City Mayoral Election of 1884 [sic]," Radical History Review, 28–30 (1984), 280–325 (the quotation is on p. 311); Peter A. Speek, The Singletax and the Labor Movement (Madison, Wis., 1917), 101–4. George had noted that in the Irish Land League also, "the best men were women." Denver Labor Enquirer, August 11, 1883.
131 Powderly to friend Dever, Sept. 22, 1883, quoted in Stuart Bruce Kaufman, Samuel

Powderly's colleague Phillips Thompson used that keynote to call not for the Single Tax but for the gradual abolition of private ownership of land. "Individualism is everywhere giving place to organized, systematized combination in the interests of capitalism," he wrote in 1893. Labor's "aim should be to substitute for the capitalist director and organizer of industry the agent of the people, and to make public convenience instead of private aggrandizement the controlling and animating principle. Public ownership of the land is an essential feature of any movement for social regeneration which keeps in view this inevitable tendency of the times."[132]

Thompson had carried the logic of the AICP's attempt to regulate the urban real estate market to a conclusion that reversed the larger economic vision of the association's leaders and sponsors. But then, every aspect of the workers' hunger for land and a home lent itself to many, often contradictory uses. The depression of the 1890s unleashed a flurry of attempts to have the unemployed colonize the land; these were sponsored by religious groups, urban reformers, the Chicago Trades and Labor Assembly, and Eugene V. Debs's Social Democracy of America. Detroit's mayor, Hazen Pingree, earned little more than ridicule from the clergy when he turned over unused land for use by the poor as "potato patches" and asked the churches to supply tools. In Massachusetts the schools did provide little gardens for the children, not to help them feed their families, but to teach them "civic virtues" and "the sense of ownership and of the institution of private property as seen from the inside."[133]

Superintendent Thomas Brown of the Chicago police found plenty of people to agree with him when he argued that "men who own the houses and lots where their families live . . . are not very likely to engage in bloody riots or in destroying the property of other people." A generation later, however, the Socialist Party's *Appeal to Reason* replied, "Socialism will enable EVERY FAMILY IN ALL THE WORLD TO OWN A HOME."[134]

The century had made clear that capitalist development, and the free market in real estate in particular, had made most wage earners

Gompers and the Origins of the American Federation of Labor, *1848–1896* (Westport, Conn., 1973), 155. On the weak enforcement of the tenement house law, see David M. Scobey, "Empire City: Politics, Culture, and Urbanism in Gilded-Age New York" (Ph.D. diss., Yale University, 1989), 347–51. On the George campaign, see Scobey, "Boycotting the Politics Factory."

132 Thompson, "Land Question," 21.

133 H. Roger Grant, *Self-Help in the 1890s Depression* (Ames, Iowa, 1983); W. T. Stead, *Chicago To-Day; Or, The Labour War in America* (London, 1894), 137–8; Nick Salvatore, *Eugene V. Debs: Citizen and Socialist* (Urbana, Ill., 1982), 163–7; Melvin G. Holli, *Reform in Detroit: Hazen S. Pingree and Urban Politics* (New York, 1969), 70–2; Ringenbach, 112.

134 Sawislak, 76–7; Fred Warren, *The Appeal's Arsenal of Facts* (Girard, Kan., 1911), 166.

into renters, not owners, of their homes. Moreover, when urban development was directed by no power other than the free market in
real estate, the result was such physical congestion and social disorder
as to make some manner of governmental planning and regulation
attractive even to the most privileged classes. Among working people,
struggles over land, rent, and housing – the physical domain of the
reproduction of daily life – provided, as Powderly said, a keynote that
did "reach the American heart" every bit as powerfully as the more
famous battles that arose directly out of working for wages.

The political struggles generated by the use of urban real estate
blended with those linked to the reorganization of police forces and
of criminal justice, to the privatization of poor relief and governmental treatment of the "wandering" population, and to the refashioning
of military power and service between the beginning and the end of
the nineteenth century. The combined effect of these changes was
both to strengthen the coercive capacity of government and to narrow
the sphere of its authority, so as to insulate the economy from democratic government while exercising a more systematic discipline over
the behavior of working people.

Max Weber argued, "A state based exclusively on money contributions, conducting the collection of the taxes (but no other economic
activity) through its own staff, and calling on personal service contributions only for political and judicial purposes, provides an optimal
environment for a rational market-operated capitalism."[135] By the end
of the nineteenth century the United States fit Weber's description.
What Weber's clear statement disguises, however, is the way in which
class rule was exercised both through governmental machinery and in
opposition to it – through business institutions and private associations that kept elected government at arm's length. Both the state and
civil society were theaters of class conflict. The democratic character
of the elected branches of government and the diversity of the nation's social life barred the way to the domination of American life by
an ideological consensus. What remains to be seen is whether the
country's political life could produce an effective alternative to "rational free-market capitalism."

---

135 Max Weber, *Economy and Society*, quoted in Hartog, 145n.

3

Political Parties

In 1880 Charles Francis Adams, Jr., reflected publicly on the nine presidential elections in which he had been actively involved since his youthful participation in antislavery parties. "I think, of the whole nine, there was but one, that of 1852, which at the time was not emphatically pronounced to be the most important election in its consequences ever held," he mused. "The issues at stake were always too tremendous to be calmly contemplated; and if the day was lost now it was lost forever." Of all those elections, he had come to believe, only one, "so far as the grand results were concerned, was really important . . . that of 1864, when we were in the midst of the Rebellion." He advised his audience that the time was overripe to put aside disputes "over the possession of a little temporal political authority," and his explanation provided a classic formulation of nineteenth-century liberalism:

> The future of this country is in the hands of our universities, our schools, our specialists, our scientific men, and our writers. Why! take in the grand results, what does Washington do but impede? As an obstacle to intelligent Progress, the National Government is an undisputable success. . . . We do not care which [party] is in office and which in opposition; we only ask that one shall be in office and one in opposition; we who manage the schools, the press, the shops, the railroads, and exchanges will take care of the rest. . . . The first object of the thinking citizen, therefore, now should be, not to keep one party or the other in power, . . . but . . . to insist on order and submission to law. That secured, all else must follow.[1]

Adams's contempt for political parties and his conviction that those who "manage[d] the schools, the press, the shops, the railroads, and exchanges" were the men best qualified to direct society's journey into the uncharted future of industrial life, while government should confine itself to securing "order and submission to law," were widely

1 Charles Francis Adams, Jr., *Individuality in Politics: A Lecture Delivered in Steinway Hall, New York, Wednesday Evening, April 21, 1880* (New York, 1880), 6, 11–13.

shared by those of his contemporaries who also enjoyed his advantages of income, status, and education. To them the republic was threatened not by the accumulation of wealth and disparities of income, which labor reformers lamented, but rather by corruption and self-interest in government. Partisan appeals to a mass electorate, in their view, encouraged self-serving aspirants to office to engage in demagoguery, "caesarism," and the "politics of class feeling." Two prints of New York polling places found in an *Illustrated London News* of 1864 encapsulated his image of American partisanship. One depicted a prosperous midtown residential district, where voting was in progress inside a livery stable. Large numbers of well-dressed men conversed soberly outside the stable. No women were in sight, and only a few boys. The other portrayed separate Lincoln and McClellan booths erected outside a liquor store in a workers' neighborhood. Shabbily attired men and women hovered around the booths. Four men were assaulting some apparent supporter of the wrong ticket while police officers approached on the run, clubs at the ready.[2]

An influential book by Stephen Skowronek has described the government of nineteenth-century America as one of parties and courts. Lacking the administrative bureaucracies that imposed governmental direction on the lives of continental Europeans and constrained by a constitution that privileged private actions, Skowronek argues, government in the United States was provided whatever coherence it possessed by the guidance of political parties and of the judiciary. Even the imposing machinery of government created by the Civil War was "simply swept aside by the party politics of the 1870s."[3]

Skowronek shares the belief, if not the values, of Anatole France's little Parisian girl, who said: "The State, Father, is a woeful, ungracious man seated behind a little window. You understand that we are not anxious to rob ourselves for him."[4] The civil service, which parliamentary regimes in continental Europe had inherited from absolutism, was conspicuously insignificant in the governing of the nineteenth-century United States, despite the conviction of Adams and his fellow liberals that merit qualifications for civil service positions and promotions would empty the trough of corruption in government. Neither Adams nor the workers were anxious to tax themselves for men and women "behind little windows," but both were keenly aware of the decisive role of parties and of courts in the daily management of the American state.

2 *Illustrated London News*, Dec. 3, 1864, reproduced in Baker, 307. On liberalism, see
  John G. Sproat, *The "Best Men": Liberal Reformers of the Gilded Age* (New York, 1968).
3 Skowronek, 30.
4 *Monsieur Bergeret à Paris*, quoted in Vandervelde, 224.

Nevertheless, the arguments offered in the previous chapters suggest a friendly amendment to Skowronek's thesis. The coercive capacity of government grew steadily throughout the century even as the authority it exercised was narrowed in scope, and undeveloped bureaucracy kept what Moisei Ostrogorski called "the spring of government" weakened.[5] Both the increase of state and local regulation of popular behavior and the ephemeral creation of the federal Leviathan that preserved the Union and destroyed slavery were indispensible if market-directed businessmen and professionals were to be able to "take care of the rest." Moreover, the use of governmental coercion to impose a new definition of "order" and popular reactions to that order played a major role in generating the "fanatical" party loyalties that Adams deplored. The primary vehicle for translating popular sentiments into governmental policy was the political party, as Skowronek contends. Nevertheless, the discourse through which parties formulated and disseminated their proposals did more than just reflect popular sentiments. It also imposed effective restraints on the expression and even the content of working people's aspirations and opinions.

Conversely, the private arrangements that had reordered economic and social life had shaped party programs and imposed sharp limits on what any party might do with governmental power. While that paradox was evident everywhere, the process by which a triumphant market system nurtured intense party loyalties while eliminating restraints on those who "manage[d] the schools, the press, the shops, the railroads, and exchanges" followed different trajectories for black workers in the South and white workers in the North. Close examination of those different trajectories also reveals how the events of that moment, in which the coercive power of the state *did* play a decisive role in reshaping the social order, provide the key to understanding the intense attachments to one or another of the existing parties that working people exhibited in both South and North long after the outcome of that bloody era's conflicts had been decided.

Black Workers and the Republicans in the South

The relationship of wage labor to democratic government, which had taken three-quarters of a century to crystallize in the North, was resolved with ferocious haste in the southern states after the Civil War. The collapse of slavery was followed in late 1865 by the enactment of state master-and-servant laws, augmented by new vagrancy statutes, in

5 Moisei Ostrogorski, *Democracy and the Organization of Political Parties,* translated by Frederick Clarke (2 vols., New York, 1902), vol. 2, 550.

special codes regulating black labor. As has already been demonstrated, the Black Codes were quickly overturned. The process by which they were abolished – and rights of citizenship secured – allied African Americans in the South to the Republican Party. In fact, no other group of working people in the history of the United States has ever linked its aspirations so tightly or with such unanimity to a political party. Nevertheless, the Republicans never became *their* party, in the sense of a party whose program and leadership were determined by black constituents.

Without a doubt the most widespread desire of former slaves was to settle on land of their own. Drafters of a petition to President Johnson from Edisto Island, South Carolina, expressed their indignation at the thought of being driven once again into their former masters' fields: "Man that have stud upon the feal of battle & have shot there master & sons now Going to ask ether one for bread or for shelter or Comfortable for his wife & children sunch a thing the u st should not aught to Expect a man."[6]

It was equally clear, however, that the land was not redistributed to its tillers. The petition just quoted came from the region covered by General William Tecumseh Sherman's famous Field Order No. 15, the only large-scale effort to settle freed people on small plots carved from plantations that had been abandoned by their owners during the war. The occasion for the petition was President Andrew Johnson's restoration of those lands to pardoned former owners. General Oliver O. Howard of the Freedmen's Bureau was dispatched to inform the sea islanders in the presence of their former masters that only those few who could produce clear titles to the land they worked would be allowed to retain their plots. At a meeting in Edisto Island's Old Stone Church a committee of black men caucused and then responded that they wished to buy or lease the lands, but would not submit to employment by their former owners. The assembly, wrote a northern reporter, "endorses by sullen silence, or bursting sobs and groans."[7]

Although many black military veterans used mustering-out pay to purchase land, even soldiers realistically feared that their discharges and their pay would arrive too late. "Run Right out of Slavery into Soldiery & we hadent nothing atoll & our wives & mothers most all of them is aperishing all about where we leave them," wrote such a soldier to his commander early in 1866. "Property & all the lands that would be sold cheap will be gone & we will have a Hard struggle to get along in the U S."[8]

6 Mary Ames, *From a New England Woman's Diary in Dixie in 1865* (Springfield, Mass., 1906), 101.
7 Berlin, *Freedom*, series 1, vol. 3, 338–40; McPherson, 36–8; *The Liberator*, Dec. 15, 1865. I am indebted to Julie Saville for this document.
8 Berlin, *Freedom*, series 2, 777–8.

Even though the depression of the 1870s threw vast tracts of southern land into state hands through tax defaults, most of that acreage made its way back to former owners, and only South Carolina and Mississippi systematically used such lands to homestead black families. By 1890, when the U.S. census first clearly distinguished patterns of land ownership and tenancy, only 14 percent of South Carolina's black farmers and 16 percent of those in Mississippi owned the land they worked. Virtually all their farms were outside the plantation regions of the states.[9]

In practice, therefore, the labor question was fought out not over ownership of the land, but over the terms of contract. Plantations remained intact, even though many were bought by new owners or were leased out to some white person with operating capital, who then hired black workers. The federal Bureau of Refugees, Freedmen and Abandoned Lands often required former slaves to contract for a full crop year, especially in Louisiana, where many sugar planters had gone over to the Union side before the war's end. The bureau also created precedents beneficial to field hands, however, because it adjudicated black workers' grievances, and it insisted that workers' claims to wages took precedence over landlords' claims for rent or merchants' claims for credit advances. The bureau's assistant commissioner for Arkansas went so far as to have the 1869 crop seized by the army in order to insure that workers received their full contracted share from the sale. Although historians are far from agreed among themselves as to the role of the bureau – Professor Leon Litwack called it the "planter's guard" – the fact remains that land-owners themselves were overwhelmingly hostile to its "interference."[10]

Worse even than the bureau, from the planters' perspective, was the presence of black soldiers. One white Mississippian explained why:

> The Negro Soldiery here are constantly telling our negroes, that for the next year, The Government will give them lands, provisions, Stock & all things necessary to carry on business for themselves, – & are constantly advising them not to make contracts with white persons, for the next year. – Strange to say the negroes believe such stories in spite of facts to the contrary told them by their ~~masters~~ [sic] employers.[11]

9 Foner, *Reconstruction*, 375; Neil R. McMillen, *Dark Journey: Black Mississippians in the Age of Jim Crow* (Urbana, Ill., 1989), 112–14.
10 Harold D. Woodman, "Post–Civil War Southern Agriculture and the Law," *Agricultural History*, 53 (Jan. 1979), 323; Litwack, *Been So Long in the Storm*, 386. For a largely favorable evaluation of the bureau, see Foner, *Reconstruction*, 144–68.
11 Berlin, series 2, 747.

The Black Codes, which were passed by every former Confederate state between late 1865 and the early months of 1866, resolved these ambiguities by openly reinstituting the law of master and servant for African Americans. All black men and women were obliged to contract by the middle of January to work for wages for the remainder of the year. Those who wished to pursue artisanal or commercial occupations were required to seek annual licenses from district courts. Civil officers were obliged to "arrest and carry back to his or her legal employer any freedman, free negro, or mulatto who shall have quit the service of his or her employer before the expiration of his or her term of service without good cause." Juries of freeholders were to assign deserters to their former employers or to new ones.[12]

No provisions of the codes caused more distress in black households than those authorizing courts to bind out orphans or those under eighteen "whose parents have not the means or who refuse to provide for and support" them, with preference in assignment to be given "the former owner of said minors." From Maryland to Mississippi black women were engaged in efforts to reclaim their own children.[13]

The practical significance of the Black Codes was revealed in a letter from twelve black soldiers in Mississippi to their commanding officer. It said:

> the Law in regard to the freedman is that they all have to have a written contract judge jones mayor of this place is enforcing of the law He says they have no right to rent a house nor land nor reside in town with[out] a white man to stand fer thim He makes all men pay Two Dollars for Licience and he will not give Licience without a written contract both women and men have to submit or go to Jail
>
> His debuty is taking people all the time men that is traverling is stoped and put in jail or Forced to contract if this is the Law of the United States we will submit but if it is not we are willing to take our musket and surve three years Longer.[14]

As we have seen, almost a year before that letter was written, General Daniel Sickles had nullified South Carolina's code and proclaimed his own elaborate rules of contract and vagrancy based on the principle that "all laws shall be applicable alike to all inhabitants." The following April, Congress enshrined that doctrine in the Civil Rights

12 Commager, *Documents*, vol. 2, 2–5; The codes of several states are paraphrased extensively in McPherson, *Poltical History*, 29–36.
13 Mississippi Apprentice Act, Commager, vol. 2, 3. On parents' battles against such laws see Tera W. Hunter, "Household Workers in the Making: Afro-American Women in Atlanta and the New South, 1861–1920" (Ph.D. diss., Yale University, 1990), 6–58; Fields, *Middle Ground*, 139–42.
14 Berlin, series 2, 821.

Act, which made it a crime for any person to deprive another individual of equal rights to make and enforce contracts. When that act
in turn was folded into the Fourteenth Amendment to the constitution later in the year, the right of all men to contract for employment
at will obtained the sanction of national law. Political economist Arthur Latham Perry summed up the ideals of the new order: "Society is
one vast hive of buyers and sellers, every man bringing something to
the market and carrying something off. . . . You do something for me,
and I will do something for you, is the fundamental law of society."[15]

Just what exertions were to be exchanged for what reward on southern plantations, however, could only be decided by sharp and sometimes bloody confrontations that in turn shaped the relationship of
field hands to the Republican Party. Planters' efforts to graft the
payment of money wages onto systems of gang labor inherited from
slavery ran afoul of two obstacles: They had little cash to advance
before sale of the year's crop, and once the driver's whip was withdrawn, gang labor maximized workers' solidarities. Planters did learn
quickly to dismiss old and infirm former slaves. Even the South Carolina Black Code departed from the customs of slavery on this score, by
requiring each black family to maintain its own "old and helpless
members." Planters also learned to lay off laborers when work was
slack. An army surgeon traveling in coastal South Carolina in June
1866 met "several troops" of freed people "who had just been discharged from plantations and were looking for work they knew not
where." After the season's final thinning and weeding, the crop had
been "laid by," and there was little work to do until harvest time, when
hands could be hired to pick cotton by the pound. Resident workers
fought this practice by greeting day laborers with great hostility so as
to drive them off and compel the planters to hire and keep year-round
hands.[16]

Workers' quest for stable employment did not, however, make them
amenable to the contractual terms the planters wanted. Some form of
wage masquerading as a share of the crop became commonplace as
early as the 1866 season, because share payment did not oblige the
employer to turn any money over to the worker until the crop was in,
and the practice also gave the worker an interest in the size of the
harvest. Always at issue, however, was the question of whose labor the
planter had hired with that share, that of one person or that of an

15 On the Codes, Sickles's order, and the Fourteenth Amendment, see this volume,
   Chapter 2. Perry is quoted in Stanley, "Contract Rights," 51.
16 Jaynes, 24–54; Joel Williamson, *After Slavery: The Negro in South Carolina during
   Reconstruction, 1861–1877* (New York, 1975), 74; Saville, "A Measure of Freedom,"
   223–4. The quotation is in ibid., 224. General Sickles's code had specified different
   treatment for jobless long-term residents of plantations than for drifters.

entire family. No issue generated more frequent personal quarrels than the refusal of married women to go to the fields. Moreover, intensive cultivation of the cash crop was best encouraged by placing many croppers on small lots; this maximized the return to the planter at the expense of the worker's standard of living. Battles over the number of families working a plantation could not be separated from disputes over the size of garden plots and the grazing area for livestock to which workers were entitled, or indeed from controversies over whether things other than cotton raised on the plantation belonged to the planter or to the worker. For that matter, to whom did the cotton itself belong before it was ginned and sold? Had the sharecropper any "interest" in the crop other than his year's pay? A major undertaking of the Ku Klux Klan was to intimidate workers from selling "what was not theirs."

In short, even on the resuscitated plantation the laborer sought to rent land by paying its owner a portion of the crop, while the employer sought to hire labor time in exchange for that same share. A Georgia freedwoman recounted a similar battle over household obligations when she returned to the plantation where she had formerly been a slave:

> my old Missus asked me if I came back to behave myself & do her work & I told her no that I came back to do my own work. I went to my own house & in the morning my old master came to me & asked me if I wouldn't go and milk the cows: I told him that my Missus had driven me off – well said he you go and do it – then my Mistress came out again & asked me if I came back to work for her like a *"nigger"* – I told her no that I was free & she said be off then & called me a stinking bitch. I afterwards wove 40 yds. of dress goods for her that she promised to pay me for; but she never paid me a cent for it . . . except give me a meal of victuals.[17]

Masters' claims to all the workers' time were thus countered by freed people's readiness to do specified tasks in exchange for money payment or a share of the crop, plus a home and earth to be used at their own discretion. This encounter was especially damaging to rice planters, whose slaves had spent much of their time in ditching and water control work, which was to the rice worker what dead work was to the coal miner – arduous and uncompensated. Such controversies put an end to rice cultivation in some coastal areas and encouraged workers there to form land-buying associations to acquire portions of former rice estates. Elsewhere, they induced sugar planters to institute

17 Berlin, series 1, vol. 1, 151.

straightforward day labor and persuaded cotton growers to divide estates into family sharecropping units.[18]

Workers quickly learned to pledge each other not to work for less than the terms to which they had agreed among themselves. Backed by sanctions of ostracism and even violence against nonconformists, former slaves increased the share of the crop offered workers from one-fourth, or the one-third specified by the Freedmen's Bureau, to one-half. Their most effective instrument was the paramilitary club, which brought men and women from various plantations together, often on Saturday market days. In response to planters' claims that six days' labor were owed, and to Black Code prohibitions against the bearing of arms by African Americans, the freed people appealed to U.S. military authorities that theirs were patriotic gatherings, defending the United States and often drilled by black army veterans. After the Reconstruction Acts of 1867 these armed contingents openly affiliated with the Union Leagues and became the most effective agencies for mobilizing Republican votes in the countryside.[19]

To put it another way: The enfranchisement of black voters by the 1867 Reconstruction Acts grafted the new state Republican parties directly onto existing networks of solidarity, which rural laborers had fashioned in daily struggles around the terms under which they would work for wages. In urban areas (especially Richmond and New Orleans) mutual aid societies and black trade unions played similar roles. Nevertheless, the black field workers neither created nor led state Republican parties. Like the Reconstruction Acts, the Republican Party had been created in the North, and had been invented for purposes different from those of the field hands. Consequently, the Republican Party simultaneously politicized and restrained the action on the plantation.

In preparation for elections of delegates to state constitutional conventions required by the Reconstruction Acts, and in the subsequent balloting for state officials, Republican activists toured the southern countryside. Among them were more than eighty "colored itinerant lecturers," financed by the party's Congressional Committee. They were welcomed by Union League clubs, which were made up not only of black field and household workers, but often of beleaguered local white loyalists as well. Local economic grievances blended with

18 On rice areas, see Saville, 242; Eric Foner, *Nothing But Freedom: Emancipation and Its Legacy* (Baton Rouge, La., 1983), 74–92. On sugar, see Jeffrey L. Gould, "Sugar Wars: The Sugar Cane Cutters' Strike of 1887 in Louisiana," *Southern Exposure,* 2 (Nov.–Dec. 1984), 45–55.

19 Saville, 232–40; Michael W. Fitzgerald, "'To Give Our Votes to the Party': Black Political Agitation and Agricultural Change in Alabama, 1865–1870," *Journal of American History,* 76 (Sept. 1989), 489–505; Jaynes, 45–53. For a wartime offer of one-fourth of the crop, see Berlin, series 1, vol. 1, 327.

state and national governmental issues in the clubs' discussions. In fact, it can be said that the distinction between economic and political questions, which was then so finely drawn by white trade unionists, made no sense in African-American organizations.[20] Although the support lent by the Republicans to the everyday struggles of rural black workers was substantial, the party never defined its policies in terms of those struggles. Moreover, former slaves representing constituencies of rural men and women never occupied major executive offices, and they appeared in significant numbers in the state legislatures only in the final years of Republican rule in states where that regime lasted past 1872: Mississippi, South Carolina, Louisiana, Alabama, and Florida.

The new states bore little resemblance to the clientelistic polities of the slave owners, which had tightly circumscribed the role of government. South Carolina's Republicans created tax-supported universal education, built asylums to shelter the aged and poor, subsidized railroad construction, protected tenants and homesteaders against eviction, outlawed payment in scrip that could be redeemed only at plantation stores, allowed election of judges, and ended imprisonment for debt. They incorporated Union League contingents into the state militia, ended the leasing of convict laborers to private employers, and inhibited mob attacks against African-American property owners. Through their power in important legislative committees, leading black Republicans ultimately won control of South Carolina's land commission and used that body to shift estates forfeited to the government during the depression of the 1870s to black smallholders.[21]

Perhaps most important of all, when disputes over work and crops led planters to charge their workers with contract violation, idleness, or theft, sheriffs and justices of the peace often lent a sympathetic ear to the former slaves. The complaint of a planter that "justice is generally administered solely in the interest of the laborer," was echoed by the editorial lament of the *Southern Argus* of Selma, Alabama: "There is a vagrant law on our statute books . . . but it is a dead letter because those who are charged with its enforcement are indebted to the vagrant vote for their offices."[22]

To be sure, the first priority of southern Republicans, just like that of their northern mentors, was capitalist economic development.

20 Foner, *Reconstruction*, 283–91; Rachleff, 39–51; Fitzgerald, 495–505.
21 Thomas Holt, *Black over White: Negro Political Leadership in South Carolina during Reconstruction* (Urbana, Ill., 1977), 95–170; Foner, *Reconstruction*, 362–79, and 539–41 on Florida. See also Francis Butler Simkins and Robert H. Woody, *South Carolina during Reconstruction* (Chapel Hill, N.C., 1932); W. McKee Evans, *Ballots and Fence Rails: Reconstruction on the Lower Cape Fear* (Chapel Hill, N.C., 1966).
22 Both quotations from Foner, *Reconstruction*, 363.

Nevertheless, the southern parties lacked the organic links to local economic elites that secured party hegemony and guided policy in the North. Quite the contrary, the vanquished elites of the South considered the new regimes illegitimate – unworthy of obedience and certainly unworthy of their taxes. In desperate need of revenues and of experienced and locally prestigious personnel, southern Republicans initially featured white candidates and extended patronage to any established political personality who would accept it. The speedy and violent removal of Republicans from power in Virginia, North Carolina, Tennessee, and Georgia showed the futility of this policy and encouraged African Americans to assert themselves more openly in party circles. Black workers from Richmond, Philadelphia, and Baltimore initiated their own National Labor Congress in 1869. It chastised the Republicans for their timidity on land redistribution, stimulated both urban and rural trade unionism, and demanded the establishment of state labor bureaus to provide wage-earners the active protection of government. A leading figure in the movement was Warwick Reed, a one-time slave, tobacco worker, and captain of a black militia unit, who was elected vice-president for Virginia by the nation's overwhelmingly white Industrial Congress in 1874.[23]

Although prominent black Republicans seized the occasion to demand a greater role in their party's affairs, they also expressed anxiety over the strikes and political demands of their constituents. The *New Orleans Tribune*, voice of the historic free black elite, counseled striking black dockers in 1867 "not to jeopardize the future by rushing into some unreasonable excitement."[24] When a South Carolina black labor convention with three hundred delegates petitioned the state legislature for land distribution, a legal nine-hour day, and labor commissioners in each county to oversee the claims of rural workers, the legislature rejected the proposals after heated debate. A white Republican from the Piedmont proclaimed, "Nobody has ever been able to legislate in regard to labor." He concluded, "The law of supply and demand must regulate the matter." William Whipper, a northern-born black lawyer and outspoken champion of civil rights who owned a rice plantation himself, agreed. He rejected the implication "that the people as a class are not able to take care of themselves." As if in

23 On "the policy" see Holt, *Black over White*, 95–109. On the National Labor Congress, see Rachleff, 55–69, 72–8; Philip S. Foner and Ronald L. Lewis, eds., *The Black Worker: A Documentary History from Colonial Times to the Present* (6 vols., Philadelphia, 1978–82), vol. 2, 37–110.
24 Eric Arnesen, *Waterfront Workers of New Orleans: Race, Class, and Politics, 1863–1923* (New York, 1991), 31. The reaction of the *Tribune* to the dock strike of 1865 had been even more hostile. Ibid., 23–25.

confirmation of his view, Whipper was taken to court by his own workers for failing to pay them.[25]

An acid test of the party's commitments arose when workers on rice plantations along the Combahee River struck against illegal scrip payment in the midst of the decisive election campaign of 1876. Although some prominent Republicans called for forceful suppression of picketing, the local militia was largely made up of strikers, and the aggressive challenge to activities in support of the strike came from an armed band of white vigilantes. The famous black congressman Robert Smalls personally intervened to separate the antagonists, and he persuaded the planters to agree to the strikers' demands that they obey the law requiring money wages. Ten arrested strikers were taken before a black trial judge in nearby Beaufort; he set them all free, to the applause of the crowd in the streets.[26]

By the end of that year, however, the hopes of black men and women throughout the rural South had been crushed. It was not the laissez-faire inclinations of the Republicans that administered the devastating blow, but the triumph of the Democratic "Redeemers." The intellectual, political, and religious leaders of the white South had quite properly envisaged themselves before, during, and after the Civil War as the true guardians of classical republicanism in North America. The "citizen with us," planter-historian William Henry Trescott of South Carolina had written, "belongs . . . to a privileged class."[27] He was a man of action who might be unequal in wealth or influence to other citizens but who shared with them recognized mastery over slaves, women, and children, and whose claim to participation in the polity was predicated on that mastery. As Stephanie McCurry has argued, racial, gender, and class hierarchies were inexorably intertwined in the belief held by defenders of the slave republic that "the restriction of political rights to a privileged few" was the region's "distinctive and superior characteristic."[28] Although the conditions of all subordinate groups could stand improvement, the eminent political writer Louisa Susana McCord had written in 1852, "Here, as in all other improvements, the good must be brought about by working with, not against – by seconding, not opposing – Nature's laws." To defy the differences in entitlements and obligations that God and nature had bestowed on each social rank would turn society into a "wrangling dog kennel," she added. "Wo to the world which seeks its

25 Holt, *Black over White*, 161–2.
26 Foner, *Nothing But Freedom*, 90–106.
27 Quoted in Stephanie McCurry, "The Two Faces of Republicanism: Gender and Proslavery Politics in Antebellum South Carolina," *Journal of American History*, 78 (March 1992), 1,263.
28 Ibid., 1,260.

rulers where it should find its drudges! Wo to the drudge who would exalt himself into the ruler!"[29]

Although southern conservatives after the war had no choice but to concede that slavery was dead, the paramilitary organizations that they mobilized against the Republican state regimes openly fought to rescue the beleaguered "natural" hierarchies of race, gender, class, and property. Senator Thomas Bayard of Delaware defended the Ku Klux Klan as "a protective arm of natural society necessary to offset the influence of blacks whose own pretensions of power were artificially and unnaturally propped up by a standing army."[30] Local black political leaders were the foremost target of killings and beatings, but not the only ones. The Klan assaulted both African Americans and white women who exhibited offensive independence, and it attacked with special venom and regularity when the two types of offenders were in some way linked, for example when black men bought or rented land from white widows. It also acted both as a labor organization for whites (fixing terms of employment or rental and driving off black competitors), and as an agency to discipline black workers. As one Georgia witness testified to Congress about the "class of people who have the old rebellious spirit in them still":

> If the negro is in their employ, they will protect him, unless they have any difficulty with him, and then they will report him to the Ku-Klux . . . Just about the time they got done laying by their crops, the Ku-Klux would be brought in upon them, and they would be run off, so that they could take their crops.[31]

Paramilitary and electoral activity were intertwined as inseparably in the conservatives' effort to restore historic "rulers" and "drudges" to their proper stations as they were in the uses made by former slaves of the Union Leagues, militia, and Republican Party. "Old men in the Tax Unions and young men in the Rifle Clubs," was the battle cry of South Carolina's Redeemers in 1876.[32] The victors shattered Repub-

29 Quoted in Elizabeth Fox-Genovese, *Within the Plantation Household: Black and White Women of the Old South* (Chapel Hill, N.C., 1988), 284–5. See Larry E. Tise, *Proslavery: A History of the Defense of Slavery in America, 1701–1840* (Athens, Ga., 1987), 224, 273–5, 345, on the influence of classical republicanism on northern defenders of slavery; and Baker, *Affairs of Party*, 143–211, on the lionizing of Edmund Burke by northern Democrats during the 1850s and 1860s.
30 Baker, *Affairs of Party*, 209.
31 U.S. Senate, *Report of the Joint Select Committee to Inquire into the Affairs of the Late Insurrectionary States*, 42d Cong., 2d sess. (13 vols., Washington, D.C., 1982), Georgia, 420. I am indebted to Kathleen Clark for her insights into the role of the Klan. Clark, "Severed Ties: Race, Sex, and Violence in Georgia, 1868–1871" (unpublished seminar paper, Yale University, 1992).
32 Simkins and Woody, 184; Robert J. Norrell, *Reaping the Whirlwind: The Civil Rights Movement in Tuskegee* (New York, 1985), 3–11.

lican political organizations, wreaking especially bloody vengeance on
party activists and on Union Leagues. They effectively suppressed the
counter-pressures of workers' solidarities in all districts but those where
the African-American population was most dense. They placed local
sheriffs and judges directly under the authority of the white-supremacist
state governments. And they festooned the statute books with legislation
regulating in detail the issues of everyday confrontation between planters
and workers: vagrancy, enticement, and criminal surety laws; laws restricting hunting rights and enclosing unimproved lands; laws declaring thefts
of livestock or sales of standing crops to be felonies; laws giving the
landlord or merchant-creditor first lien on the crop; and laws for leasing
out to labor the thousands of African Americans sentenced under the
new statutes. "The lords of the soil," concluded defeated Republican
Albion Tourgee, "are the lords of the labor still."[33]

Disfranchisement followed. "It is certain," the *Memphis Daily Avalanche* predicted in 1889, "that many years will elapse before the bulk
of the Negroes will reawaken to an interest in elections, if relegated to
their proper sphere, the corn and cotton fields."[34]

Southern black workers were driven from the political arena while
legislation clamped tight judicially enforced controls on their terms of
contract. The states had imposed labor discipline on a free market
system. State courts and many local sheriffs outdid the legislatures.
Although statute law in every state limited the enforcement of crop
liens to advances made to the worker against the current year's crop,
courts in Alabama and Mississippi allowed the accumulation of lien
indebtedness from year to year, while those of Georgia and North
Carolina allowed creditors to seize personal tools and possessions if
the crop proved insufficient to cover the debt. Arkansas's judges even
approved confiscation of a sharecropper's sewing machine. In effect,
distress judgments, which had disappeared from the North early in
the century, had returned to the South. So did specific enforcement
of contracts. Mississippi's legislature enacted laws in 1900 and 1906
making a tenant who left his landlord during a crop year subject to
imprisonment for fraud. A coal miner from the Birmingham region
described less formal sanctions faced by newly recruited miners who
attempted to quit their jobs:

33 [Albion Tourgee], *A Fool's Errand by One of the Fools* (New York, 1880), 342.
34 *Memphis Daily Avalanche*, March 27, 1889, quoted in J. Morgan Kousser, *The Shaping
   of Southern Politics: Suffrage Restrictions and the Establishment of the One-Party South* (New
   Haven, Conn., 1974), 111. The best account of Redeemers' legislation is Michael
   Perman, *The Road to Redemption: Southern Politics, 1869–1879* (Chapel Hill, N.C.,
   1984), 237–63. See also Steven Hahn, *The Roots of Southern Populism: Yeoman Farmers
   and the Transformation of the Georgia Upcountry, 1850–1890* (New York, 1983), 239–
   68; W. E. B. DuBois, *Black Reconstruction in America, 1860–1880* (New York, 1935),
   670–711.

lo! and behold! [The mine superintendent] touches the button, and smooth and smiling 'Squire Wingo appears as the heavy villain in this almost every-day transaction, and they (the transports) are placed under arrest, remanded to the mines, and are worked, guarded the same as convicts, until the Sloss Iron & Steel Company . . . has been sufficiently compensated for the trouble and expense of increasing the population of Alabama.[35]

Although the southern Republican Party continued to battle the worst excesses of the new regime, such as the unrestrained exploitation of convict labor and the shrinking budgets of public schools, and to enjoy the active support of those black men who could still vote, it had been reduced to little more than an agency for distribution of federal offices, except perhaps in North Carolina, Virginia, and the Appalachian Mountain region. Black plantation laborers asked of their party above all else that it persuade Congress to protect those in the South who wished to exercise their rights of citizenship, while millenarian dreams inspired Exodusters along the lower Mississippi to flock to the riverbanks in hopes of finding a boat that would let them escape to Kansas.[36]

The Democrats won and retained control of the South by proclaiming themselves the one legitimate "white man's party." Their ability to overawe rebellious political movements after the 1870s with the warning that any break in the ranks of white voters threatened to restore "Negro rule" provided a heavy ballast for property and for white supremacy that would guide the course of the national Democratic Party until the 1940s.[37] Editor Patrick Ford of the *Irish World,* who worshiped at the shrine of Thomas Jefferson, protested in 1876 that if one asked a "Regular Democrat," "*What is a Democrat?* The instant answer from him would be: *A man who hates niggers!* . . . Never before was common sense so impudently outraged. Never before were words so recklessly twisted from their true meaning. Never!"[38]

35 Woodman, 331–6; McMillen, 142–3; Birmingham *Labor Advocate,* Aug. 3, 1895, quoted in Daniel L. Letwin, "Race, Class, and Industrialization in the New South: Black and White Coal Miners in the Birmingham District of Alabama, 1878–1897" (Ph.D. diss., Yale University, 1991), 298–9. The U.S. Supreme Court ruled in 1897 (*Robertson* v. *Baldwin*) that one may contract into servitude for a time without violating the Thirteenth Amendment, but its important *Bailey* v. *Alabama* decision of 1911 ruled decisively against bound labor. Finkin, Goldman, and Summers, 33–4; Forbath, 138–9.

36 Painter, 108–201.

37 John Hope Franklin, *Reconstruction: After the Civil War* (Chicago, 1961), 218–27. See also John R. Lynch, *The Facts of Reconstruction* (New York, 1913); Rachleff, 86–178; C. Vann Woodward, *Origins of the New South, 1877–1913* (Baton Rouge, La., 1951); Michael R. Hyman, "Taxation, Public Policy, and Political Dissent: Yeoman Disaffection in the Post-Reconstruction Lower South," *Journal of Southern History,* 55 (Feb. 1989), 49–76; Jonathan H. Wiener, *Social Origins of the New South: Alabama, 1860–1885* (Baton Rouge, La., 1978).

38 Editorial, *Irish World,* Oct. 21, 1876.

Industrial Workers and Party Politics

Unlike black workers in the South, the northerners to whom Ford addressed those words were welcomed into the polity by all political parties. They too, however, had played visible roles in the party controversies that reshaped the Union, abolished slavery, and redrafted the framework of government to suit the industrious "hive of buyers and sellers," which Arthur Latham Perry had celebrated and Louisa McCord had denounced as a "wrangling dog kennel." But the triumph of market capitalism eventually minimized the impact of those parties on everyday affairs and encouraged white workers to mobilize their social power independently of the two parties. A comparison of workers' political involvement in the Democratic stronghold of New York and such Republican bastions as Philadelphia and Pittsburgh may help explain this process.

During the 1840s the Democratic, Whig, and Native American parties of New York had all integrated voters into their organizations through ward committees, usually of thirteen to twenty-five members each, which nominated candidates for aldermen, tax assessors, and constables, and also organized vigilance committees of neighborhood activists to mobilize friendly voters and scrutinize unfriendly ones on election day. Ward committees selected delegates to a city general committee, which established a slate for citywide, state, and Congressional offices and oversaw periodic conventions where formal nominations were made. Although prominent figures from business and professional life (especially lawyers) dominated top party offices during the 1840s, tradesmen and artisans contributed the bulk of Democratic and Nativist ward representatives.[39]

Clubs that grouped men by nationality or occupation sponsored social activities and public spectacles, as did neighborhood fire companies. Licensed cartmen, who were virtually all native-born whites, and who often paraded on behalf of Whig nominees, continued a centuries-old tradition of personal ties to leading political figures. Newer contingents in public displays upheld particular causes. Among them were Shiffler Clubs, named in honor of the Philadelphia Morocco-dresser apprentice who had been killed fighting Catholics in 1844, and the Empire Club, dedicated to the annexation of Texas and Oregon, whose members were notorious for charging their opponents on horseback. Paramilitary formations appeared with the white-hatted contingents of Wide Awakes created by the Know-Nothings and continued as regular features of Re-

39 Anthony Gronowicz, "Revising the Concept of Jacksonian Democracy: A Comparison of New York City's Democrats in 1844 and 1884" (Ph.D. diss., University of Pennsylvania, 1981), 127–50; Bridges, *City in the Republic;* Pessen, "Who Governed?" 242–60.

publican parades, but then more ominously equipped with muskets and field uniforms. After the Civil War every party sported its contingents of uniformed veterans – including labor reform parties – and Chicago's socialists displayed their *Lehr-und-Wehr Vereine*.[40]

The English hatter James Burn, who claimed to have been cured of his youthful Chartist illusions by observing universal suffrage at work in New York, conceded, "It is true the people are amused with processions, illuminations, musical serenades, and other public demonstrations." More than one observer confirmed such descriptions of election night as George Lippard provided for Philadelphia when he wrote, "Bonfires were blazing in every street, crowds of voters collected around every poll, and every grocery and bar room [was] packed with drunken men."[41]

But the political pageantry did more than just amuse voters. It also served to define the nation and its social boundaries. Patriotism was trumpeted by all processions of vote seekers. Flags, soldiers, war heroes, and stirring march music were indispensable. Women were restricted to ceremonial or allegorical roles in these thoroughly masculine rituals, in contrast to their appearance in temperance and trade-union processions as marchers (albeit in decorous attire and flanked by contingents of dignified-looking men). As Jean H. Baker has argued persuasively, partisan ceremonies and the public schools reinforced each other's indoctrination into the wondrous heritage and awesome might of a republic, which coupled individual advancement to community bondings and obligations. The rhetoric and symbolism of elections defined the terms on which propertyless men took part in the governance of the republic.[42] The respectability of the citizenry was underscored by the studious exclusion of African Americans. In fact, for those deemed fit to be slaves to appear even in their own parades for temperance or in celebration of Britain's Emancipation Day was to invite ridicule and often physical attack.[43]

Electioneering was also expensive, and the funds needed to finance it were generated by the role of municipal government in the city's

40 Gronowicz; Montgomery, "Shuttle and the Cross," 432. On the Wide Awakes, see McMaster, vol. 8, 85–7. On Chicago socialists, see Nelson, *Beyond the Martyrs*, 138–51.
41 [James D. Burn,] *Three Years among the Working-Classes of the United States during the War* (London, 1865), 251; [Lippard,] 29.
42 Davis, *Parades*, 47, 149, 157; Michael E. McGerr, *The Decline of Popular Politics: The American North, 1865–1928* (New York, 1986); Baker, *Affairs of Party*, 71–107. See also Paula Baker, "The Domestication of Politics: Women and American Political Society, 1780–1920," *American Historical Review*, 89 (June 1984), 620–47; Mary H. Blewett, *Men, Women, and Work: Class, Gender, and Protest in the New England Shoe Industry, 1780–1910* (Urbana, Ill., 1988), 130–62.
43 Such attacks have been most closely examined in Philadelphia. See Davis, *Parades*, 46; Gary B. Nash, *Forging Freedom: The Formation of Philadelphia's Black Community, 1720–1840* (Cambridge, Mass., 1988), 172–211, 253–9. For New York, see Blackmar, 52–3, 172–5.

physical expansion. Two crucial innovations of the 1850s had attached New York's contractors and developers securely to the dominant Democratic Party. First, the financial district emerged as one of the world's leading capital markets. Prominent bankers, shippers, and railroad developers, like August Belmont, John A. Dix, and Samuel Tilden, based their activities in the city and linked their fortunes to the Democratic Party and its policies of expansionism, free trade, and conciliation of slavery. Second, the same securities markets provided the means for urban development through deficit financing – a practice the Tweed Ring ultimately developed into a fine art. In 1852 the city began funding its streets, sewers, gas works, wharves, schools, and other construction through bond issues. This meant that contractors could be paid before a project was completed and local assessments collected. As a result, smaller firms could bid for projects that would previously have required much greater capital resources. In addition, taxes could be kept down while expenditures swelled. Municipal improvements raced ahead, and competing contractors scrambled to improve their chances by donations to party coffers and by employment of workers recommended by party leaders.[44]

In 1863 William Curtis Noyes lamented that the character of city government was shaped "not by the best men in the city, not by the best women in the city, but by the dangerous classes, who are permitted to dominate, because men are so much occupied in their private affairs, and in the making of money that they will not attend to governmental affairs." His assessment was strongly endorsed at the end of the century by European scholars such as James Bryce and Moisei Ostrogorski. More recently, historians like Amy Bridges and Robin Einhorn have insisted that, although the wealthiest men of affairs were less likely to hold local governmental offices after 1840 than they had been before, they remained deeply involved in party leadership, either personally or through family members, in all major cities. They devoted close personal attention not only to the administration of police and public charities, as we have seen, but also to the development of urban real estate, to tax policies and municipal regulations that affected major industrial enterprises, and to the introduction of electrical and gas power and lighting. Much of their involvement in local politics was aimed at securing access to state and federal decision making. Although the daily hands-on direction of urban government had largely been assumed in the last half of the century by

44 Bernstein, 200–1; Alfred B. Chandler, Jr., *The Visible Hand: The Managerial Revolution in American Business* (Cambridge, Mass., 1977), 92–4. New York City did not adopt the plan of the Industrial Congress – that the government employ workers at union scales – to construct its own improvements. See Bernstein, 88–9.

professional politicians who were not from the economic and social elites, just as Noyes declared, the men who directed private business and professional life had by no means withdrawn from municipal politics. And certainly the "dangerous classes" did not "dominate" it.[45]

Despite New York's distinctiveness as the country's leading port, similar developments occurred in other cities, though often with different partisan implications. In Philadelphia, for example, the Republican Party played the developer's role and mustered even the Irish-American building contractors to its side. After the consolidation of its manufacturing suburbs into Philadelphia in 1854, the city was governed by mayors from various competing parties, but all with impeccable upper-class credentials, and all committed to strengthening the police force and to fending off dissolution of the United States. Eminent families with close business and marriage ties to the southern states provided leadership to the Buchanan Democrats and could count on large angry crowds to intimidate "black abolitionists."

It was the war itself, and especially the defeat of Lee's invasion of Pennsylvania in 1863, that allowed the consolidation of Republican rule. Despite its long history of race riots and widespread resistance to the state draft of 1862, the "Great Loyal City," as it came to be called, did not erupt when conscription was imposed after the battle of Gettysburg, and the Union (Republican) Party trounced the anti-emancipationist Democrats in the ensuing mayoral, gubernatorial, and presidential elections. Factory owners running for political office and mustering military units out of their own workers provided the new party with direct links to the working class; Irish Democrats with a prowar stance effectively challenged their party's elite leaders; and a spectacular Great Central Fair initiated by the Union League in 1864 mobilized the city's major churches and voluntary societies in support of the new political order. Although the Democrats recaptured city hall in 1871, the refusal of their new mayor to unleash the police against crowds that savagely attacked black voters, killing Octavious Catto, leader of the suffrage struggle, and two other men, and injuring hundreds of others, rallied both upper-class reformers and most workers to the cause of William Stokely, founder of the Republican machine that would dominate the city until the middle of the next century.[46]

45 Noyes reported by *New York Tribune*, Dec. 28, 1863, quoted in Bridges, 36. James Bryce, *The American Commonwealth,* edited and abridged by Louis Hacker (2 vols., New York, 1959); Ostrogorski; Einhorn, "Civil War and Municipal Government."
46 Dennis Clark, *The Irish in Philadelphia: Ten Generations of Urban Experience* (Philadelphia, 1973), 138–42; A. K. McClure, *Old Time Notes of Pennsylvania* (2 vols., Philadelphia, 1905); Russell F. Weigley, "'A Peaceful City': Public Order in Philadelphia from Consolidation through the Civil War," in Davis and Haller, 155–73; William Dusinberre, *Civil War Issues in Philadelphia, 1856–1865* (Philadelphia, 1965); J. Matthew Gallman, "Voluntarism in Wartime: Philadelphia's Great Central Fair," in Vinovskis, 93–116; Steinberg, 207–8.

In manufacturing and mining towns throughout New England and the Middle Atlantic states large numbers of old stock and British immigrant workers moved through life in networks of Protestant chapels, temperance associations, and reading and discussion societies, which drew them into the orbit of the Know-Nothing and Republican parties. Like other Republicans they espoused active use of the government's coercive, financial, and administrative powers to "improve" social life. Philadelphia's champions of the imprisoned poor, William Mullen and William D. Kelley, were labor reform activists who were drawn through self-improvement networks into Republican circles, as were John Sedden, Frederick Turner, James L. Wright, Thomas Phillips, and other leaders of the city's labor movement who had begun their careers as Chartists in England.

Elsewhere, the future socialist Judson Grenell, who swore off the bottle lest he become another "blear-eyed bum printer," and moved west to Detroit at the invitation of his brother, a Baptist preacher (who provided a job in the composing room of the *Michigan Christian Herald*), followed this political path. So did the first secretary of the United Mine Workers, Robert Watchorn, whose every step from Derbyshire to Pennsylvania was guided by contacts in the Primitive Methodist Church, and who ended his days a prosperous businessman and benefactor of Methodist charities. In Boston, George McNeill and Edward Rogers were prominent among workers who inspired the party with their Christian activism. Such men guided the numerous, though volatile, working-class Republican clubs of the 1860s.[47]

The working-class adherents of the Republican Party were more mecurial than those of the Democrats for two reasons. First, most of the former believed that the energetic use of governmental power by which their party had enlarged police forces, expanded and systematized the public schools, curbed liquor dealers, opened the public domain to homesteaders, subsidized railroad construction, and encouraged manufacturers with tariffs, national banks, and an expanded currency – not to mention waging war to preserve the Union and emancipate slaves, imposing new governments on the rebellious states, and codifying citizens' rights in amendments to the federal constitution – provided a valuable precedent for legislative action to reform industrial employment and urban living conditions as well. No

---

47 Judson Grenell, "Autobiography" (unpublished manuscript, Michigan State University Archives and Historical Collections); Robert Watchorn, *The Autobiography of Robert Watchorn*, edited by Herbert Faulkner West (Oklahoma City, 1958); Steinberg, 112–3, 157–61; Montgomery, *Beyond Equality*, 201–10, 249–51; Ken Fones-Wolf, *Trade Union Gospel: Christianity and Labor in Industrial Philadelphia, 1865–1915* (Philadelphia, 1989), 68–9.

sooner had the war ended than state legislatures were bombarded
with petitions to establish a legal eight-hour day, petitions that bore
the signatures of many well-known Republicans. Ward clubs and Republican legislators in industrial constituencies often viewed with
favor proposals to substitute for privately owned national banks a
federally managed currency that would provide credit on easy terms,
regulate tenement-house construction, mandate mine and factory
safety codes, charter workers' cooperatives, cleanse city streets and
canals, and create state bureaus of labor statistics. Their enthusiasm
for high tariffs was no less vigorous than that of their employers.
Workers have "brought the political leaders to their feet," lamented
Republican editor E. L. Godkin in 1867. "Now no convention ever
draws up a platform without inserting in it a small parcel of twaddle on
the 'rights of labor.'"[48]

Second, in the century's final decades entrenched Republican city
machines could be as lax as their Democratic counterparts in the
suppression of saloons, prostitution, and Sunday commerce and en-
tertainment. Enforcement of blue laws by police magistrates in
Philadelphia, Pittsburgh, Denver, and Kansas City was notoriously
capricious, in spite of the periodic law-and-order campaigns of Protestant reformers. Businesses that operated on the margins of the law
were a rich source of revenues for government, party, and police
officials. Labor reformers were reluctant to attack taverns and beer
gardens because they often provided space for movement gatherings
and a livelihood for blacklisted militants. Many labor activists took the
temperance pledge, labor reform parties formed occasional local
alliances with prohibitionist parties, and the Knights of Labor praised
the Women's Christian Temperance Union in the late 1880s and
circulated its petitions for laws to protect women against seduction
and abuse. But the very qualities that made saloon life obnoxious to
labor activists – its social pressures for excessive drinking, its suscep-
tibility to the politics of patronage that flourished there, and its am-
bience of strictly male sociability – were all highly desirable in the eyes
of machine politicians, Democrat or Republican.[49]

Christopher L. Magee and William Flinn, who forged a Republican
ring "safe as a bank" in the Pittsburgh region, astutely coupled favors
to local business leaders (including sale of the city's poor farm to

48 E. L. Godkin, "The Labor Crisis," *Nation*, 4 (April 15, 1867), 335; Daniel Walker
   Howe, *The Political Culture of American Whigs* (Chicago, 1979); Montgomery, *Beyond
   Equality*, 230–368.
49 Thomas J. Noel, *The City and the Saloon: Denver, 1858–1916* (Lincoln, Neb., 1982);
   Ruth Bordin, *Woman and Temperance: The Quest for Power and Liberty, 1873–1900*
   (Philadelphia, 1981). On the Knights and the WTCU's petitions, see Frances E.
   Willard, *Glimpses of Fifty Years: The Autobiography of an American Woman* (Chicago,
   1889), 423–4.

Andrew Carnegie at half its market value for expansion of his Home-stead mill), with construction contracts providing many jobs awarded to their own companies. The practice of financing civic improvements by taxation levied on immediate recipients funneled almost all city services into more prosperous neighborhoods and left working-class women toting water from unreliable hydrants up unpaved streets in an unending struggle to keep homes and families clean, but it kept taxes low for landlords and shopkeepers. The party also assiduously cultivated popular faith in high tariffs as the guarantee of good profits and steady work, while the justices of the peace, in John Ingham's words, "acted as an important buffer in the working-class community, protecting immigrant, largely Roman Catholic workers, from the evan-gelical predilections of the upper-class Presbyterian Republicans."[50]

The running battle over Sunday closing laws saw the labor move-ment joining with religious organizations to insist that shop clerks and factory workers be given the day off, while employers insisted that their services could not be spared. When it came to closing public institutions and privately-operated shops, however, evangelists and labor activists parted company. Robert Layton of the Knights de-nounced ordinances that kept libraries, parks, and athletic grounds closed on Sunday as obstacles to workers' self-improvement. Journals as self-consciously respectable as Pittsburgh's *Commoner and Glass Work-er* ridiculed the arrest of widows who sold cigars, newspapers, or drinks in their little shops on Sunday. "Arrest her quick in the interests of public peace and morality," proclaimed an editor, "and add another to the list of persecuted cripples and orphans."[51]

Workers, businessmen, evangelists, and intellectuals who shared deep hostility to the Democratic Party, therefore, were also locked into recurrent battles with each other during the final decades of the nineteenth century. Republican city bosses like Philadelphia's Stokely, Pittsburgh's Magee, and Cincinnati's George B. Cox catered to what-ever sources of political power capitalism produced, pursuing a style of government little different from that practiced by New York's Dem-ocrats. Republican labor activists often bolted to Greenback Labor, Populist, Socialist Labor, or occasionally Prohibition parties, while

50 Ingham, 164; Krause, 97–136, 278–81; Paul Kleppner, "Government, Parties, and Voters in Pittsburgh," in Samuel P. Hays, ed., *City at the Point: Essays on the Social History of Pittsburgh* (Pittsburgh, Pa., 1989), 151–80; Kleinberg, 84–93.
51 Fones-Wolf, 22–3, 50–1, 60–6; Jürgen Kocka, *White Collar Workers in America, 1890–1940: A Social-Political History in International Perspective,* translated by Maura Kealey (London, 1980), 55–9; Henry F. May, *Protestant Churches and Industrial America* (New York, 1949); *Commoner and Glass Worker,* Nov. 6, 1887, quoted in Kleinberg, 247–8. The outstanding study of class conflict over the regulation of social life is Roy Rosenzweig, *Eight Hours for What We Will: Workers and Leisure in an Industrial City, 1870–1920* (New York, 1983).

business, professional, and religious leaders harassed both Republican and Democratic machines with citizens' associations, law and order leagues, and "committees of one hundred." Prominent men of letters like Godkin and Charles Francis Adams rallied to the cause of municipal reform out of fear that "the passionate pursuit of equality of conditions on which the multitude seems now entering, and the elevation of equality of conditions into the rank of the highest political good, will eventually prove fatal to art, to science, to literature, and to law."[52] Republican rule was often secure, but it was never sedate.

Workers and Tammany Hall

All this meant little to New York, however, because the peculiar society created by the nation's dominant port had confined the Republicans to a permanent minority position and focused political activity on rival clubs within the Democratic fold. During the 1830s and 1840s voter turnout remained noticeably lower in municipal than in presidential elections, and control of local government was often wrested from the Democrats by coalitions of Whigs and nativists. By the 1850s, however, participation in mayoral elections had risen almost to the level of voting for president, and Democratic dominance of local government was endangered only by factionalism within the party. Few white Republican workers were found in the city. Even those worker advocates of land and housing reform in Manhattan who collaborated with prominent Republicans on specific issues proclaimed their personal independence of all "party thralldom." Some neighborhoods, like the large shipbuilding area along the East River where employers still resided alongside predominantly native ship carpenters and caulkers, had lent strength to nativist parties; but the huge enterprises where metal ships were fabricated just to the north were staffed entirely by immigrants, who were ardent Democrats – and their products were rendering the wooden ships obsolete.[53]

It was to the Democratic Party that New Yorkers flocked, in Mike Walsh's words, to "get a taste of the equality which they hear so much preached, but never, save there, see even partially practiced."[54] They subscribed to the Jeffersonian doctrines of the prominent editor of

52 E. L. Godkin, "The Danger of Playing Tricks with the Labor Question," *Nation*, 15 (Sept. 5, 1872), 148.
53 Bridges, 14–15, 34–5; Blackmar, 101; Leonard A. Swann, *John Roach, Maritime Entrepreneur: The Years as Naval Contractor, 1862–1886* (Annapolis, Md., 1965). On New York's working-class land reformers, see Lewis Masquerier, *Sociology: Or, The Reconstruction of Society, Government, and Property, upon the Principles of Equality . . . Giving All the Liberty and Happiness to Be Found on Earth* (New York, 1877); Helene S. Zahler, *Eastern Workingmen and National Land Policy, 1829–1862* (New York, 1941).
54 Quoted in Gutman, *Work, Culture, and Society*, 56.

the *Democratic Review,* John L. O'Sullivan: "It is under this word *government,* that the subtle danger lurks." The party that upheld the personal and property rights of the street vendor, the holiday reveler, the patron of the Bowery Theater, the celebrator of Saint Monday, the volunteer fireman, the Catholic schoolchild, the family relaxing in a German beer garden, the striker, the merchant, and the slave owner mustered their support in opposition to the active-government party of the Protestant industrialists.

> Government [wrote O'Sullivan] should have as little as possible to do with the general business and interests of the people. . . . Its domestic action should be confined to the administration of justice, for the protection of the natural equal rights of the citizen, and the preservation of social order. In all other respects, the VOLUNTARY PRINCIPLE . . . affords the true "golden rule."[55]

As champions of "strict construction" of state and federal constitutions to limit the scope of governmental authority, and of a scrupulously secular state that would respect the diversity of popular beliefs and customs, the Democrats attracted both immigrants and many labor reformers to their fold. Nevertheless, they adamantly repudiated political discourse and mobilization that pivoted on social class or class struggle. Their leaders condemned the "one-ideaism" of socialism, women's rights, free soil, and vegetarianism, as well as abolitionism. "The spirit of harmony," editorialized the party's *New York Post,* was "essential to a republican form of government." By the 1860s, in fact, the fury of their battles against the "abolitionist conspirators" of the Republican Party had led these spiritual descendants of Thomas Jefferson to elevate Edmund Burke to the position of a favored oracle and forebearer while they identified the doctrines of the Republican Party with the Jacobins and with Thomas Paine.[56]

In neither of his presidential election campaigns did Abraham Lincoln obtain as many as 35 percent of New York's votes. Republicans dominated the areas of central uptown Manhattan, where the bourgeoisie had clustered their new homes, and they reached deep into the fabric of daily life through such institutions as the Association for Improving the Condition of the Poor. The prominent young men of the publishing world who joined forces with scions of the city's oldest mercantile families during the war to form the Union League Club, called by founder Frederick Law Olmsted the "club of the true

55 *United States Magazine and Democratic Review,* 1 (Jan. 1838), 2–15, reprinted in Edwin C. Roswencz, ed., *Ideology and Power in the Age of Jackson* (Garden City, N.Y., 1964), 300–19. The quotations are on pp. 306, 308.
56 Baker, *Affairs of Party,* 143–211, 320–1; *New York Post,* April 20, 1844, quoted in ibid., 320; Montgomery, *Beyond Equality,* 48–59.

American aristocracy," shaped the thinking of the reading public across the land.[57] To obtain the police force, poor laws, and morals legislation they desired to regulate their own city, however, the Republicans had to appeal to the state government in Albany. In the Astor Place theater riot of 1849, the police attacks on striking tailors in 1850, and the war of the "Bloody Oulde Sixth" ward against the metropolitan police in 1857, those impositions had produced violent clashes with the impoverished residents of the tenement neighborhoods where clothing and shoes were fabricated.[58]

In July 1863 these antagonisms erupted in the bloodiest urban violence in the country's history, with consequences that significantly changed the relationship between workers and the Democratic Party. Enforcement of the federal conscription law provoked a violent popular assault on Republican notables, on the agencies through which they governed city affairs from Albany and Washington, and on African Americans, whose cause of emancipation the Republicans had embraced. The law, which made "able-bodied male citizens" eligible for conscription but allowed commutation for a fee of $300 and the purchase of substitutes, came in the wake of the futile battlefield carnage of the winter of 1862–3 and the president's announcement of emancipation for slaves behind Confederate lines. A provost-marshall in each conscription district was empowered to administer the law, to imprison obstructionists and deny them the writ of habeas corpus, and, if need be, to call upon detachments of the army to impose martial law. Some coal-producing areas of Pennsylvania were under martial law for a year and a half. The future member of Parliament, John Wilson of Durham, later recalled mining near such a region. Someone who uttered "a word of praise of Lincoln," he wrote, "if not sure of his company, need not have been surprised if he was called upon to look into the barrel of a revolver or a rifle." In those mining towns Lincoln's assassination evoked only cheers and mockery.[59]

As Iver Bernstein's splendid account of the New York uprising reveals, the battle developed through three successive but overlapping phases. It began early Monday morning with a general strike, rolling out of the riverside industrial areas of the upper West Side, and spread by marchers who toured Manhattan closing down work. The Black

57 Bernstein, 55–6, 129–31.
58 Wilentz, 358–9, 378–80; Lawrence Levine, *Highbrow, Lowbrow: The Emergence of Cultural Hierarchy in America* (Cambridge, Mass., 1988), 63–8; Richard Moody, *The Astor Place Riot* (Bloomington, Ind., 1958); Carol Groneman, "The 'Bloody Oulde Sixth': A Social Analysis of a New York City Working-Class Community in the Mid-Nineteenth Century" (Ph.D. diss., University of Rochester, 1973). On the battle against the metropolitans, see this volume, Chapter 2.
59 Palladino, 95–120; John Wilson, *Memories of a Labour Leader* (Firle, Sussex, 1980), 172, 178–80.

Joke fire company, whose leader was a Democratic alderman and municipal contractor, led an assault that destroyed the district provost-marshall's office while other groups vandalized the homes of prosperous Republicans. Late in the day the character of the crowds began to change. The infamous assault on the Colored Orphanage Asylum, which destroyed the building (though the children escaped), inaugurated three days of lynchings of black men and women and devastation of their dwellings. At the same time, the fire companies, including the Black Joke, reversed course and began extinguishing fires, often in defiance of people by whose sides they had attacked buildings earlier.

Having made their protest against the draft and effectively halted it, the fire companies and most trade unions (with the notable exception of the largest, the Longshoremen's Association) withdrew from the action. So too did the impoverished outworkers of the Bloody Oulde Sixth – leaving the historic heartland of New York riots remarkably quiet. Moreover, the workers of Kleindeutschland, the German neighborhood above the eastern bulge of lower Manhattan, barricaded and patrolled their district against all outsiders. They were subsequently to provide decisive votes for the victory of the anti-Tammany Democrat C. Godfrey Gunther in the fall mayoral elections. Their newspaper, the *New York Arbeiter Zeitung* expressed animosity toward their Irish neighbors that was as virulent as their own opposition to the draft: "These [Tammany voters], nine-tenths of them Irish, stand, as everyone knows, at no higher a cultural level than Russian peasants. . . . Their drunkenness makes them in most instances willing tools of the most coarse and depraved swindlers."[60]

The battle, which raged on through Tuesday and Wednesday, was sustained by two main groups. Waterfront workers killed black men and women or drove them from their neighborhoods, and sacked brothels and taverns. There was vicious irony in the fact that local crowds were cleansing their communities of the interracial sociability and vice that reformers had long described as signs of those districts' degradation. Farther north, in the newer manufacturing areas along the two riverfronts, industrial workers and their families pummeled policemen to death, sacked wealthy midtown homes and the offices of Republican periodicals, and systematically erected barricades to seal off their parts of the city.

These were the barricades smashed on Wednesday and Thursday by the five regiments of soldiers withdrawn from the Gettysburg front. Some of their antagonists shouted cheers for Jeff Davis; others waved

60 *Arbeiter-Zeitung,* Sept. 10, 1864. My translation.

American flags. In their final assault, soldiers fought house-to-house eastward along Twenty-second street, clearing the streets with grapeshot and driving tenement dwellers from their rooftops with bayonets. New York City had been retaken by the federal government.[61]

The riots reshaped New York's politics so that control of the Democratic Party, and of the city government, belonged for the next eight years to the Tweed Ring. Its rule permanently changed the relationship between the party and workers in a manner that typified the new urban politics. Tweed and his cohorts dressed themselves in patriotic garb, while calling for an end to Republican "tyranny." In 1864 their Tammany Hall Political Club ardently supported the nomination of General George B. McClellan for president and featured soldiers in blue at its public manifestations. But it also effectively exempted the city of New York from the draft for the rest of the war by having the city council appropriate more than a million dollars to pay the $300 commutation for any needy conscript who applied. At the same time, not only did Tammany celebrate the example of Alderman Peter Masterson of the Black Joke fire company, who had protested the draft but then safeguarded his community's property, but its own future mayor A. Oakey Hall vigorously prosecuted scores of arrested rioters. Claims of black victims were studiously ignored by the city, leaving assistance for the city's rapidly diminishing black population up to the Union League.

The support Tammany had long enjoyed from building contractors was now augmented by that of immigrant manufacturers and proprietors downtown, whom the war had enriched. For the rest of the century, American-born voters of Irish descent remained the Tammany stalwarts, not the recent immigrants. Moreover, artisans and other workers, whose presence had been so noteworthy in the 1840s, virtually disappeared from the membership of party committees. By reinvigorating construction with deficit spending on an unprecedented scale, Tweed not only kept employment levels high but even dulled the antagonism of the Republican elite, while he traded patronage appointments with the Republican-controlled customs house, which employed a thousand people and accounted for more than half the revenues of the federal government. Tammany also marginalized the former mayor and Peace Democrat Fernando Wood. Wood did not leave politics, but he did leave his former bailiwick, the Bloody

61 Except where citations specify otherwise, this account is based on Bernstein, 17–42, and Montgomery, *Beyond Equality*, 101–7.

Oulde Sixth, to return to Congress with votes from the shantytowns on the periphery of New York's northward growth.[62]

The trade unions grew rapidly after the war, providing an organized voice for workers that Tammany Hall was obliged to court. The unions were coordinated by two citywide delegate bodies: an English-language Workingmen's Union and a German-speaking *Arbeiter-Union*. They were spurred on not only by the prosperity of the construction, shipping, and consumer-goods industries, but also by the fact that the new edifices expanded the city and redesigned its commercial heart without breaking up the working-class neighborhoods, which had stood behind the barricades of 1863. When Republican Governor Reuben Fenton refused to apply his party's doctrine of the active state to enforcement of the "legal eight-hour day" recently enacted by the state legislature, the bricklayers struck in 1868, and contractors responded with conspiracy prosecutions of the unions. Tammany leader Peter B. Sweeney assured a reporter that his party was "sound on all questions affecting the laboring interests," considered the limitation of working hours to eight for the sake of "moral and intellectual improvement . . . an established maxim," and would urge repeal of the "odious and absurd" conspiracy law. "Submission to strikes," he added, "will, after a while, be a necessity, and the excesses, if any, in the claims made for the time being must be left to the after good sense and sober second thought of the unions." Small wonder the attempt by union leaders and socialists to challenge Tammany at the polls in 1869 had pathetic results. Sensing that its opposition to black enfranchisement was by then costing more votes than it was winning, especially among German workers, however, the Tweed Ring switched its target to the Chinese. In 1870 it joined the unions in a huge rally against the immigration of "coolie labor" to the United States.[63]

Nevertheless, the ability of an exuberantly nationalistic party – with business and professional leaders cultivating a lucrative real estate market by deficit financing – to retain the benevolent neutrality of manufacturers and bondholders, as well as the loyalty of an increasingly well-organized working class, did not survive beyond the fall of 1871. It was then that a parade of Orangemen, inspired by the Belfast

62 Bernstein, 52–7, 196–9, 205–8, 215–16; Montgomery, *Beyond Equality*, 107–13; Martin Shefter, "The Electoral Foundations of the Political Machine: New York City, 1884–1897," in Joel H. Silbey, Allan G. Bogue, and William Flanigan, eds., *The History of American Electoral Behavior* (Princeton, N.J., 1978), 263–98; Gronowicz; Skowronek, 61. On immigrant manufacturers, see Gutman, *Work, Culture, and Society*, 211–33. It was only after the Civil War that the Democratic Party secured a building for its national headquarters and housed permanent staff and commissions there. Baker, *Affairs of Party*, 139.
63 Montgomery, *Beyond Equality*, 189–90, 323–6; Bernstein, 211–15, 225–6. The quotation from Sweeney is on pp. 214–15.

militancy of 1867–8, brought bloody collision between soldiers and workers back to the city's streets and enraged the Protestant establishment against the Tweed Ring. In the following months an Executive Committee of Citizens and Taxpayers for Financial Reform organized a concerted refusal by a thousand leading property owners to pay taxes until the city's books were audited. A strike of stonecutters inspired a procession for the eight-hour day, which traversed the march route made familiar by the draft rioters, between the industrial neighborhoods of the upper East Side and city hall, and was greeted by an estimated twenty-five thousand people. The ideological distance the city's labor movement had traveled since 1863 was evident in the report of a correspondent, who observed, "The centers of attraction appeared to be section 2 of the Internationals, carrying the red flag, and the colored men, both of whom were enthusiastically cheered by citizens at every point." The marchers denounced the reckless developers of the city for forcing workers into "tenement rookeries," and ended with a thunderous vote to "throw off all allegiance to the Democratic party." Simultaneously, the *Staats-Zeitung*, the *Times,* and the *Tribune* all attacked the ring. The latter two papers collaborated in circulating an anti-Tweed pamphlet, on the cover of which the feminine figure of "Reform" beckoned New Yorkers away from a hideous mob of murders and pillagers, who were waving flags emblazoned "Commune," "Hibernia," and "Socialism, Robbery, Arson."[64]

Attacked from many sides, the previously invincible Tweed Ring was abruptly toppled from power. Not only did the city's Democrats dissolve into half a dozen competing clubs for the rest of the century, but the major social confrontations of the next fifteen years were fought outside the arena framed and controlled by political parties. With city expenditures pared to the bone during the 1870s and larger factories leaving for more spacious surroundings, unemployment soared, while the provision of relief came effectively under the control of the Association for Improving the Condition of the Poor and its offspring, the Charity Organization Society. No major efforts were made to plan city development through government agencies during the next twenty-five years. The future of trade unions and the eight-hour day were decided by the strikes of a hundred thousand workers in 1872, when concurrent cessations of work by construction, wood, and metal workers were successfully challenged by the city's largest employers,

64 Montgomery, *Beyond Equality,* 378–9; Bernstein, 233–4; *Workingman's Advocate,* Sept. 23, 1871; [anon.,] *Civil Rights. The Hibernian Riot and the "Insurrection of the Capitalists."* A History of Important Events in New York in the Midsummer of 1871 (New York, 1871). On Belfast see Peter Gibbon, *The Origins of Ulster Unionism: The Formation of Popular Protestant Politics and Ideology in Nineteenth Century Ireland* (Manchester, 1975), 99–102.

organized in an Employers' Central Committee against what one leader called "the spirit of communism behind this movement." No politician had any influence on the outcome.[65]

The formidable resurgence of New York's labor movement during the 1880s prompted the city's Democratic leaders to respond within the ideological parameters established in the 1860s, but without the managed-growth policies of Tweed's days. They appointed many trade union leaders to patronage jobs, just like their counterparts did in Detroit and Chicago, where city payrolls contributed significantly to financing a labor officialdom. They blamed low wages on specific groups of people who personified "cheap labor" – convicts, tenement house producers, "Negro labor," the Chinese, and "contract labor." The campaign handbook of the Democratic National Committee in 1884 laid special emphasis on the last two. "If it became necessary to protect the American workingmen on the Pacific slope from the disastrous and debasing competition of Coolie labor, the same argument now applied with equal force and pertinency to the importation of pauper labor from southern Europe." The success of workers' organizations in drawing the votes of both first- and second-generation immigrant workers away to Henry George in the 1886 mayoral campaign revived the Democrats' passion for their old reliable causes: Irish nationalism, Catholic worship in public institutions, and patronage appointments for trade unionists.[66]

Simultaneously, the party's traditional devotion to "the voluntary principle" led it to lend its voice to the chorus of labor protest against the routine clubbing of strikers by uniformed police and the wave of injunctions with which courts suppressed labor's favorite new weapon, the citywide boycott. Jeffersonian doctrines restraining state interference against "private arrangements" assumed renewed importance to workers during the increasingly violent industrial conflict of the last quarter of the century, even though the party that espoused those doctrines was firmly in the control of professional politicians and beholden to mercantile and planter elites. As Samuel T. McSeveny has pointed out, even when the nomination of William Jennings Bryan and the adoption of a platform denouncing "government by injunc-

---

65 John W. Pratt, "Boss Tweed's Public Welfare Program," *New York Historical Society Quarterly*, 45 (Oct. 1961), 396–411; [E. L. Godkin,] "Labor and Politics," *Nation*, 14 (June 13, 1872), 386–7. On the end of planning in New York see Scobey, "Empire City," 450–90. On employers' resistance to the eight-hour–day strikes, see [Adam S. Cameron,] *The Eight Hour Question* (n.p., n.d.). The quotation is on p. 7.

66 Shefter, 264–91; Gwendolyn Mink, *Old Labor and New Immigrants in American Political Development: Union, Party, and State, 1875–1920* (Ithaca, N.Y., 1986), 107; Scobey, "Boycotting the Politics Factory"; Samuel T. McSeveny, *The Politics of Depression: Political Behavior in the Northeast, 1893–1896* (New York, 1972), 16; William L. Riordan, *Plunkitt of Tammany Hall* (New York, 1948).

tion as a new and highly dangerous form of oppression" prompted the upstanding Cleveland Democrats to desert the party, the controlling positions they had formerly occupied were quickly filled not by labor reformers but by party loyalists like those of Tammany Hall. No matter how many workingmen deposited their party ballots, neither the Democrats nor the Republicans were nor could become a workers' party.[67]

Labor Reform and Electoral Politics

Between the mid-1840s and the mid-1870s the capacity of government to police and reshape social life had grown prodigiously at the municipal, state, and federal levels. City ordinances, state legislation, constitutional amendments, court rulings, professionalized law enforcement, private initiatives in poor relief, and a huge conscription-fed army had all played important roles in creating the social order in which daily affairs were directed by those who managed its schools, press, factories, railroads, and exchanges within parameters fixed by market competition, and with a minimum of guidance from governmental officials.

The elected officials of government were linked to the large, male electorate by political parties, and voters displayed intense loyalty to their parties. Rapid industrial growth, urbanization, immigration, civil war, and the destruction of chattel slavery had generated intense, sometimes violent, controversies over public policy at the municipal, state, and federal levels, and the parties had found their most consistent supporters among the members of social groupings that were aligned on opposing sides of those controversies. As the arena within which crucial decisions about the reshaping of the economic and social order moved increasingly away from the purview of elected governmental officials, however, contestants in the fierce social conflicts that characterized the last quarter of the century increasingly denounced party loyalties as obstacles to effective resolution of those conflicts.

Champions of the laissez-faire regime like Charles Francis Adams, Jr., feared that professional politicians, competing for the votes of a largely propertyless electorate, might prove unable to resist the temptation to relax police supervision of popular behavior, and also to extend the functions of government into the preserve of private interests and market forces in order to placate the wishes of the

67 Forbath, 81–94; McSeveney, 173–81; the Democratic platform of 1896 in Commager, *Documents*, vol. 2, 179. One of the few polls of voters in 1896, conducted in a Brooklyn factory, found 58.7 percent of the workers for Bryan and 41.3 percent for McKinley, while among the office staff, 86.3 percent were for McKinley, 7.8 percent for Bryan, and 5.9 percent for the Gold Democrat Palmer. McSeveney, 304, n. 44.

multitude. "Universal suffrage," he had written in 1869, "can only mean in plain English the government of ignorance and vice: – it means a European, and especially Celtic, proletariat on the Atlantic Coast; an African proletariat on the shores of the Gulf; and a Chinese proletariat on the Pacific."[68] Despite well-publicized efforts during the 1870s to restrict voting in New York's municipal elections to property owners, and despite ruthless attacks on African-American activists and organizations in the South, formal voting rights for adult men remained intact, at least until the last decade of the nineteenth century. Moreover, courtship of popular support by political parties lost none of its ardor or its patriotic trappings, and the turnout of voters for national elections remained high.[69]

The leading protagonists of the post–Civil War labor movement extolled those democratic attributes of the polity that Adams feared. They did share his anxiety that the republic was in peril, but they located the source of the danger in the concentration of wealth and power in the hands of private individuals and in the triumph of selfish manipulation of a market economy over the community welfare. Paradoxically, labor reformers also expressed hostility toward political officeholders and their parties as often as upper-class reformers did. In fact, alliances between bourgeois citizens' committees and labor activists against incumbent political machines were not uncommon during the last quarter of the century, though they seldom survived more than a single election campaign. Andrew Cameron, the prominent labor editor from Chicago, admonished Republican workers to "have no more of this wicked as well as silly cant about loyalty," while he asked of Democrats that "our ears be no longer daily saluted with the disloyal outcries of unholy prejudice against 'the nigger.'" Workers needed, he said, to "turn to political pursuits, more befitting the loyalty, due God and our families," if they wished a future "of honesty and fair dealing, in and out of politics, of rewarded labor, and of comfortable homes for tired toil."[70]

68 Quoted in Foner, *Reconstruction*, 497.
69 On the New York state commission, see editorial, *Irish World*, April 14, 1877. On elite opinion regarding African-American suffrage, see James G. Blaine, James A. Garfield, Montgomery Blair, L. Q. C. Lamar, Alexander H. Stephens, Thomas A. Hendricks, Wade Hampton, and Wendell Phillips, "Ought the Negro to Be Disfranchised? Ought He to Have Been Enfranchised?" *North American Review*, 268 (March 1879), 225–83 and 269 (April, 1879), 337–51. On voting participation, see Kleppner, *Cross of Culture;* McSeveney; McGerr, 12–45; Baker, *Affairs of Party.* A good critique of recent studies of political behavior can be found in Richard Oestreicher, "Urban Working-Class Political Behavior and Theories of American Electoral Politics, 1870–1940," *Journal of American History,* 74 (March 1988), 1,257–86.
70 Editorial, *Workingman's Advocate,* April 9, 1870.

One decade later, a ruling by General Master Workman Powderly prohibited "electioneering for any candidate in the Sanctuary" of a Knights of Labor Assembly. "Our order," he explained, "teaches MAN his duty by educating him on the great question of labor." Warnings against the corrupting influence of party shibboleths were no less frequent at the end of the century. Go "into a ward room rally," advised Secretary August McCraith of the International Typographical Union, and there anyone would find "that sectarian prejudice reigned supreme, that the average voter casting his ballot is not a free man, but a one idead, corked up zealot on the old questions that were fought over in the days of [Queens] Mary and Elizabeth."[71]

No matter if the participating worker was a Democrat or a Republican, a Catholic, a freethinker or a Methodist, a member of the Hibernians or of the Elks, a frequenter of saloons or a member of an antisaloon league, the labor movement sought to draw him or her into a network of associations based on the common interests of people whose livelihood depended on wages. Self-organization, lectures, reading rooms, debating clubs, cooperatives, union rules and boycotts to impose a mutualistic morality on the marketplace, and strikes when all else failed – these became the favored weapons of the workers' movement. To be sure, unions often directed successful appeals to parties and officeholders for expressions of support for strikes, for pardons of workers sentenced for conspiracy or disorder, for the employment of union printers on party publications or of local, union tradesmen on municipal projects, and for making government agencies exemplary adherents to union wages and hours. Even the effectiveness of these appeals, however, depended on their success in building a movement independent of the professional politicians.[72]

When Republicans and Democrats failed to respond to labor's demands, local conventions dominated by trade unionists nominated their own slates of candidates for office in Pittsburgh, Cincinnati, Boston, and other cities during the late 1860s, initiating a challenge to the established parties that culminated in the campaigns of the Greenback-Labor (or National) Party between 1876 and 1882. In coal-mining regions from Pennsylvania to Alabama that party not only won legislative offices for some of its candidates, but also provided a vehicle for the organization of workers under the shelter of election campaigns mandated by law at a time when depression conditions and

71 Decisions of the Grand Master Workman, No. 65, *Fourth General Assembly, 1880*, 258; August McCraith to (Boston) *Labor Leader*, Dec. 23, 1893.
72 George A. Stevens, *New York Typographical Union No.6: Study of a Modern Trade Union and Its Predecessors* (Albany, N.Y., 1913) contains many accounts of efforts by union printers to influence politicians, sometimes with success and sometimes without.

conspiracy prosecutions had left workers afraid to gather publicly in union meetings.[73]

In mines near Homestead, Pennsylvania, Welsh-born David R. Jones headed the Thad Stevens Greenback-Labor Club until a successful strike in 1879 made possible the open formation of a district of the Miners National Union with Jones as president. In Detroit and among the Germans of Chicago the Socialist Labor Party played the role of the open agency through which unions and Knights assemblies were discretely organized. In 1882, however, General Master Workman Powderly set out to distance the Knights from both the Greenbackers and the Socialists in the belief that too close an association had begun to hamper the order's growth once economic conditions more hospitable to union activity had returned. After suffering a crushing defeat in his campaign for governor on the Greenback-Labor ticket in 1882, even Pittsburgh's longtime enthusiast of electoral action Thomas A. Armstrong conceded, "It is evident that whatever shall be accomplished for labor through politics must be done indirectly, by the agitation of questions in which labor may be interested with a view to compelling an established party to adopt them."[74]

Pressure on the established parties had already proven somewhat effective. In Pennsylvania some statute regulating conditions in coal mines had been enacted almost every year between 1868 and 1881. Checkweighmen were permitted and later required at mines, safety regulations and inspections were mandated, payment was allowed only in lawful money, company stores were forbidden, and a state hospital was established for the anthracite region. Most of those measures had had little impact on mining practice in the absence of unions, and two successive statutes proclaiming an end to conspiracy prosecutions of striking miners were virtually nullified by the state's courts. Nevertheless, the pattern of bipartisan support for bills introduced into the legislature by representatives who were usually miners themselves continued into the early twentieth century.[75]

During the 1880s and 1890s the scope of unions' legislative demands expanded. Lobbying for bills creating state bureaus of labor

73 Montgomery, *Beyond Equality*, 261–76, 296–310, 389–94, 425–41; Herbert G. Gutman, *Power & Culture: Essays on the American Working Class,* Ira Berlin, ed. (New York, 1987), 117–212; Letwin, 106–53; John D. French, "'Reaping the Whirlwind': The Origins of the Allegheny County Greenback Labor Party in 1877," *Western Pennsylvania Historical Magazine,* 64 (April 1981), 97–119; Ralph R. Ricker, "The Greenback-Labor Movement in Pennsylvania" (Ph.D. diss., Pennsylvania State University, 1955), 61–152.
74 Krause, 120–35, 196; Oestreicher, *Solidarity and Fragmentation,* 79–89; Nelson, *Beyond the Martyrs,* 26–76; *National Labor Tribune,* Nov. 18, 1882, quoted in Krause, 201.
75 Pennsylvania Bureau of Industrial Statistics, *Report, 1880/1881* (Harrisburg, Pa., 1881), 581–635.

statistics, restricting child labor, providing free textbooks for public schools, outlawing the importation of strikebreakers or armed guards from out of state, obliging factories to construct fire escapes, prohibiting home or tenement-house manufacturing, restricting manufacturing, printing, or mining by convict labor, installing railroad safety appliances, prescribing ten-hour workdays for women in factories, forbidding employers to punish their workers with fines, making Labor Day an official holiday, and regulating terms of apprenticeship proved successful in a variety of industrial states. Four states had also provided for mediation of industrial disputes (usually called "arbitration") by state boards, or more often by judges or mayors, before 1886, and ten others followed suit in the next four years. Demands that women be excluded from night work, underground mining, and selling liquor had produced a handful of such laws by 1900, though the flourishing of "protective legislation," designed to keep women out of a variety of occupations was to come only after that date.

Both the Knights and the AFL favored the substitution of Australian ballots (listing all candidates on an official sheet) for the familiar colored ballots distributed at the polls by the parties, and they pushed vigorously to allow voters to initiate and vote on laws outside of the legislative process, or "direct legislation," as it was then called. Both organizations had endorsed the campaign for women's suffrage by the end of the 1880s. During the 1890s Pennsylvania established state licensing of coal miners and levied direct (and ineffective) financial sanctions against employment of immigrants, while southern states enacted color bars for jobs in hotels, restaurants, and train crews. Less successful were union proposals for government hiring halls, special courts of claims for injured workers, and a ban on the dismissal of workers for union membership or voting.[76]

It is important to note that all these demands were addressed to state legislatures, not to the federal government. Washington was asked to do only what labor organizations considered properly within its realm: restrict immigration by the Chinese, and later by "contract labor" and those who could not pass literacy tests; create a federal

76 The full scope of union lobbying has yet to be examined by historians, and Victoria Hattam's categorical distinction between the lobbying objectives of the Knights and that of the unions is misleading. Hattam, 82–128. For a partial list of union-supported legislative demands, see "Michael McKettrick," *Labor Leader*, Oct. 24, 1891; Knights of Labor, *Proceedings of D.A. 16 held at Scranton, July 28th and 29th 1890* (manuscript, no pagination, Powderly Papers, reel 66). On arbitration laws, see Gerald Friedman, "Worker Militancy and Its Consequences: Political Responses to Labor Unrest in the United States, 1877–1914," *International Labor and Working-Class History*, 40 (Fall 1991), 8–9. On nineteenth-century protective legislation for women, see Alice Kessler-Harris, *Out to Work: A History of Wage-Earning Women in the United States* (New York, 1982), 180–94.

bureau of labor statistics; provide its own employees with an eight-hour day, standard wages, and civil service protection; and substitute a managed "greenback" currency for national banks. In the 1890s some unions added nationalization of railroads, coal mines, and telegraph systems to this list. Demands for national systems of social insurance, such as Austria and Germany had initiated, were conspicuously absent. Even socialists did not ask for insurance of workers by a capitalist government. No mention of welfare legislation in the twentieth-century sense appeared in the Political Programme of 1893–4, whose sponsors sought without success to commit the AFL to "the collective ownership by the people of all means of production and distribution." Although social insurance loomed large among the immediate demands of the Socialist Party after 1901, the tireless discussion of poverty among socialists before that time had focused directly and uncompromisingly on the need to end exploitation.[77]

More important, all the hard-won state laws belonged to what Elizabeth Brandeis called "the pre-enforcement stage," which continued to characterize labor legislation long after it had ended in criminal law. They were of three types, she explained. Some explicitly permitted workers to agree to a contract in violation of the law's provisions – most notably those which made eight or ten hours a "legal day's work" but enabled courts to consider any work in excess of those hours voluntary. The second type specified certain rights (like payment of earnings in cash or compensation for injury), which could be enforced only by a civil suit brought by the offended worker. The third, and most common type, prescribed some fine for violation of the law, but left it up to the worker or some other interested party to initiate prosecution. Although courts might find employers guilty in such cases and might even award part of the fine to the "informer," the judicial doctrine of employment at will made it perfectly legal for the convicted boss to fire a worker who had acted to enforce the law.[78]

When statutes did threaten to impinge on companies' control of their own business affairs, the courts usually found them unconstitu-

77 For socialist demands, see "Manifesto of the International Working People's Association" in Richard T. Ely, *The Labor Movement in America* (New York, 1886), 358–63; "Political Programme" in Kaufman, *Gompers Papers*, vol. 3, 616–17; Ira Kipnis, *American Socialist Movement, 1897–1912* (New York, 1952), 152. George Steinmetz has shown that the Socialist delegates in the German parliament opposed every one of the government's famous social insurance measures, and James E. Cronin and Peter Weiler argued that the Labour Representation Committee's members in the British Parliament were also hostile to the Liberal Party's welfare state plans. George Steinmetz, "Workers and the Welfare State in Imperial Germany," *International Labor and Working-Class History*, 40 (Fall 1991), 18–46; James E. Cronin and Peter Weiler, "Working-Class Interests and the Politics of Social Democratic Reform in Britain, 1900–1940," ibid., 47–66.
78 Elizabeth Brandeis, "Labor Legislation," in Commons, *History*, vol. 3, 626–7.

tional. William Forbath has cataloged sixty state labor laws invalidated by courts between 1881 and 1900. Most of them, not surprisingly, dealt with coal mining. Others had restricted hours of labor, outlawed workplace fines, prohibited dismissal for union membership or voting, required union labor on public works, or allowed workers suing employers to be awarded attorneys' fees. Important measures that *were* upheld were often construed so narrowly as to nullify their intended effect. For example, although two-thirds of all states had enacted laws by 1877 securing married women's claims to wages they had earned themselves, the courts limited that protection to what the women had clearly acquired outside of the household. As Amy Stanley has written, "Taking in boarders, nursing the sick, canning fruit, working [at home] as a seamstress for five dollars a week, running a hotel – such diverse enterprises were all deemed part of the domestic labor the wife owed as the 'helpmate of her husband,'" and to which any enforcement of her claim might result in "frauds upon the creditors."[79]

The courts also threw their weight decisively against efforts by workers' organizations to impose social standards through their own collective action in the market. Fines levied on employers for violations of union rules were successfully prosecuted as extortion, and public exposure of working conditions by the labor press brought suits for libel. The courts' primary weapon, however, was the injunction, an order issued by a judge forbidding some action he considered illegal or injurious. Any violation of an injunction would be prosecuted before the same judge in a juryless trial as contempt of court. After years of confrontation with state legislatures over conspiracy laws – which New York, Pennsylvania, and other states rewrote to put an end to the prosecution of strikers while courts defiantly continued to hear such cases – the legal profession fashioned the injunction into a more effective device, which could be elaborated and applied under its own control without interference by elected officials.[80]

Court orders were issued with increasing frequency between 1885 and 1887 against boycotts of employers who were deemed unfair by labor organizations. The citywide boycott, by which all residents were mobilized to "leave severely alone" a particular firm that persecuted or defied its own workers, had developed into the most effective weapon of the Knights of Labor. The boycott, said Knights, was an "arbitration persuader," which would bring miscreant employers to the negotiating table. While workers defended their hundreds of local boycotts as the sort of private arrangements to promote the common welfare that

79 Forbath, 38n, 177–87; Stanley, "Contract Rights," 283–303. The quotation is on p. 302.
80 Hattam, 117–28; Tomlins, *The State and the Unions*, 44–90.

was favored by America's Jeffersonian legacy, courts impugned them precisely because their motivation was not self-interested but "sympathetic." By introducing community moral standards into economic behavior, they charged, boycotts were "combinations of irresponsible cabals or cliques" that threatened to bring "an end of government." By the end of the 1890s, courts were even issuing injunctions against city officials who aided workers during their strikes.[81]

It would be misleading, however, to depict the judiciary as the bulwark of capitalists' interests, single-handedly defending the unfettered marketplace against persistent attempts by elected officials to aid the workers. Most of the legislation sought by labor organizations never passed the state legislatures, and much of what did pass was so poorly drafted and difficult to enforce as to suggest that legislators of both parties had voted for the measures with an eye to improving their voting records for the folks back home without injuring business interests. The accusation by liberals like Godkin and Adams that politicians were "playing tricks with the labor question" and cultivating disrespect for the law contained more than a little truth. Other forums proved no more responsive to union initiatives than were the court-obstructed legislatures. When New York's constitutional convention met in 1894, for example, it incorporated in the new organic law a ban on prison labor, which was advocated by the AFL and supported by numerous businesses, but it voted down all other proposals that had come from the unions, among them free meals for school children, limits to the working hours of women and children, municipal home rule, public ownership of utilities, an industrial arbitration court, and restriction of tenement-house manufacturing. As the president of Alabama's mine workers concluded, "We could go on voting and voting, but the results would never benefit us one iota if we do not organize."[82]

In fact, the influence workers could exert on the major parties in any locality was directly proportional to the level of organization accomplished there by the trade unions and the Knights of Labor. It also helped if the concentration of wage earners was large, and Democrats appeared more likely to favor labor's demands if the town had many Germans. A close and unstable balance of power between the major parties often made both of them more attentive to workers' voices, and the presence of an effective Greenback-Labor or Socialist Labor party in the community made them much more attentive. In fact, it was the socialist presence in German communities that ac-

81 Norman J. Ware, *The Labor Movement in the United States, 1860–1895* (New York, 1929), 334–5; Grimes, 44; *Crump* v. *Commonwealth,* 84 Va., 927, 946 (1888), quoted in Forbath, 84.
82 McSeveny, 80–1; Birmingham *Labor Advocate,* Dec. 1, 1894, quoted in Letwin, 282.

counted for the appeal of labor legislation to local Democrats. Homestead, Pennsylvania, which the Republicans usually carried by a narrow margin, benefited from all those attributes on the eve of the great strike of 1892. The result was that workers nominated by one party or another had increased their grip on local offices and legislative seats election by election until they had established what Paul Krause called "a worker's republic," which was brought to an end only when Carnegie Steel crushed the unions.[83]

Although workers' political influence was most clearly apparent in the response of local governments to industrial disputes, as it was in Homestead, it is very misleading to consider working-class politics only as an adjunct to union struggles. Every one of the five successful mobilizations of workers in municipal politics of the 1880s studied by Leon Fink was made possible by a strong presence of the Knights of Labor and trade unions in local manufacturing and construction, to be sure. The focal point of political struggle, however, was the workers' effort to rescue their cities from the squalor and neglect produced by the capitalist market. The town officials elected by the United Labor Party of Rochester, New Hampshire, did little to alter the structure of government, but they did shift municipal expenditures away from private claims for public favors into increased appropriations for schools, poor relief, a reading room, and road paving, all of which had suffered long neglect.

The story was similar in every other case Fink examined. While the coercive power of government had roused the anger of labor organizations, the diminished scope of governmental action, where social priorities had been fixed by market economics, had left urban life a shambles, except for those individuals with sufficient wealth to provide for themselves. In Kansas City, Kansas, where mayor Thomas Hannan had channeled labor's strength into the Republican fold, thus facilitating a most unusual alliance between white and black workers, his administration wrung the funds needed for parks, a library, and a sewer system from the city's businesses. There and in other manufacturing towns the public institutions that wealthy philanthropists donated to cities after their workers' movements had been defeated had first been introduced through municipal action on the initiative of the workers themselves. To be sure, the scale of public projects was less grandiose, because no town government had as much money at its disposal as Andrew Carnegie had. Moreover, civic and patriotic festivities flourished as never before under the regime of labor reformers.

83 Krause, 188, 382.

Nowhere did municipal efforts to regenerate civil society flourish more than they did in Milwaukee, where the evolution of the United Labor party into the Social Democracy produced three decades of continuous elaboration of worker-oriented programs. Schools became community centers; public bath houses and municipal pawn shops dotted workers' neighborhoods; and free legal and medical services and even symphony concerts became part of urban life. In short, effective labor politics was not simply a matter of urging labor legislation on governments, but also an effort by workers to provide an infrastructure of services to family life that the free market had denied them.[84]

Municipal government, therefore, had become an arena of decisive importance in the political mobilization of the working class. This was not the case only in the United States, but also in Britain, France, and Germany, where the appeal of socialism to workers spread not only union by union, but also city by city. The brutality of an industrial life shaped only by market forces was evident not only on the job, but also in the apartments, washrooms, and streets where men and women carried on their daily lives. The promise and the failures of party politics were also manifested there.[85] Despite the veto power of the judiciary, therefore, and despite the parties' "playing tricks with the labor question," the negative assessment, shared by many scholars and well expressed by John Cumbler, that "political parties . . . had little effect on low-income groups," and that worker activists' participation in politics "often failed to contribute to the workers' daily struggle for dignity and bread," is misleading.[86] That conception of class and politics focuses its definition of "dignity and bread" too narrowly on workplace struggles and male experience.

The fact remains, however, that in none of the two hundred towns and cities where the labor movement fielded its own candidates in the

84 Fink, 58, 131, 208. See also Holli, 30–65; Zane L. Miller, *Boss Cox's Cincinnati: Urban Politics in the Progressive Era* (New York, 1968), 89–90, 125–6; Richard Schneirov, "The Knights of Labor in the Chicago Labor Movement and in Municipal Politics, 1877–1887" (Ph.D. diss., Northern Illinois University, 1984), 498–508; Elmer A. Beck, *The Sewer Socialists: A History of the Socialist Party of Wisconsin, 1897–1940* (2 vols., Fennimore, Wis., 1982), vol. 1, 68–94.
85 Joan Wallach Scott, "Social History and the History of Socialism: French Socialist Municipalities in the 1890's," *Le Mouvement Social*, 111 (April–June 1980), 145–53; Daisy E. Devreese, "Belgium," in van der Linden and Rojahn, vol. 1, 39–49; Jacques Kergoat, "France," in ibid., vol. 1, 171–80; Klaus Tenfelde, "Germany," in ibid., vol. 1, 266–8; E. P. Thompson, "Homage to Tom Maguire," in Asa Briggs and John Saville, eds., *Essays in Labour History* (London, 1960), 276–316. German Social Democrats, who scorned Bismarckian social insurance and repudiated the state as "an instrument of domination," nevertheless considered the municipality, in the words of Karl Kautsky, "an administrative organization, a mechanism for the administration of *things by men.*" Steinmetz, 37.
86 John T. Cumbler, *Working Class Community in Industrial America: Work, Leisure, and Struggle in Two Industrial Cities, 1880–1930* (Westport, Conn., 1979), 10.

1880s did labor retain its grip on municipal offices after the defeat of union organization in the locality's major enterprises. In most urban areas the effective employers' counterattack against the Knights and the trade unions between 1887 and 1894 destroyed the organizational base without which propertyless individuals could not forge themselves into an effective political force.[87]

As union power declined, the regular Republicans and Democrats trumpeted the slogans that rallied their traditional followers back to the fold. Tariffs, state funding of parochial schools, liquor licensing, and pensions for veterans who had saved the Union reemerged as the central issues of political debate in the industrial states despite the rising tide of Farmers' Alliance strength in southern and western states, which posed a major challenge to the two-party system. When Senator Henry Cabot Lodge introduced his Force Bill to provide federal protection for the voting rights of African Americans in national elections, Democratic protests supplied a major campaign theme for the next decade, and persuaded even General Master Workman Powderly that there was "more intimidation contained in four lines of that [proposed] law than in all the Southern outrages that have taken place since the war." An Australian ballot would eliminate the need "for the supervision of Congressional watch-dogs," Powderly argued, and he went on to use the republicanism of the Order to undermine the aspirations of its own black members: "If there is a body of men in this land who do not know enough to do their own voting, if they lack the manhood to defend their ballots with their lives at the polls, then that body of men are not the kind to be privileged to vote for those who make laws for others."[88]

Simultaneously both parties courted the endorsements of individual union officers avidly. In Detroit, for example, the Democrats creamed off the leadership of the city's Knights of Labor, appointing District Master Workman J. D. Long city assessor, executive board member John Haire sidewalk inspector, and his prominent colleague John Devlin United States consul in Winsor, Ontario, where Devlin in turn found jobs for twenty-three of his colleagues in the customs house. During the election of 1888, the Republicans found themselves for the first time in a generation facing a presidential campaign without federal patronage at their disposal. To secure their historic bases of support, the party's national platform pledged to increase tariff protection against the competition of foreign manufactures and

87 David Montgomery, "Labor and the Republic in Industrial America," *Le Mouvement Social*, 111 (April–June 1980), 208–15; Commons, *History*, vol. 2, 439–520.
88 Kleppner, *Cross of Culture*, 130–78; Goodwyn, 177–272; T. V. Powderly, "The Federal Election Bill," in *Journal of United Labor*, July 31, 1890. See also Powderly's Cleveland speech against the bill, ibid., April 10, 1890.

to provide by generous pensions "against the possibility that any man who honorably wore the Federal uniform shall be the inmate of an almshouse, or dependent upon private charity." Party leaders established fund-raising business advisory committees across the land, recruited secretary Charles Litchman of the Knights of Labor, former president John Jarrett of the Iron and Steel Workers, incumbent president John Campbell of the Glass Workers, and the eminent one-time Chartist and Greenbacker Thomas W. "Beeswax" Taylor to stump for Harrison in Pennsylvania. They also made Judith Ellen Foster, a prominent prohibitionist who opposed the Prohibition Party, chair of the Women's National Republican Committee.[89]

Whether labor's political influence was strong or weak, there remained one essential product of free-market capitalism that was beyond the capacity of national parties, workers' own organizations, or municipal government to remedy: unemployment. Although the specter of being without work haunted every worker and his or her family, the depression of the 1890s made it a reality on a scale that overwhelmed every attempt to deal with the problem. While Jacob Coxey's army of unemployed traversed the country from west to east and "Count" Joseph Rybakowski's Industrial Army enjoyed the overwhelming support of Buffalo's Polish community during its violent clashes with the city police, many trade unionists attempted self-help on a massive scale. The Trades and Labor Assembly of Denver ran Camp Relief with quasi-military discipline for more than seventeen thousand workers who flocked to the city from the idle mining camps of the region, until both the unions and the local church relief missions ran out of funds. In Danbury, Connecticut, locked-out hat workers simply assembled in the town meeting and voted $50,000 for their own relief, only to be overruled by the town's selectmen. Mayor Carter Harrison of Chicago, after his police had broken up meeting after meeting of the unemployed, responded to a huge rally addressed by Gompers, Henry George, and others, by transferring city funds to public works, which were administered by a Labor and Temporary Relief Committee. There again the available money was soon exhausted, and the dispensation and control of relief to the needy fell back on private agencies.[90]

So severe was the crisis, however, that even the Charity Organization Society of New York, flagship of the movement for privatization of

---

89 Oestreicher, *Solidarity and Fragmentation*, 186–7; Skowronek, 74–5; Skocpol, 125; McClure, vol. 2, 570–5; Commons, *History*, vol. 2, 468; Krause, 252–66; Ginzberg, 185.

90 Carlos A. Schwantes, *Coxey's Army: An American Odyssey* (Lincoln, Neb., 1985); Closson, "Unemployed in American Cities"; Harring, "Class Conflict," 895–906. See also Keyssar, 222–31; John A. Garraty, *Unemployment in History: Economic Thought and Public Policy* (New York, 1978), 116–28.

poor relief, called on Mayor Thomas F. Gilroy to create a special fund for jobs improving Central Park. In a reversal of roles from Boss Tweed's day, the mayor established a Citizens' Relief Committee of elite figures to raise contributions and disperse funds to private and religious agencies for aid to the needy. The most far-reaching governmental assistance was provided by Republican Mayor Hazen Pingree of Detroit, who enjoyed the ardent support of the city's German and Polish workers and was reelected in 1893 with the endorsement of the Populists and the tacit support of the Socialist Labor Party. In addition to participating personally in a direct action campaign against the traction company to reduce streetcar fares, Pingree borrowed money to the legal limit for public works, forced the city's salaried employees to contribute regularly to poor relief funds, drove down the price of bread, commandeered land for potato patches so that the poor could feed themselves, and sent commissioners out to find people in need, rather than obliging supplicants to appeal for aid.[91]

Probably no other American mayor of the nineteenth century had attacked the whole complex of grievances that urban life aroused among working people more systematically than did this man, who paradoxically was a shoe manufacturer brought into politics by liberal good-government reformers to oust the Irish Democrats from power, in a city that was then a stronghold of labor organization. By 1893 he was despised by his initial supporters, but he had shown working people what a city might do even with the limited resources at its disposal. Nevertheless, his experience made Pingree keenly aware of the way public assumption of the human costs of capitalism can serve to reinforce the very system that generated the suffering. "I think I see where methods of charity lessen wages," he said, as if anticipating the course of twentieth-century welfare politics, "where capitalists are secure from the demands of economic justice behind a public tax for the support of the so-called unfortunates; where charity, in short, is the handmaiden of economic oppression."[92]

Citizenship and the Unseen Hand

In the first years of the twentieth century, Alfred Kolb, a city councillor from the German Rhineland, spent many months in Chicago investigating the lives and thoughts of emigrants from Germany, among whom he "heard and saw almost nothing of Social Democracy." On many an evening when men gathered to smoke pipes and share a pitcher of beer (far less, Kolb noted, than their counterparts in Ger-

91 Ringenbach, 93–7; Holli, 63–72.
92 Holli, 73.

many imbibed), they expressed their admiration for the new country
where they could speak their minds without fear of the police, where
they ate meat frequently, where even their cramped housing seemed
spacious in comparison to workers' residences in the old country, and
where "nobody looks down on the manual worker" or treats "the pen
pusher . . . like a lord." They had also found, however, that the "only
law here is money," and the pace of work was so intense that older men
who were unemployed blackened their hair before setting out in
search of jobs. Moreover, the immigrants constantly emphasized the
contrast between the "unblemished hands" of officials who inspected
factories and administered social insurance in Germany, and the bla-
tant venality of politicians and officeholders in Chicago. Those who
had arrived in America the most recently seemed to Kolb to be the
most vociferous expressing the fear shared by all, that available jobs
were being taken up by "the quarter of a million hungry Europeans,
who come here every year."[93]

   Worker citizens of 1900 still found much to cherish in the Jeffersonian legacy that had earlier inspired Thomas Devyr and John Binns.
The right to quit remained the badge of one's independence, even
though it resembled a cruel joke to men whose family responsibilities
and advanced age made them hesitant to exercise it, and to women
who combined wage-earning and household obligations only by means
of arrangements that would be difficult to duplicate elsewhere. Black
sharecroppers, coal miners, and tracklayers in the South were often so
deeply ensnared in debts and so closely watched by sheriffs and gang
bosses that they were as likely as working people of the 1790s to risk
being locked up for "absconding from their masters." Police enforcement of vagrancy and tramp acts reminded everyone that the worker
with no employer at all was a criminal. Nevertheless, rates of labor
turnover and geographical mobility were notoriously high. Though
up-to-date managers would soon direct their attention systematically
to slowing down the pace of voluntary departures from their payrolls,
workers could readily understand and agree with Cornelia Parker's
exclamation, "Praise be the labor turnover!"[94]

   Individual migration from one job to another, however, was most
unlikely to effect changes in the conditions under which people
worked as extensively as collective action did. Consequently, the ability
to associate openly to advance their own interests, and to act together
to regulate their own lives, was the most precious of all liberties.
Without it, constitutional rights that had historically been conceived

93 Alfred Kolb, *Als Arbeiter in Amerika. Unter deutsch-amerikanischen Großstadt Proletariern*
   (Berlin, 1904). The quotations are on pp. 3, 91, 94, 95.
94 Cornelia Straton Parker, *Working with the Working Woman* (New York, 1922), 43. On
   turnover and attempts to deter it, see Montgomery, *Fall*, 236–44.

and elaborated in terms of the attributes of property, the exchange of commodities, and the protection of privileged minorities from majoritarian government, had little to offer those who worked for others in exchange for wages. Only group solidarities to enforce wage demands, uphold workers' codes of behavior on the job, and establish mechanisms for the negotiation of grievances could offer workers some shelter from the vicissitudes of the market. On occasion joint action could even enable them to manipulate labor markets to their own advantage. And group self-help, whether exercised through unions, fraternal lodges, women's associations, or religious bodies, permitted men and women not only to survive when the market provided no work, but also sometimes to escape the cruel regime of the charity reformers. To Samuel Gompers the libertarian side of the republican heritage, which allowed people to act for themselves, was far more important than formal rights to elect governmental officials. "It is ridiculous to imagine that the wage-workers can be slaves in employment and yet achieve control at the polls," said Gompers in one of his most famous statements. "There never yet existed coincident with each other autocracy in the shop and democracy in political life."[95]

As Gompers never hesitated to point out, however, judicial treatment of union rules, fines, boycotts, and sympathetic strikes as illegal, coupled with the elaboration of employers' authority in common law, had placed the machinery of government on the side of "autocracy in the shop," at times even in defiance of state legislatures. The treatment of workers' street life, public meetings, marches, and strikes by municipal police also triggered many a campaign for control of the mayor's office, as well as confrontations between elected mayors and police chiefs selected by state-appointed commissioners. By the 1890s workers engaged in large strikes were overawed by the armed forces of state and federal governments with increasing regularity. Although all workers despised such hired agents of company power as the Pinkertons and Pennsylvania's Coal and Iron Police, both the overwhelming might and the patriotic symbolism of the army posed troubling dilemmas. No easy answer appeared to whether workers should try to democratize the armed forces or to shun them.

The problem facing workers at the century's end, however, was not simply to restrain the coercive authority of the courts, police, and army, so that working people might more freely form their own associations and inform market activities with their codes of mutual assistance and community welfare, but also to use the machinery of government, to

95 [American Federation of Labor,] *Report of the Proceedings of the Fourteenth Annual Convention of the A. F. of L. held at Denver, Col., Dec. 1894* (Bloomington, Ind., 1905), 14.

which democracy gave them access, to rescue urban life from the squalor
and neglect left by a market system that funneled its benefits to those best
able to purchase them. Many an opponent of committing the AFL to a
national agenda of electoral politics, like John Lennon, the tailors' leader
from Denver, agreed that "the proper development of this movement for
political action is first in municipal affairs," where "partisanship can be
eliminated and should be eliminated."[96]

During the last quarter of the nineteenth century, civic consciousness in urban politics materialized first among working people, while
bourgeois "good government" reformers remained spellbound by
political corruption as though it were the fountainhead of evil in a
society best regulated by market and domestic relationships. The
battle over public sanitation, low fares and extended service on streetcar lines, health centers, public libraries, free textbooks and lunches
in schools, and public works to feed the unemployed grew out of the
experienced needs of working-class families and shaped the most
durable and influential local political movements based on workers'
votes, whatever party label they sported. Civic-minded men and wom-
en of property were still trying to meet social needs by charitable
donations of relief, libraries, museums, colleges, and parks, returning
to the community a fraction of the wealth they had extracted from it
on terms they could specify.

The conflict over the purpose of government reopened controversy over who should participate in the polity. In the name of
reducing political corruption, elite reformers of the North joined
white supremacists of the South in campaigning for the restitution
of property, residency, poll tax and literacy qualifications for
voting, for the imposition of requirements that the prospective
voter register personally with the authorities at some date well in
advance of the voting, and for the reduction in the number of
government officials chosen by elections. Although such reforms
seriously changed voting patterns in the North only after the turn
of the century, they had been imposed with devastating effect by
the end of the 1890s on black voting in the South, and on the
participation of poor white voters there as well. A pamphlet written
by George Gunton for the AFL in 1889 denounced the various
measures then being espoused for "imposing property, educational
and other qualifications for voting, lengthening the terms and
increasing the appointing powers of executive officers, making
popular elections less frequent, . . . taking public offices out of the
reach of politics, etc." These measures, Gunton contended, were

96 Kaufman, *Gompers Papers*, vol. 3, 647.

"simply attempts to whittle away our democratic institutions in order to sustain a pernicious industrial policy."[97]

That did not mean that he or anyone else in labor's ranks found the status quo satisfactory. Trade unionists, Knights, and socialists were as hostile as Adams and Godkin to the "spoils system," which inspired the cynicism reported by Alfred Kolb. They located the source of political corruption, however, in the ability of men of great wealth to buy influence in government and in the protection provided that wealth by the judiciary. By far the strongest faction in the union movement rallied behind Gompers in opposition to proposals to nationalize industry or launch a workers' party, believing that such measures would only enmesh labor more deeply in the clutches of government, while their advocacy would subject the movement to ferocious attacks. A minority, which was to grow significantly as World War I approached, sought the remedy in overt economic and political struggle to wrest command of both industry and government from the employers and their two political parties.

One proposed reform, proudly bearing the pedigree of a century of claims to citizenship, still enjoyed widespread support across the various ideological divisions of the labor movement: the institution of popular rights of initiative and referendum for legislation and recall of elected officials. As Youngstown's "puddler poet," Michael Mc-Govern, put the case:

> When parties you've elected to
>   Direct (and rob) the nation,
> Had not your interest in view,
>   'Tis time to try what you can do
>   Through Direct Legislation.
>
> On this reformers can unite
>   And vote for reformation.
> Then wrongs which judges will call "right"
>   Will disappear before the light
>   Of Direct Legislation.[98]

Working people were reminded each day that market regulation of social production and urban habitation had submerged industry's promise of abundance in waters where the big fish devoured the small. When at work, as George McNeill had written, they were "continually under surveillance," and when out of work, were "the pariah[s] of society." The rapid concentration of control within industry, which

97 George Gunton, *The Economic and Social Importance of the Eight-Hour Movement* (AFL Eight-Hour Series, No. 2, Washington, D.C., 1889), 23. Cf. Frank K. Foster's reference to "the rising wrath of American Democracy" as one of the world's many currents of popular protest. Gutman, *Work, Culture, and Society*, 87.
98 McGovern, 66–7.

resulted from the merger movement at the turn of the century, had
subjected the market itself to the manipulation of corporate oligop-
olies, while rendering the capacity of workers' organizations to impose
their mutualistic standards tenuous at best.[99] A generation of efforts by
the labor movement to lobby for reform legislation and to redirect
municipal affairs had placed those issues high on the nation's political
agenda, but its outcome to date had also left workers, such as those
whom Kolb interviewed, awed by the power of the judiciary to shield
business from both community solidarities and elected legislatures,
and contemptuous of the actual practitioners of urban government.

   The most urgent question facing workers' movements in both
North America and Europe as the new century dawned, therefore, was
whether democracy could be rescued by extending its scope into the
forbidden gardens of the market itself. Henry Demarest Lloyd defined that issue precisely in a widely circulated speech to a trade union
picnic on July 4, 1889. The "mission of the labour movement," he
declared, was "to free mankind from the superstitions and sins of the
market, and to abolish the poverty which is the fruit of those sins." To
achieve that goal, he argued in a clarion call to the 1893 AFL convention, was to extend the principles on which the polity was based to the
direction of the economy as well. "It is by the people who do the work
that the hours of labour, the conditions of employment, the division
of the produce is to be determined," Lloyd proclaimed. "It is by them
the captains of industry are to be chosen, and chosen to be servants,
not masters. It is for the welfare of all that the coordinated labour of
all must be directed. . . . This is democracy."[100]

99 On the merger movement and workplace struggles, see Montgomery, *Fall*, 257–
    329. The quotations from McNeill are in *Labor Movement*, 455.
100 Henry Demarest Lloyd, *Men, The Workers* (New York, 1909), 14, 91.

Bibliography

Abbott, Grace. *The Child and the State* (2 vols., Chicago, 1938).

"Account of the Grand Federal Procession," *American Museum,* 4 (July 1788) 57–58.

Adams, Charles Francis, Jr. *Individuality in Politics: A Lecture Delivered in Steinway Hall, New York, Wednesday Evening, April 21, 1880* (New York, 1880).

Alexander, Winthrop. "Ten Years of Riot Duty," *Journal of the Military Service Institution of the United States,* 19 (July 1896), 1–62.

Altgeld, John Peter. *Live Questions* (Chicago, 1890).

[American Federation of Labor.] *Report of the Proceedings of the Fourteenth Annual Convention of the A. F. of L. held at Denver, Col., Dec. 1894* (Bloomington, Ind., 1905).

Ames, Mary. *From a New England Woman's Diary in Dixie in 1865* (Springfield, Mass., 1906).

Appleby, Joyce. *Capitalism and a New Social Order: The Republican Vision of the 1790s* (New York, 1984).

Arnesen, Eric. *Waterfront Workers of New Orleans: Race, Class, and Politics, 1863–1923* (New York, 1991).

Avrich, Paul. *The Haymarket Tragedy* (Princeton, N.J., 1984).

Baker, Jean H. *Affairs of Party: The Political Culture of Northern Democrats in the Mid–Nineteenth Century* (Ithaca, N.Y., 1983).

Baker, Paula. "The Domestication of Politics: Women and American Political Society, 1780–1920," *American Historical Review,* 89 (June 1984), 620–47.

Barron, Hal S. *Those Who Stayed Behind: Rural Society in Nineteenth-Century New England* (New York, 1984).

Beck, Elmer A. *The Sewer Socialists: A History of the Socialist Party of Wisconsin, 1897–1940* (2 vols., Fennimore, Wis., 1982).

Bennett, John. "The Iron Workers of Woods Run and Johnstown: The Union Era" (Ph.D. diss., University of Pittsburgh, 1977).

Berlin, Ira. *Freedom: A Documentary History of Emancipation, 1861–1867* (5 vols., Cambridge, 1982–).

Bernstein, Iver. *The New York City Draft Riots: Their Significance for American Society and Politics in the Age of the Civil War* (New York, 1990).

Binns, John. *Recollections of the Life of John Binns: Twenty-Nine Years in Europe and Fifty-Three in the United States* (Philadelphia, 1854).

Birkhimer, W. E. "The Army: Its Employment during Time of Peace, and the Necessity for Its Increase," *Journal of the Military Service Institution of the United States,* 19 (July 1896), 188–9.

Bishop, Joel. *New Commentaries on the Criminal Law* (2 vols., Chicago, 1892).

Blackburn, David, and Geoff Eley. *Peculiarities of German History: Bourgeois Society and Politics in Nineteenth-Century Germany* (Oxford, 1984).

Blackmar, Elizabeth. *Manhattan for Rent* (Ithaca, N.Y., 1989).

Blaine, James G., James A. Garfield, Montgomery Blair, L. Q. C. Lamar, Alexander H. Stephens, Thomas A. Hendricks, Wade Hampton, and Wendell Phillips. "Ought the Negro to Be Disfranchised? Ought He to Have Been Enfranchised?" *North American Review,* 268 (March 1879), 225–83, and 269 (April 1879), 337–51.

Blatchly, Cornelius C. *Some Causes of Popular Poverty, Arising from the Enriching Nature of Interest, Rents, Duties, Inheritances, and Church Establishments. Investigated in Their Principles and Consequences* (Philadelphia, 1817).

Blewett, Mary H. *Men, Women, and Work: Class, Gender, and Protest in the New England Shoe Industry, 1780–1910* (Urbana, Ill., 1988).

[Bolles, John A.] *The Affairs of Rhode Island, By a Member of the Boston Bar* (Boston, 1842).

Bordieu, Pierre. *Distinction: A Social Critique of the Judgment of Taste* (Cambridge, Mass., 1984).

Bordin, Ruth. *Woman and Temperance: The Quest for Power and Liberty, 1873–1900* (Philadelphia, 1981).

Boyer, Paul. *Urban Masses and Moral Order in America, 1820–1920* (Cambridge, Mass., 1978).

Brandeis, Elizabeth. "Labor Legislation," in John R. Commons, et al., *History of Labour in the United States* (4 vols., New York, 1918–35), vol. 3, 399–700.

Braudel, Fernand. *Civilization and Capitalism, 15th–18th Century* (3 vols., translated by Sian Reynolds, New York, 1981–4).

Brennan, Brother Joseph, F.S.C. *Social Conditions in Industrial Rhode Island, 1820–1860* (Washington, D.C., 1940).

Bridge, James Howard. *The Inside History of the Carnegie Steel Company. A Romance of Millions* (New York, 1903).

Bridges, Amy. *A City in the Republic: Antebellum New York and the Origins of Machine Politics* (Cambridge, 1984).

Bryce, James. *The American Commonwealth,* edited and abridged by Louis Hacker (2 vols., New York, 1959).

[Burn, James D.] *Three Years among the Working-Classes of the United States during the War* (London, 1865).

Byington, Margaret F. *Homestead: The Households of a Mill Town* (New York, 1910).

Byrdsall, Fitzwilliam. *The History of the Loco-Foco or Equal Rights Party* (New York, 1842).

[Cameron, Adam S.] *The Eight Hour Question* (n.p., n.d.).

Carey, Mathew. *Appeal to Common Sense and Common Justice* (Philadelphia, 1822).

Essays on the Public Charities of Philadelphia (Philadelphia, 1829).

Appeal to the Wealthy of the Land (Philadelphia, 1833).

Carroll, Anna Ella. *The Great American Battle; Or, The Contest between Christianity and Political Romanism* (New York, 1856).

Catterall, Helen T. *Judicial Cases Concerning American Slavery and the Negro* (5 vols., Washington, D.C., 1936).

Chandler, Alfred D., Jr. *The Visible Hand: The Managerial Revolution in American Business* (Cambridge, Mass., 1977).

Charters and Legislative Documents, Illustrative of Rhode Island History (Providence, R.I., 1844).

Chauncey, George A., Jr. "Gay New York: Urban Culture and the Making of a Gay Male World, 1890–1940" (Ph.D. diss., Yale University, 1989).

Cheng, Lucie and Edna Bonacich. *Labor Immigration under Capitalism: Asian Workers in the United States before World War II* (Berkeley and Los Angeles, 1984).

Christman, Henry M. *Tin Horns and Calico: A Decisive Episode in the Emergence of Democracy* (New York, 1945).

Civil Rights. The Hibernian Riot and the "Insurrection of the Capitalists." A History of Important Events in New York in the Midsummer of 1871 (New York, 1871).

Clark, Dennis. *The Irish in Philadelphia: Ten Generations of Urban Experience* (Philadelphia, 1973).

Clark, Kathleen. "Severed Ties: Race, Sex, and Violence in Georgia, 1868–1871" (unpublished seminar paper, Yale University, 1992).

Clement, Priscilla Ferguson. "The Transformation of the Wandering Poor in Nineteenth-Century Philadelphia," in Eric H. Monkkonen, ed., *Walking to Work: Tramps in America, 1790–1935* (Lincoln, Neb., 1984), 59–66.

Closson, Carlos C., Jr. "The Unemployed in American Cities," *Quarterly Journal of Economics,* 8 (Jan. 1894), 168–217, 257–8.

Cohen, Lizabeth. *Making a New Deal: Industrial Workers in Chicago, 1919–1939* (Cambridge, 1990).

Cohen, Patricia Cline. "Unregulated Youth: Masculinity and Murder in the 1830s City," *Radical History Review,* 52 (Winter 1992), 33–52.

Coleman, Peter J. *The Transformation of Rhode Island, 1790–1860* (Providence, R.I., 1963).

  Debtors and Creditors in America: Insolvency, Imprisonment for Debt, and Bankruptcy, 1607–1900 (Madison, Wis., 1974).

Colley, Linda. "Whose Nation? Class and National Consciousness in Britain, 1750–1830," *Past and Present,* 113 (Nov. 1986), 97–117.

Commager, Henry Steele. *Documents of American History* (2 vols. in one, 3rd edition, New York, 1947).

Commons, John R., et al. *Documentary History of American Industrial Society* (10 vols., Cleveland, Ohio, 1910–11).

  History of Labour in the United States (4 vols., New York, 1918–35).

Cottereau, Alain. "Justice et injustice ordinaire sur les lieux de travail d'après les audiences prud'homales (1806–1866)," *Le Mouvement Social,* 141 (Oct.–Dec. 1987), 25–60.

Cox, LaWanda F. "The American Agricultural Wage Earner, 1865–1900," *Agricultural History,* 22 (April 1948), 95–114.

Cronin, James E., and Peter Weiler. "Working-Class Interests and the Politics of Social Democratic Reform in Britain, 1900–1940," *International Labor and Working-Class History,* 40 (Fall 1991), 47–66.

Cumbler, John T. *Working Class Community in Industrial America: Work, Leisure, and Struggle in Two Industrial Cities, 1880–1930* (Westport, Conn., 1979).

Cunliffe, Marcus. *Soldiers and Civilians: The Martial Spirit in America, 1775–1865* (Boston, 1968).

[Curtis, George T.] *The Merits of Thomas W. Dorr, and George Bancroft as They Are Politically Connected, By A Citizen of Massachusetts* (Boston, n.d.).

Dacus, J. A. *Annals of the Great Strikes in the United States* (Chicago, 1877).

David, Henry. *History of the Haymarket Affair: A Study in the American Social Revolutionary and Labor Movements* (New York, 1936).

Davis, Allen F., and Mark H. Haller, eds. *The Peoples of Philadelphia: A History of Ethnic Groups and Lower-Class Life, 1790–1940* (Philadelphia, 1973).

Davis, David Brion. "The Significance of Excluding Slavery from the Old Northwest," *Indiana Magazine of History,* 84 (March 1988), 75–89.

Davis, Susan G. *Parades and Power: Street Theater in Nineteenth-Century Philadelphia* (Philadelphia, Pa., 1986).

Dawley, Alan. *Class and Community: The Industrial Revolution in Lynn* (Cambridge, Mass., 1976).

Denning, Michael. *Mechanic Accents: Dime Novels and Working-Class Culture in America* (London, 1987).

Devyr, Thomas Ainge. *The Odd Book of the Nineteenth Century, or, "Chivalry" in Modern Days* (Greenpoint, N.Y., 1882).

Dublin, Thomas. *Women at Work: The Transformation of Work and Community in Lowell, Massachusetts, 1826–1860* (New York, 1979).

Du Bois, W. E. B. *Black Reconstruction in America, 1860–1880* (New York, 1935).

Dunn, Richard S. "Servants and Slaves: The Recruitment and Employment of Labor," in Jack P. Greene and J. R. Pole, eds., *Colonial British America: Essays in the History of the Early Modern Era* (Baltimore, 1984), 157–94.

Dusinberre, William. *Civil War Issues in Philadelphia, 1856–1865* (Philadelphia, 1965).

Einhorn, Robin L. "The Civil War and Municipal Government in Chicago," in Maris A. Vinovskis, ed., *Toward a Social History of the American Civil War: Exploratory Essays* (Cambridge, 1990), 117–38.

Eley, Geoff. *Reshaping the German Right: Radical Nationalism and Political Change after Bismarck* (New Haven, 1980).

Ellis, David M. *Landlords and Farmers in the Hudson-Mohawk Region, 1790–1850* (Ithaca, N.Y., 1946).

Ely, Richard T. *The Labor Movement in America* (New York, 1886).

Emmons, David M. *The Butte Irish: Class and Ethnicity in an American Mining Town, 1875–1925* (Urbana, Ill., 1989).

"'Refuge of the Exile': The Social Welfare Policies of Butte's Ancient Order of Hibernians, 1880–1925" (unpublished paper).

Ets, Marie Hall. *Rosa, the Life of an Italian Immigrant,* with forward by Rudolph Vecoli (Minneapolis, 1970).

Evans, Peter B., Dietrich Rueschemeyer, and Theda Skocpol. *Bringing the State Back In* (Cambridge, 1985).

Evans, W. McKee. *Ballots and Fence Rails: Reconstruction on the Lower Cape Fear* (Chapel Hill, N.C., 1966).

Facts Involved in the Rhode Island Controversy with Some Views upon the Rights of Both Parties (Boston, 1842).

Faler, Paul G. *Mechanics and Manufacturers in the Early Industrial Revolution: Lynn, Massachusetts, 1780–1860* (Albany, N.Y., 1981).

Fields, Barbara Jeanne. *Slavery and Freedom on the Middle Ground: Maryland during the Nineteenth Century* (New Haven, Conn., 1985).

 Review of Steven Hahn, *Roots of Southern Populism,* in *International Labor and Working-Class History,* 28 (Fall 1985), 135–9.

Fink, Leon. *Workingmen's Democracy: The Knights of Labor and American Politics* (Urbana, Ill., 1983).

Finkin, Matthew W., Alvin L. Goldman, and Clyde W. Summers. *Legal Protection for the Individual Employee* (St. Paul, Minn., 1989).

Fitzgerald, Michael W. "'To Give Our Votes to the Party': Black Political Agitation and Agricultural Change in Alabama, 1865–1870," *Journal of American History,* 76 (Sept. 1989), 489–505.

Fitzpatrick, Tara. "Reared by Industry: Labor Discipline and Prison Discipline in the New York House of Refuge" (unpublished seminar paper, Yale University, 1981).

Fitzroy, Herbert William Keith. "Punishment of Crime in Provincial Pennsylvania," *Pennsylvania Magazine of History and Biography,* 60 (July 1936), 242–69.

Flinn, John J. *History of the Chicago Police Force* (Chicago, 1887).

Floy, Michael, Jr. *The Diary of Michael Floy, Jr. Bowery Village, 1833–1837,* edited by R. A. E. Brooks (New Haven, Conn., 1941).

Foner, Eric. *Nothing But Freedom: Emancipation and Its Legacy* (Baton Rouge, La., 1983).

 Reconstruction: America's Unfinished Revolution, 1863–1877 (New York, 1988).

Foner, Philip S., ed. *The Factory Girls* (Urbana, Ill., 1977).

Foner, Philip S. *The Great Labor Uprising of 1877* (New York, 1977).

Foner, Philip S., and Ronald L. Lewis, eds. *The Black Worker: A Documentary History from Colonial Times to the Present* (6 vols., Philadelphia, 1978–82).

Fones-Wolf, Ken. *Trade Union Gospel: Christianity and Labor in Industrial Philadelphia, 1865–1915* (Philadelphia, 1989).

Forbath, William E. *Law and the Shaping of the American Labor Movement* (Cambridge, Mass., 1991).

Forbes, Robert S. *An Appeal to Merchants and Ship Owners on the Subject of Seamen* (Boston, 1854).

Fox-Genovese, Elizabeth. *Within the Plantation Household: Black and White Women of the Old South* (Chapel Hill, N.C., 1988).

Franklin, John Hope. *Reconstruction: After the Civil War* (Chicago, 1961).

Freifeld, Mary Ellen. "The Emergence of the American Working Classes: The Roots of Division, 1865–1885" (Ph.D. diss., New York University, 1980).

French, Adela Haberski, ed. *The Social Reform Papers of John James McCook: A Guide to the Microfilm Edition* (Hartford, Conn., 1977).

French, John D. "'Reaping the Whirlwind': The Origins of the Allegheny County Greenback Labor Party in *1877*," *Western Pennsylvania Historical Magazine,* 64 (April 1981), 97–119.

Friedman, Gerald. "Worker Militancy and Its Consequences: Political Responses to Labor Unrest in the United States, 1877–1914," *International Labor and Working-Class History,* 40 (Fall 1991), 5–17.

Gallman, J. Matthew. "Voluntarism in Wartime: Philadelphia's Great Central Fair," in Vinovskis, 93–116.

Garraty, John A. *Unemployment in History: Economic Thought and Public Policy* (New York, 1978).

Geary, Dick. *European Labour Protest, 1848–1939* (London, 1981).

Genovese, Eugene D. *Roll, Jordan, Roll: The World the Slaves Made* (New York, 1972).

George, Henry. *Progress and Poverty: An Inquiry into the Cause of Industrial Depression and of Increase of Want with Increase of Wealth* (New York, 1935, first edition 1879).

Gettleman, Marvin E. *The Dorr Rebellion: A Study in American Radicalism, 1833–1849* (New York, 1973).

Gibbon, Peter. *The Origins of Ulster Unionism: The Formation of Popular Protestant Politics and Ideology in Nineteenth Century Ireland* (Manchester, 1975).

Gilje, Paul A. *Road to Mobocracy: Popular Disorder in New York City, 1763–1834* (Chapel Hill, N.C., 1987).

Ginzberg, Lori D. *Women and the Work of Benevolence: Morality, Politics, and Class in the Nineteenth-Century United States* (New Haven, Conn., 1990).

Glettler, Monika. *Pittsburg-Wien-Budapest: Programm und Praxis der Nationalitatenpolitik bei der Auswanderung der ungarischen Slowaken nach Amerika um 1900* (Vienna, 1980).

[Godkin, E. L.] "The Labor Crisis," *Nation,* 4 (April 15, 1867), 335.

"Labor and Politics," *Nation,* 14 (June 13, 1872), 386–7.

"The Danger of Playing Tricks with the Labor Question," *Nation,* 15 (Sept. 5, 1872), 148.

Goodell, William. *The Rights and Wrongs of Rhode Island* (*Christian Investigator,* No. 8, Whitesboro, N.Y., Sept. 1842).

Goodenow, John Milton. *Historical Sketches of the Principles and Maxims of American Jurisprudence, in Contrast with the Doctrines of English Common Law on the Subject of Crimes and Punishments* (Steubenville, Ohio, 1819).

Goodwyn, Lawrence. *Democratic Promise: The Populist Moment in America* (New York, 1976).

Gorn, Elliott J. "'Good-Bye Boys, I Die a True American': Homicide, Nativism, and Working-Class Culture in Antebellum New York City," *Journal of American History,* 74 (Sept. 1987), 388–410.

Gould, Benjamin A. *Investigations in the Military and Anthropological Statistics of American Soldiers* (New York, 1869).

Gould, Jeffrey. "Sugar Wars: The Sugar Cane Cutters' Strike of 1887 in Louisiana," *Southern Exposure,* 2 (Nov.–Dec. 1984), 45–55.

Gramsci, Antonio. *Selections from the Prison Notebooks of Antonio Gramsci* (translated and edited by Quintin Hoare and Geoffrey N. Smith, New York, 1971).

Grant, H. Roger. *Self-Help in the 1890s Depression* (Ames, Iowa, 1983).

Grenell, Judson. "Autobiography" (unpublished manuscript, Michigan State University Archives and Historical Collections).

Grimes, Mary C. *The Knights in Fiction: Two Labor Novels of the 1880s,* with afterword by David Montgomery (Urbana, Ill., 1986).

Griscom, John H. *The Sanitary Condition of the Laboring Population of New York* (New York, 1845).

Groh, Dieter. *Negative Integration und Revolutionärer Attentismus: Die deutsche Sozialdemokratie am Vorabend des Ersten Weltkrieges* (Frankfurt/M, 1973).

Groneman, Carol. "The 'Bloody Oulde Sixth': A Social Analysis of a New York City Working-Class Community in the Mid-Nineteenth Century" (Ph.D. diss., University of Rochester, 1973).

Gronowicz, Anthony. "Revising the Concept of Jacksonian Democracy: A Comparison of New York City's Democrats in 1844 and 1884" (Ph.D. diss., University of Pennsylvania, 1981).

Gunn, L. Ray. *The Decline of Authority: Public Economic Policy and Political Development in New York, 1800–1860* (Ithaca, N.Y., 1988).

Gunton, George. *The Economic and Social Importance of the Eight-Hour Movement* (AFL Eight-Hour Series, No. 2, Washington, D.C., 1889).

Gutman, Herbert G. "The Tompkins Square 'Riot' in New York City on January 13, 1874," *Labor History,* 6 (Winter, 1965), 44–70.

   Work, Culture, and Society in Industrializing America: Essays in Working-Class and Social History (New York, 1976).

   Power & Culture: Essays on the American Working Class, edited by Ira Berlin (New York, 1987).

Hahn, Steven. *The Roots of Southern Populism: Yeoman Farmers and the Transformation of the Georgia Upcountry, 1850–1890* (New York, 1983).

Hamilton, Howard D. "The Legislative and Judicial History of the Thirteenth Amendment," *National Bar Journal,* 9 (March 1951), 26–134.

Hansen, Marcus Lee. *The Atlantic Migration, 1607–1860: A History of the Continuing Settlement of the United States* (New York, 1961).

Harring, Sidney L. "Class Conflict and the Suppression of Tramps in Buffalo, 1892–1894," *Law and Society Review,* 11 (Summer 1977), 873–911.

   Policing a Class Society: The Experience of American Cities, 1865–1915 (New Brunswick, N.J., 1983).

Harris, David. *Socialist Origins in the United States: American Forerunners of Marx, 1817–1842* (Assen, Netherlands, 1966).

Hartog, Hendrick. *Public Property and Private Power: The Corporation of the City of New York in American Law, 1730–1870* (Chapel Hill, N.C., 1983).

Hattam, Victoria. "Economic Visions and Political Strategies: American Labor and the State, 1865–1896," *Studies in American Political Development,* vol. 4, ed. Karen Orren and Stephen Skowronek (New Haven, Conn. 1990), 82–129.

Headley, Joel T. *The Great Riots of New York, 1712–1873* (New York, 1873).

Herrick, Cheesman A. *White Servitude in Pennsylvania: Indentured and Redemption Labor in Colony and Commonwealth* (Philadelphia, 1926).

Hobsbawm, E. J. *Nations and Nationalism since 1780: Programme, Myth, Reality* (Cambridge, 1990).

Holli, Melvin G. *Reform in Detroit: Hazen S. Pingree and Urban Politics* (New York, 1969).

Holmes, Amy E. "'Such Is the Price We Pay': American Widows and the Civil War Pension System," in Vinovskis, 171–95.

Holt, Thomas. *Black over White: Negro Political Leadership in South Carolina during Reconstruction* (Urbana, Ill., 1977).

Holt, Wythe. "Recovery by the Worker Who Quits: A Comparison of the Mainstream, Legal Realist, and Critical Legal Studies Approaches to a Problem of Nineteenth Century Contract Law," *Wisconsin Law Review*, 4 (1986), 677–732.

Horowitz, Morton J. *The Transformation of American Law, 1780–1860* (Cambridge, Mass., 1977).

Howe, Daniel Walker. *The Political Culture of American Whigs* (Chicago, 1979).

Hunter, Tera W. "Household Workers in the Making: Afro-American Women in Atlanta and the New South, 1861–1920" (Ph.D. diss., Yale University, 1990).

Hurst, James Willard. *Law and the Conditions of Freedom in the Nineteenth Century United States* (Madison, Wis., 1956).

Hyman, Michael R. "Taxation, Public Policy, and Political Dissent: Yeoman Disaffection in the Post-Reconstruction Lower South," *Journal of Southern History*, 55 (Feb. 1989), 49–76.

Ingham, John W. *Making Iron and Steel: Independent Mills in Pittsburgh, 1820–1920* (Columbus, Ohio, 1991).

International Workingmen's Association. *La Première Internationale. Recueil de documents publié sous la direction de Jacques Fréymond* (2 vols., Geneva, 1962).

Jaynes, Gerald D. *Branches without Roots: Genesis of the Black Working Class in the American South, 1862–1882* (New York, 1986).

Jentz, John B., and Hartmut Keil. "From Immigrants to Urban Workers: Chicago's German Poor in the Gilded Age and Progressive Era, 1883–1908," *Vierteljahrschrift für Sozial- und Wirtschaftsgeschichte*, 68 (1981), 52–97.

Jones, Maldwyn A. *American Immigration* (Chicago, 1960).

Journal of the Military Service Institution of the United States.

Kaelble, Hartmut. *Industrialisation and Social Inequality in 19th-Century Europe* (Leamington Spa, 1986).

Karsten, Peter. "'Bottomed on Justice': A Reappraisal of Critical Legal Studies Scholarship Concerning Breaches of Labor Contracts by Quitting or Firing in Britain and the U.S., 1630–1880," *American Journal of Legal History*, 34 (1990), 213–61.

Katz, Michael. *In the Shadow of the Poorhouse: A Social History of Welfare in America* (New York, 1986).

Kaufman, Stuart Bruce. *Samuel Gompers and the Origins of the American Federation of Labor, 1848–1896* (Westport, Conn., 1973).

Kaufman, Stuart B., ed. *The Samuel Gompers Papers* (4 vols., Urbana, Ill., 1986–91).

Keil, Hartmut, ed. *German Workers' Culture in the United States, 1850 to 1920* (Washington, D.C., 1988).

Keil, Hartmut, and Heinz Ickstadt. "Elemente einer deutschen Arbeiterkultür in Chicago zwischen 1880 und 1890," *Geschichte und Gesellschaft*, 5 (1979), 103–24.

Kelly, Alfred. *The German Worker: Working-Class Autobiographies from the Age of Industrialization* (Berkeley, Cal., 1987).

Kent, James. *Commentaries on American Law*, 2d ed. (2 vols., New York, 1832).

Kerber, Linda K. *Women of the Republic: Intellect and Ideology in Revolutionary America* (Chapel Hill, N.C., 1980).

Kessler-Harris, Alice. *Out to Work: A History of Wage-Earning Women in the United States* (New York, 1982).

Keyssar, Alexander. *Out of Work: The First Century of Unemployment in Massachusetts* (Cambridge, 1986).

Kipnis, Ira. *American Socialist Movement, 1897–1912* (New York, 1952).

Klebaner, Benjamin J. "The Home Relief Controversy in Philadelphia, 1782–1861," *Pennsylvania Magazine of History and Biography*, 78 (Oct. 1954), 413–23.

Kleinberg, S. J. *The Shadow of the Mills: Working-Class Families in Pittsburgh, 1870–1907* (Pittsburgh, Pa., 1989).

Kleppner, Paul. *The Cross of Culture: A Social Analysis of Midwestern Politics, 1850–1900* (New York, 1970).

Continuity and Change in Electoral Politics, 1893–1928 (Westport, Conn., 1987).

"Government, Parties, and Voters in Pittsburgh," in Samuel P. Hays, ed., *City at the Point: Essays on the Social History of Pittsburgh* (Pittsburgh, Pa., 1989), 151–80.

Knights of Labor. *Record of the Proceedings of the Fourth Regular Session of the General Assembly, Held at Pittsburgh, Pa., Sept. 7–11, 1880* (n.p., n.d.).

Proceedings of D.A. 16 held at Scranton, July 28th and 29th 1890 (manuscript, no pagination, Powderly Papers, reel 66).

Kocka, Jürgen. *White Collar Workers in America, 1890–1940: A Social-Political History in International Perspective*, translated by Maura Kealey (London, 1980).

Kolb, Alfred. *Als Arbeiter in Amerika: Unter deutsch-amerikanischen Großstadt Proletariern* (Berlin, 1904).

Kousser, J. Morgan. *The Shaping of Southern Politics: Suffrage Restrictions and the Establishment of the One-Party South* (New Haven, Conn., 1974).

Krause, Paul. *The Battle for Homestead, 1880–1892: Politics, Culture, and Steel* (Pittsburgh, Pa., 1992).

Kull, Nell, ed. "'I Never Can Be Happy In There Among So Many Mountains': The Letters of Sally Rice," *Vermont History*, 38 (Winter 1970), 49–57.

"The Labor Question," *American Catholic Quarterly Review*, 3 (Oct. 1878), 721–46.

Lanard, Thomas S. *One Hundred Years with the State Fencibles . . . 1813–1913* (Philadelphia, 1913).

Laurie, Bruce. *Working People of Philadelphia, 1800–1850* (Philadelphia, 1980).

"Law and Labor," *Galaxy*, 6 (Oct. 1868), 566–7.

Lefebvre, Georges. *The French Revolution,* translated by Elizabeth Moss Evanson (two vols., London, 1962–4).

Letwin, Daniel L. "Race, Class, and Industrialization in the New South: Black and White Coal Miners in the Birmingham District of Alabama, 1878–1897" (Ph.D. diss., Yale University, 1991).

Levey, Jane "The New Haven Mothers' Aid Society and the Day Nursery Idea, 1885–1904" (unpublished seminar paper, Yale University, 1990).

Levine, Lawrence. *Highbrow, Lowbrow: The Emergence of Cultural Hierarchy in America* (Cambridge, Mass., 1988).

Linderman, Gerald F. *Embattled Courage: The Experience of Combat in the American Civil War* (New York, 1987).

[Lippard, George.] *Life and Adventures of Charles Anderson Chester, the Notorious Leader of the Philadelphia "Killers," Who Was Murdered, While Engaged in the Destruction of the California House, on Election Night, October 11, 1849* (Philadelphia, 1849).

Litwack, Leon F. *North of Slavery: The Negro in the Free States, 1790–1860* (Chicago, 1961).

Been So Long in the Storm: The Aftermath of Slavery (New York, 1979).

Lloyd, Henry Demarest. *Men, The Workers* (New York, 1909).

Lonn, Ella. *Foreigners in the Union Army and Navy* (Baton Rouge, La., 1951).

Lownes, Caleb. *An Account of the Alteration and Present State of the Penal Laws of Pennsylvania, also, an Account of the Gaol and Penitentiary House of Philadelphia* (Boston, 1799).

Luther, Seth. *Address on the Right of Free Suffrage* (Providence, R.I., 1833).

Address to the Working Men of New England on the State of Education and on the Condition of the Producing Classes in Europe and America (New York, 1833).

Lynch, John R. *The Facts of Reconstruction* (New York, 1913).

McClure, A. K. *Old Time Notes of Pennsylvania* (2 vols., Philadelphia, 1905).

McConnell, Stuart. "Who Joined the Grand Army? Three Case Studies in the Construction of Union Veteranhood, 1866–1900," in Vinovskis, 139–170.

McCurry, Stephanie. "The Two Faces of Republicanism: Gender and Proslavery Politics in Antebellum South Carolina," *Journal of American History*, 78 (March 1992), 1,245–1,264.

[McDougall, Frances H. Greene.] *Might and Right; By A Rhode Islander* (Providence, R.I., 1844).

McGerr, Michael E. *The Decline of Popular Politics: The American North, 1865–1928* (New York, 1986).

McGovern, Michael. *Labor Lyrics, and other Poems* (Youngstown, Ohio, 1899).

McMaster, John Bach. *A History of the People of the United States, From the Revolution to the Civil War* (8 vols., New York, 1910).

McMillen, Neil R. *Dark Journey: Black Mississippians in the Age of Jim Crow* (Urbana, Ill., 1989).

McNeill, George E. *Argument on the Hours of Labor. Delivered before the Labor Committee of the Massachusetts Legislature* (New York, n.d.).

The Labor Movement: The Problem of To-day (New York, 1887).

McPherson, Edward. *The Political History of the United States of America during the Period of Reconstruction* (Washington, D.C., 1875).

McSeveny, Samuel T. *The Politics of Depression: Political Behavior in the Northeast, 1893–1896* (New York, 1972).

Mahon, Richard. "Wage Labor and Seasonal Migration in the Wheat Belt of the Upper Mississippi Valley, 1860–1875" (unpublished paper presented to the Chicago Area Labor History Group, Dec. 9, 1988).

Marsh, Margaret. "From Separation to Togetherness: The Social Construction of Domestic Space in American Suburbs, 1840–1915," *Journal of American History,* 76 (Sept. 1989), 506–27.

Marx, Karl. *Capital: A Critique of Political Economy* (3 vols., Chicago, 1906).

Selected Works (2 vols., New York, n.d.).

Masquerier, Lewis. *Sociology: Or, The Reconstruction of Society, Government, and Property, upon the Principles of Equality . . . Giving All the Liberty and Happiness to Be Found on Earth* (New York, 1877).

Massachusetts. House of Representatives, unpassed legislation files. Massachusetts State Archives.

Matthews, Albert. "Hired Man and Help," *Publications of the Colonial Society of Massachusetts,* 5 (Transactions, 1897, 1898).

May, Henry F. *Protestant Churches and Industrial America* (New York, 1949).

Middlesex Society of Husbandmen and Manufacturers. *Transactions,* 1851 (Lowell, Mass., 1851).

Miller, Perry, ed. *Legal Mind in America: From Independence to the Civil War* (Garden City, N.Y., 1962).

Miller, Zane L. *Boss Cox's Cincinnati: Urban Politics in the Progressive Era* (New York, 1968).

Milton, John. *"Paradise Lost," The Complete Poems of John Milton, with Complete Notes by Thomas Newton. D.D., Bishop of Bristol* (New York, 1936).

Mink, Gwendolyn. *Old Labor and New Immigrants in American Political Development: Union, Party, and State, 1875–1920* (Ithaca, N.Y., 1986).

Mitchell, Reid. "The Northern Soldier and His Community," in Vinovskis, 78–92.

Mohl, Raymond. "Poverty in Early America, a Reappraisal: The Case of Eighteenth-Century New York City," *New York History,* 50 (Jan. 1969), 5–27.

Monkkonen, Eric H. "From Cop History to Social History: The Significance of the Police in American History," *Journal of Social History,* 15 (Summer 1982).

Monkkonen, Eric H., ed. *Walking to Work: Tramps in America, 1790–1935* (Lincoln, Neb., 1984).

Montgomery, David. *Beyond Equality: Labor and the Radical Republicans, 1862–1872* (New York, 1967).

"The Shuttle and the Cross: Weavers and Artisans in the Kensington Riots of 1844," *Journal of Social History,* 5 (Spring 1972), 411–46.

"Strikes in Nineteenth-Century America," *Social Science History,* 4 (Feb. 1980), 81–104.

"Labor and the Republic in Industrial America," *Le Mouvement Social,* 111 (April–June 1980), 201–15.

The Fall of the House of Labor: The Workplace, the State, and American Labor Activism, 1865–1925 (New York, 1987).

"William H. Sylvis and the Search for Working-Class Citizenship," in Melvyn Dubofsky and Warren Van Tine, eds., *Labor Leaders in America* (Urbana, Ill., 1987).

Moody, Richard. *The Astor Place Riot* (Bloomington, Ind., 1958).

Moore, Albert B. *Conscription and Conflict in the Confederacy* (New York, 1924).

Morris, Richard B. *Government and Labor in Early America* (New York, 1946).

"Labor Controls in Maryland in the Nineteenth Century," *Journal of Southern History,* 14 (Aug. 1948), 385–400.

Murphy, Teresa Anne. *Ten Hours' Labor: Religion, Reform, and Gender in Early New England* (Ithaca, N.Y., 1992).

Nash, Gary B. *The Urban Crucible: Social Change, Political Consciousness and the Origins of the American Revolution* (Cambridge, Mass., 1979).

Forging Freedom: The Formation of Philadelphia's Black Community, 1720–1840 (Cambridge, Mass., 1988).

Nelson, Bruce C. "'We Can't Get Them to Do Aggressive Work': Chicago's Anarchists and the Eight-Hour Movement," *International Labor and Working-Class History,* 29 (Spring 1986), 1–13.

Beyond the Martyrs: A Social History of Chicago's Anarchists, 1870–1900 (New Brunswick, N.J., 1988).

Noel, Thomas J. *The City and the Saloon: Denver, 1858–1916* (Lincoln, Neb., 1982).

Noiriel, Gérard. *Les ouvriers dans la société française* (Paris, 1986).

Norrell, Robert J. *Reaping the Whirlwind: The Civil Rights Movement in Tuskegee* (New York, 1985).

Oestreicher, Richard J. *Solidarity and Fragmentation: Working People and Class Consciousness in Detroit, 1875–1900* (Urbana, Ill., 1986).

"Urban Working-Class Political Behavior and Theories of American Electoral Politics, 1870–1940," *Journal of American History,* 74 (March 1988), 1,257–86.

Ostrogorski, Moisei. *Democracy and the Organization of Political Parties,* translated by Frederick Clarke (2 vols., New York, 1902).

Painter, Nell Irvin. *Exodusters: Black Migration to Kansas after Reconstruction* (New York, 1976).

Palladino, Grace. *Another Civil War: Labor, Capital, and the State in the Anthracite Regions of Pennsylvania, 1840–68* (Urbana, Ill., 1990).

Palmer, Bryan D. *Descent into Discourse: the Reification of Language and the Writing of Social History* (Philadelphia, 1990).

Parker, Cornelia Straton. *Working with the Working Woman* (New York, 1922).

Pennsylvania Bureau of Industrial Statistics. *Report, 1880/1881* (Harrisburg, 1881).

Pennsylvania. *Journal of the Senate of Pennsylvania,* 1878 (Harrisburg, 1879).

Perman, Michael. *The Road to Redemption: Southern Politics, 1869–1879* (Chapel Hill, N.C., 1984).

Perrot, Michelle. *Les ouvriers en grève. France, 1871–1890* (2 vols., Paris, 1974). "The Three Ages of Industrial Discipline in Nineteenth-Century France," in John M. Merriman, ed., *Consciousness and Class Experience in Nineteenth-Century Europe* (New York, 1979), 149–68.

Pessen, Edward. "Who Governed the Nation's Cities in the 'Era of the Common Man?'" in Pessen, ed., *The Many-Faceted Jacksonian Era: New Interpretations* (Westport, Conn., 1977).

Peterson, Merrill D., ed. *Democracy, Liberty, and Property: The State Constitutional Conventions of the 1820's* (Indianapolis, Ind. 1966).

Philadelphia. Mayor's Court of the City of Philadelphia, Appearance Docket (Philadelphia City Archives, RG 20.2).

Philadelphia County Prison. Prisoners for Trial Docket, March 1790 to December 1797 (Philadelphia Archives, RG 38.39).

  Prisoners for Trial Docket, March 17, 1796, to March 5, 1802 (RG 38.38).

  Prisoners for Trial Docket, Feb. 1, 1819, to March 2, 1821 (RG 38.38).

  Prisoners for Trial Docket, Oct. 21, 1831, to Jan. 28, 1834, (Philadelphia Archives, RG 38.38).

Philadelphia Prison Vagrants Docket. May 31, 1790, to Dec. 29, 1797. Inspectors of the Jail and Penitentiary House, County Prison (RG 38).

  June 1, 1817, to July 12, 1822 (RG38).

Philadelphia Society for Alleviating the Miseries of Public Prisons. *A Statistical View of the Operation of the Penal Code of Pennsylvania* (Philadelphia, 1819).

[Pitman, John.] *A Reply to the Letter of the Hon. Marcus Morton by One of the Rhode-Island People* (Providence, R.I., 1842).

Pitman, Joseph S. *Report of the Trial of Thomas Wilson Dorr for Treason against the State of Rhode Island* (Boston, 1844).

Pocock, J. G. A. *The Machiavellian Moment: Florentine Political Thought and the Atlantic Republican Tradition* (Princeton, N.J., 1975).

Powderly, Terence V. "The Federal Elections Bill," *Journal of United Labor* (July 31, 1890).

  Papers (microfilm edition).

Powderly, Terence V., and A.W. Wright, eds. *Labor Day Annual* (Toronto, 1893).

Pratt, John W. "Boss Tweed's Public Welfare Program," *New York Historical Society Quarterly,* 45 (Oct. 1961), 396–411.

Prude, Jonathan. *Coming of Industrial Order: Town and Factory Life in Rural Massachusetts, 1810–1860* (Cambridge, 1983).

Quill, Charles [pseud.] *The Working-Man* (Philadelphia, 1839).

Rachleff, Peter J. *Black Labor in the South: Richmond, Virginia, 1865–1890* (Philadelphia, 1984).

Randall, Edwin T. "Imprisonment for Debt in America: Fact or Fiction," *Mississippi Valley Historical Review,* 39 (June 1952), 89–102.

Reeve, Tapping. *The Law of Baron and Femme, of Parent and Child, Guardian and Ward, Master and Servant and of the Powers of the Courts of Chancery* (Albany, N.Y., 1862).

Reinders, Robert. "Militia and Public Order in Nineteenth-Century America," *Journal of American Studies,* 11 (April 1977), 81–101.

Rhodes, James Ford. *History of the United States from the Compromise of 1850 to the Final Restoration of Home Rule at the South in 1877* (5 vols., New York, 1893–1904).

Richmond, Rev. John Francis. *New York and Its Institutions* (New York, 1871).

Ricker, Ralph R. "The Greenback-Labor Movement in Pennsylvania" (Ph.D. diss., Pennsylvania State University, 1955).

Ringenbach, Paul T. *Tramps and Reformers, 1873–1916: The Discovery of Unemployment in New York* (Westport, Conn., 1973).

Riordan, William L. *Plunkitt of Tammany Hall* (New York, 1948).

Roberts, Kenneth, and Anna M. Roberts. *Moreau de St. Méry's American Journal [1793–1798]* (Garden City, N.Y., 1947).

Rochefoucault-Liancourt, François Alexandre Frédéric, duc de La. *On the Prisons of Philadelphia* (Philadelphia, 1796).

Rock, Howard B. *Artisans of the New Republic: The Tradesmen of New York City in the Age of Jefferson* (New York, 1979).

Roediger, David R. *The Wages of Whiteness: Race and the Making of the American Working Class* (London, 1991).

Rosenzweig, Roy. *Eight Hours for What We Will: Workers and Leisure in an Industrial City, 1870–1920* (New York, 1983).

Rosenzweig, Roy, and Elizabeth Blackmar. *The Park and the People: A History of Central Park* (Ithaca, N.Y., 1992).

Ross, Steven J. "Workers on the Edge: Work, Leisure, and Politics in Industrializing Cincinnati, 1830–1890" (Ph.D. diss., Princeton University, 1980).

   Workers on the Edge: Work, Leisure, and Politics in Industrializing Cincinnati, 1788–1890 (New York, 1985).

Roswencz, Edwin C., ed. *Ideology and Power in the Age of Jackson* (Garden City, N.Y., 1964).

Rowe, G. S. "Black Offenders, Criminal Courts, and Philadelphia Society in the Late Eighteenth Century," *Journal of Social History,* 22 (Summer 1981), 687–712.

   "Women's Crime and Criminal Administration in Philadelphia, 1763–1790," *Pennsylvania Magazine of History and Biography,* 109 (June 1985), 335–68.

Rowe, G. S., and Billy G. Smith. "The Prisoners for Trial Docket for Philadelphia County, 1795," *Pennsylvania History,* 53 (Oct. 1986), 289–319.

Rubinow, I. M. *Social Insurance, With Special Reference to American Conditions* (New York, 1913).

Ryan, Mary P. *Cradle of the Middle Class: The Family in Oneida County, New York, 1790–1865* (Cambridge, 1981).

Salinger, Sharon V. "Colonial Labor in Transition: The Decline of Indentured Servitude in Late Eighteenth-Century Philadelphia," *Labor History,* 22 (Spring 1981).

   "To Serve Well and Faithfully": Labor and Indentured Servants in Pennsylvania, 1682–1800 (Cambridge, 1987).

Salvatore, Nick. *Eugene V. Debs: Citizen and Socialist* (Urbana, Ill., 1982).

Saville, Julie. "A Measure of Freedom: From Slave to Wage Labor in South Carolina, 1860–1868" (Ph.D. diss., Yale University, 1986).

Sawislak, Karen Lynn. "Smoldering City: Class, Ethnicity, and Politics in Chicago at the Time of the Great Fire, 1867–1871" (Ph.D. diss., Yale University, 1990).

Saxton, Alexander. *The Rise and Fall of the White Republic: Class Politics and Mass Culture in Nineteenth Century America* (London, 1990).

Schiller, Dan. *Objectivity and the News: The Public and the Rise of Commercial Journalism* (Philadelphia, 1981).

Schneirov, Richard. "The Knights of Labor in the Chicago Labor Movement and in Municipal Politics, 1877–1887" (Ph.D. diss., Northern Illinois University, 1984).

Schob, David E. *Hired Hands and Plowboys: Farm Labor in the Midwest, 1815–60* (Urbana, Ill., 1975).

Schwantes, Carlos A. *Coxey's Army: An American Odyssey* (Lincoln, Neb., 1985).

Scobey, David. "Boycotting the Politics Factory: Labor Radicalism and the New York City Mayoral Election of 1884," *Radical History Review*, 28–30 (1984), 280–325.

"Empire City: Politics, Culture, and Urbanism in Gilded-Age New York" (Ph.D. diss., Yale University, 1989).

Scott, Joan Wallach. "Social History and the History of Socialism: French Socialist Municipalities in the 1890's," *Le Mouvement Social*, 111 (April–June 1980), 145–53.

Gender and the Politics of History (New York, 1988).

Scranton, Philip. *Proprietary Capitalism: The Textile Manufacture at Philadelphia, 1800–1885* (New York, 1983).

Sewell, Rev. Benjamin T. *Sorrow's Circuit, or Five Years' Experience in the Bedford Street Mission, Philadelphia* (Philadelphia, 1860).

Shapiro, Karin A. "The Tennessee Coal Miners' Revolts of 1891–92: Industrialization, Politics, and Convict Labor in the Late Nineteenth-Century South" (Ph.D. diss., Yale University, 1991).

Shefter, Martin. "The Electoral Foundations of the Political Machine: New York City, 1884–1897," in Joel H. Silbey, Allan G. Bogue, and William Flanigan, eds., *The History of American Electoral Behavior* (Princeton, N.J., 1978), 263–98.

Shelton, Cynthia J. *The Mills of Manayunk: Industrialization and Social Conflict in Philadelphia, 1787–1837* (Baltimore, Md. 1986).

Simkins, Francis Butler, and Robert H. Woody. *South Carolina during Reconstruction* (Chapel Hill, N.C., 1932).

Simon, Daphne. "Master and Servant," in John Saville, ed., *Democracy and the Labor Movement* (London, 1954), 160–200.

Simon, Jean-Claude. "Textile Workers, Trade Unions, and Politics: Comparative Case Studies, France and the United States, 1885–1914" (Ph.D. diss., Tufts University, 1980).

Skocpol, Theda. *Protecting Soldiers and Mothers: The Political Origins of Social Policy in the United States* (Cambridge, Mass., 1992).

Skowronek, Stephen. *Building a New American State: The Expansion of National Administrative Capacities, 1877–1920* (Cambridge, 1982).

Smith, Adam. *An Inquiry into the Nature and Causes of the Wealth of Nations* (New York, 1937).

Smith, Billy G. *The "Lower Sort": Philadelphia's Laboring People, 1750–1800* (Ithaca, N.Y., 1990).

Smith, Billy G., and Cynthia Shelton. "The Daily Occurrence Docket of the Philadelphia Almshouse: Selected Entries, 1800," *Pennsylvania History*, 52 (April 1985), 86–116.

"The Daily Occurrence Docket of the Philadelphia Almshouse: Selected Entries, 1800–1804," *Pennsylvania History*, 52 (July 1985), 183–205.

Smith, Merritt Roe. *Harpers Ferry Armory and the New Technology: The Challenge of Change* (Ithaca, N.Y., 1977).

Speek, Peter A. *The Singletax and the Labor Movement* (Madison, Wis., 1917).

Sproat, John G. *The "Best Men": Liberal Reformers of the Gilded Age* (New York, 1968).

Stanley, Amy Dru. "Contract Rights in the Age of Emancipation: Wage Labor and Marriage after the Civil War" (Ph.D. diss., Yale University, 1990).

"Beggars Can't Be Choosers: Compulsion and Contract in Postbellum America," *Journal of American History*, 78 (March 1992).

Stansell, Christine. *City of Women: Sex and Class in New York, 1789–1860* (New York, 1986).

Stead, W. T. *Chicago To-Day; Or, The Labour War in America* (London, 1894).

Steinberg, Allen. *The Transformation of Criminal Justice: Philadelphia, 1800–1880* (Chapel Hill, N.C., 1989).

Steinfeld, Robert J. "Property and Suffrage in the Early American Republic," *Stanford Law Review*, 41 (Jan. 1989), 335–76.

Invention of Free Labor: The Employment Relations in English and American Law and Culture, 1350–1870 (Chapel Hill, N.C., 1991).

Steinmetz, George. "Workers and the Welfare State in Imperial Germany," *International Labor and Working-Class History*, 40 (Fall 1991), 18–46.

Stevens, George E. *New York Typographical Union No. 6: Study of a Modern Trade Union and Its Predecessors* (Albany, N.Y., 1913).

Stevens, Sylvester K. *Pennsylvania: Birthplace of a Nation* (New York, 1964).

Stoddard, William Osborn. *The Volcano under the City, by a Volunteer Special* (New York, 1887).

Sutherland, John F. "Housing the Poor in a City of Homes: Philadelphia at the Turn of the Century," in Allen F. Davis and Mark H. Haller, eds., *The Peoples of Philadelphia: A History of Ethnic Groups and Lower-Class Life, 1790–1940* (Philadelphia, 1973), 175–201.

Swann, Leonard A. *John Roach, Maritime Entrepreneur: The Years as Naval Contractor, 1862–1886* (Annapolis, Md., 1965).

Swisher, Carl B. *Roger B. Taney* (New York, 1935).

Sylvis, James C. *Life, Speeches, Labors and Essays of William H. Sylvis* (Philadelphia, 1872).

Therborn, Göran. "The Rule of Capital and the Rise of Democracy," *New Left Review*, 103 (May–June 1977), 11–17.

Thernstrom, Stephan. *The Other Bostonians: Poverty and Progress in the American Metropolis, 1880–1970* (Cambridge, Mass., 1973).

Thompson, E. P. "Homage to Tom Maguire," in Asa Briggs and John Saville, eds., *Essays in Labour History* (London, 1960), 276–316.

The Making of the English Working Class (New York, 1963).

"Time, Work Discipline, and Industrial Capitalism," *Past and Present*, 39 (December 1967), 56–97.

Thompson, Phillips. "The Land Question," in Terence V. Powderly and A.W. Wright, eds., *Labor Day Annual* (Toronto, 1893), 18–22.

Tise, Larry E. *Proslavery: A History of the Defense of Slavery in America, 1701–1840* (Athens, Ga., 1987).

Tocqueville, Alexis de. *Democracy in America*, translated by Henry Reeve (New York, 1838).

Tomlins, Christopher L. *The State and the Unions: Labor Relations, Law, and the Organized Labor Movement in America, 1880–1960* (Cambridge, 1985).

"The Ties that Bind: Master and Servant in Massachusetts, 1800–1850," *Labor History*, 30 (Spring 1989), 193–227.

Law, Labor and Ideology in the Early American Republic (New York, 1993).

Topalov, Christian. "Régulation publique du capitalisme et propriété de masse du logement: la 'révolution hypothecaire' des années 1930 aux Etats-Unis," *Economie et Société*, 5 (1988), 51–99.

[Tourgee, Albion.] *A Fool's Errand by One of the Fools* (New York, 1880).

Trautman, Frederic. "Pennsylvania Through a German's Eyes: The Travels of Ludwig Gall, 1819–1820," *Pennsylvania Magazine of History and Biography*, 105 (Jan. 1981), 35–65.

Tuckerman, Joseph. *An Essay on the Wages Paid to Females for Their Labour* (Philadelphia, 1830).

Typographical Union No. 2 [Philadelphia.] Minutes.

U.K. *Parliamentary Sessional Papers, 1867*, xxxii, c 3952, "Fourth Report of the Commissioners Appointed to Inquire into the Organization and Rules of Trades Unions and Other Associations" (London, 1867).

U.S. Department of Commerce, Bureau of the Census. *Historical Statistics of the United States. Colonial Times to 1970* (2 vols., Washington, D.C., 1975).

U.S. Senate. *Report of the Joint Select Committee to Inquire into the Affairs of the Late Insurrectionary States*, 42d Cong., 2d sess. (13 vols., Washington, D.C., 1982).

Van der Linden, Marcel, and Jürgen Rojahn, eds. *The Formation of Labour Movements, 1870–1914* (two vols., Leiden, 1990).

Vandervelde, Emile. *Socialism Versus the State*, translated by Charles H. Kerr (Chicago, 1919).

VanderVelde, Lee S. "The Labor Vision of the Thirteenth Amendment," *University of Pennsylvania Law Review*, 138 (Dec. 1989), 437–504.

Vinovskis, Maris A., ed. *Toward a Social History of the American Civil War: Exploratory Essays* (New York, 1990).

Walker, Samuel A. "Terence V. Powderly, the Knights of Labor and the Temperance Issue," *Societas* 5 (Autumn 1975), 279–93.

Walsh, Walter J. "Redefining Radicalism: A Historical Perspective," *The George Washington Law Review*, 59 (March 1991), 636–682.

Ware, Norman J. *The Labor Movement in the United States, 1860–1895* (New York, 1929).

Warner, Sam B., Jr. *Streetcar Suburbs: The Process of Growth in Boston, 1870–1900* (Cambridge, Mass., 1962).

Warren, Fred. *The Appeal's Arsenal of Facts* (Girard, Kans., 1911).

Watchorn, Robert. *The Autobiography of Robert Watchorn*, edited by Herbert Faulkner West (Oklahoma City, 1958).

Way, Peter. "Shovel and Shamrock: Irish Workers and Labor Violence in the Digging of the Chesapeake and Ohio Canal," *Labor History*, 30 (Fall 1989), 489–517.

Webb, Frank J. *The Garies and Their Friends* (London, 1857).

Weber, Eugene. *Peasants into Frenchmen: The Modernization of Rural France, 1870–1914* (Stanford, Cal., 1976).

Weigley, Russell F. "'A Peaceful City': Public Order in Philadelphia from Consolidation through the Civil War," in Davis and Haller, 155–73.

Weinbaum, Paul O. "Temperance, Politics, and the New York City Riots of 1857," *New-York Historical Society Quarterly*, 59 (July 1975).

Weiner, Lynn. *From Working Girl to Working Mother: The Female Labor Force in the United States, 1820–1980* (Chapel Hill, N.C., 1985).

White, Shane. *Somewhat More Independent: The End of Slavery in New York City, 1770–1810* (Athens, Ga., 1991).

Whiteside, Aaron. Brief of Aaron Whiteside, *Richmond* v. *Brown* (Providence, R.I., Court of Common Pleas, November term 1832).

Whittaker, Capt. Fred. "Larry Locke, The Man of Iron; Or, A Fight for Fortune. A Story of Labor and Capital," *Beadle's Weekly*, 1–2 (1883–4).

Wiener, Jonathan H. *Social Origins of the New South: Alabama, 1860–1885* (Baton Rouge, La., 1978).

Wilentz, Sean. *Chants Democratic: New York City and the Rise of the American Working Class, 1788–1850* (New York, 1984).

Willard, Frances E. *Glimpses of Fifty Years: The Autobiography of an American Woman* (Chicago, 1889).

Williams, Raymond. *Marxism and Literature* (Oxford, 1977).

Williamson, Joel. *After Slavery: The Negro in South Carolina during Reconstruction, 1861–1877* (New York, 1975).

Wilson, Harold F. *The Hill Country of Northern New England: Its Social and Economic History, 1790–1930* (New York, 1936).

Wilson, John. *Memories of a Labour Leader* (Firle, Sussex, 1980).

Woodman, Harold D. "Post–Civil War Southern Agriculture and the Law," *Agricultural History*, 53 (Jan. 1979), 319–37.

Woodward, C. Vann. *Origins of the New South, 1877–1913* (Baton Rouge, La., 1951).

Wright, Frances. *Views of Society and Manners in America*, edited by Paul R. Baker (Cambridge, Mass., 1963).

Young, Alfred F. "The Mechanics and the Jeffersonians: New York, 1789–1801," *Labor History*, 5 (Fall 1964), 247–76.

"George Robert Twelves Hewes (1752–1840): A Boston Shoemaker and the Memory of the American Revolution," *William and Mary Quarterly*, 3d series, 38 (Oct. 1981), 561–623.

Zahler, Helene S. *Eastern Workingmen and National Land Policy, 1829–1862* (New York, 1941).

Zelnik, Reginald E. *Labor and Society in Tsarist Russia: The Factory Workers of St. Petersburg* (Stanford, Cal., 1971).

Zieren, Gregory R. "The Propertied Worker: Working Class Formation in Toledo, Ohio, 1870–1900" (Ph.D. diss., University of Delaware, 1981).

Zonderman, David A. *Aspirations and Anxieties: New England Workers and the Mechanized Factory System, 1815–1850* (New York, 1992).

Index